*Twayne's English Authors Series*

Sylvia E. Bowman, *Editor*

INDIANA UNIVERSITY

*Sir Thomas Malory*

(TEAS) 35

# Sir Thomas Malory

By EDMUND REISS

*The Pennsylvania State University*

Twayne Publishers, Inc.   ::   New York

*To Dot*
*who was interested*
*and*
*to Kathy and Geoff*
*who some day might be*

# *Preface*

Although many articles, pamphlets, editions, and monographs have been written on Malory and his *Morte Darthur,* books on the man and his work have been few. Indeed, since Vida Scudder's study in 1917 and Eugène Vinaver's in 1929, the only books of literary criticism of Malory to appear have been three collections of essays, all published since 1963. While these collections by J. A. W. Bennett, R. M. Lumiansky, and Charles Moorman are very useful and represent, along with Vinaver's forthcoming revised version of his Oxford edition, a renaissance of sorts for Malory studies, they are still no substitute for a full-length, unified critical examination of Malory's work, emphasizing the artistic and thematic relationships of the parts of the *Morte Darthur* to each other and to the whole formed by them.

In the present work I have tried, therefore, to provide a commentary on Malory's work that is primarily concerned with how it functions as a work of literary art. I could have proceeded by analyzing according to subject: for example, one chapter on Malory's idea of chivalry, another on his concept of love, and so forth. Such a method is valuable, and many recent studies have approached the *Morte Darthur* in this way. Instead, I have preferred to discuss the work as it stands and to show Malory's concepts as they arise and function in his developing narrative.

In my discussion I have made use of many ideas of my predecessors, but I have not tried to repeat everything written on the subject or to say everything about Malory that can be said. Rather, I have attempted to suggest how the *Morte Darthur* can and should be read; and I hope to have provided within one cover a work that is both an introduction to Malory and a new analysis of his work.

After an introduction about general problems, the commentary begins. Chapter 2 represents a detailed examination of the first part of the *Morte,* the section showing the birth of Arthur and his early struggles as king. This section is discussed in detail because many ideas found throughout the whole book first appear here. Chapter 3 is an analysis of the bulk of the *Morte,* those parts represented by Arthur's fight with Lucius, emperor of Rome; by the adventures of Lancelot and Gareth; and by the story of Tristram and Isode. These episodes, detailing the glorious adventures of the Knights of the Round Table, represent the halcyon days of Arthur's realm. Chapter 4 is limited to a study of the Quest of the Holy Grail, representing the turning point of Malory's Arthur story; and Chapter 5 discusses the final decline and destruction of Arthur and his Order.

Because of the nature of this commentary, I have not presented the backgrounds of Arthurian romance. Likewise, in noting relationships between Malory's work and his sources, I have had to be brief and selective; and, in bringing medieval religious ideas to bear on the work, I have had to be suggestive rather than inclusive. Generally, for authority on points of Christian doctrine, I have limited my references to the New Testament and to the writings of St. Augustine. Even though scores of references closer to the fifteenth century could ordinarily have been included, these two sources are sufficient to give definitive statements of Malory's spiritual concepts.

I thank Oxford University Press for permission to quote from *The Works of Sir Thomas Malory,* ed. Eugène Vinaver, 1947, 3 vols., and 1954, 1 vol.; and from *Essays on Malory,* ed. J. A. W. Bennett, 1963. I also gratefully acknowledge the assistance of time and money given to me by the Graduate School of Western Reserve University to facilitate the preparation of this book.

EDMUND REISS

*Cleveland, Ohio*

# Contents

# Chronology

c. 1400– Thomas Malory is born, son of Sir John Malory, of New-
1410  bold Revel, Warwickshire.
1434  Sir John dies; Sir Thomas inherits family estate.
1436  Thomas fights at siege of Calais in retinue of Richard
      Beauchamp, Earl of Warwick.
1443  Thomas's first indictment, for theft.
1444  Member of Parliament for Warwickshire.
 or
1445
1450– Supposedly involved in attempted murder, robbery, rape,
1451  extortion, and cattle raids. Imprisoned at Coleshill; escapes;
      robs Cistercian monastery.
1452  Arrested.
1454  Released on bail, apparently steals cattle and personal
      property. Imprisoned in Colchester; escapes; is recaptured
      and sent to the Marshalsea.
1456  Released through royal pardon; sent to Ludgate, normally
      a debtor's prison.
1457  Released on bail; returned to prison, again at the Marshal-
      sea.
1460  Last recorded arrest; sent to Newgate Prison.
1468  Excluded from two general pardons granted by Edward IV.
1469– In prison, finished last tale in the *Morte Darthur*.
1470
1471  Died on March 14, perhaps due to plague; perhaps while
      still in prison.
1485  William Caxton published the *Morte Darthur* on July 31.

# CHAPTER 1

## Introduction: The Man and the Work

FOR many readers the *Morte Darthur* of Sir Thomas Malory is synonymous with Arthurian romance, and, for the English-speaking world of today at least, the work can truly be called "the fountainhead of Arthurian fiction." [1] Now approximately five hundred years old, the book itself has had a general and continuing popularity and at present is probably better known than any other English work of the Middle Ages except Chaucer's *Canterbury Tales*. The *Morte Darthur* exists in several scholarly and expensive multivolumed editions; it appears in expurgated and modernized collections as a standard work for children and adolescents; it is available in new paper-covered renditions for a general public; and recently it has appeared as a selection of at least one American book club titillatingly described as containing in unexpurgated form the famous love stories of Tristan and Iseult and of Lancelot and Guinevere.

The work seems to have been popular from the time of its printing at William Caxton's press in Westminster on July 31, 1485. It has, moreover, survived both attacks on its morality and slavish imitations of its contents. When Roger Ascham, for example, a hundred years after Malory, attacked the work as delighting in "open mans slaughter, and bold bawdrye" and lamented that he knew "when Gods Bible was banished the Court, and *Morte Arthure* receiued into the Princes chamber,"[2] he not only attested to the popularity of the book but revealed some of the misunderstandings readers have had of it. In like manner, when Tennyson and the Pre-Raphaelites sentimentalized and romanticized Malory's work, changing its action and meaning, and transforming, as Sir Herbert Read has said, its "muscular prose into watery verse," [3] they were still not able to replace the *Morte Darthur* with their own compositions.

Although existing for an English-speaking audience as a source book of stories of the days when knighthood was in flower, as a vehicle for political allegories, as a repository of motifs and designs for such writers as E. A. Robinson, T. S. Eliot, Charles Williams, and John Steinbeck; as the basis of parodies and satires by Mark Twain and T. H. White; and as the source of musical comedies and movies, the *Morte Darthur* has still continued to exist in its own right as a standard work for the general reading public, as a key work in fifteenth-century English literature, and, most important, as a work of literary art. As one recent critic has stated, from the time of its publication the *Morte Darthur* "has stood at the centre of English literature." [4] It is truly remarkable that this work, itself based on several Arthurian romances in French and English of the late Middle Ages, should have outlived its sources and not in turn have been outlived by the scores of works based on it. Eugène Vinaver, dean of Malory scholars and important interpreter of medieval French romances, has commented on the longevity of the *Morte Darthur:* "Many writers had worked on the French Arthurian prose romances between the thirteenth and the fifteenth centuries; there had been adaptations of it in Spain and in Germany. All this is now dead and buried, and Malory alone stands as a rock defying all changes of taste and style and morals; not as a grand paradox of nature, but as a lasting work of art." [5]

For centuries the man who wrote the *Morte Darthur* existed as only a name. In an *explicit*—words taking leave of the reader—at the end of the work, the author apparently identified himself: "this book was ended the ninth yere of the reygne of King Edward the Fourth, by Syr Thomas Maleoré, Knyght" (883). [6] In the Preface to his edition of Malory, Caxton also referred to a "Syr Thomas Malorye" who took the story of Arthur "out of certeyn bookes of Frensshe and reduced it into Englysshe" (xvii). Along with the name and the indication that the author of the *Morte Darthur* was a knight, there appeared the suggestion that he may have been a prisoner; for also in the final *explicit* Malory asked the reader to "praye for me whyle I am on lyve that God sende me good delyveraunce" (883). Such a suggestion implies that Malory may have written at least part of the *Morte Darthur* while in prison.

[ 14 ]

## Introduction: The Man and the Work

Despite the continuing fame of the work, nothing more was known of the man who wrote it until the end of the nineteenth century. At this time, George Lyman Kittredge, searching for a Sir Thomas Malory who was alive in the ninth year of Edward IV's reign—that is, from March 4, 1469, to March 3, 1470—and who was old enough at that time to have written a book, found in Sir William Dugdale's *Antiquities of Warwickshire*, published in 1656, a Sir Thomas Malory of Newbold Revel in Warwickshire, who fit the requirements.[7] Subsequent discoveries, primarily in the Public Records Office in London by Edward Hicks and Albert C. Baugh, have brought to light the following information about the man who seems to have been the writer of the *Morte Darthur*.[8]

Sir Thomas Malory was born about the turn of the fifteenth century; and, following the death in 1434 of his father, John, he inherited the family estate in Warwickshire. He served in France in the retinue of Richard Beauchamp, Earl of Warwick; and he apparently fought at the siege of Calais in 1436, when the city was besieged by the Burgundians. A few years later he married a woman named Elizabeth, who bore him a son, Robert, who died before Sir Thomas; in 1444 or 1445, he was a member of Parliament for Warwickshire; in 1462, he may have accompanied Warwick on an expedition to Northumberland; and on March 14, 1471, he died, perhaps due to the plague. Along with this account that suggests a noble public figure, however, are other records indicating that Malory led a life somewhat less than respectable and certainly less than conventional.

In 1443 Malory was charged by Thomas Smythe of Sprotton, Northamptonshire, with theft of his property. The facts of this case are vague, but later records are more specific as to the charges brought against Malory. On January 4, 1450, he, along with twenty-six men, allegedly lay in ambush in the woods of Combe Abbey for the purpose of murdering Humphrey, Duke of Buckingham. On May 25 of the same year he supposedly broke into the house of Hugh Smyth of Monks Kirby and feloniously raped his wife, Joan. Ten weeks later, on August 6, he again apparently broke into the same house, again raping Joan; but this time he also carried off personal property belonging to Hugh. In May and August, 1450, Malory and John Appleby extorted money by threats and oppression from Margaret Kyng, William Hales, and John Mylner at Monks Kirby. In June and July, 1451, he made extensive cattle raids at Cosford and Caludon, and on one, on June 4, he carried off to Newbold Revel seven cows, two calves, a cart, and three hundred thirty-five sheep belonging to William Rowe and William Dowde of Shawell, Leicestershire. Finally, on July 23, 1451, he was arrested and imprisoned at Coleshill in Warwickshire. Two days later he escaped from his imprisonment by swimming a moat at night; and three days after this, with the help of John Appleby and other accomplices, Malory apparently broke into the Abbey of the Blessed Mary of Combe, a Cistercian monastery midway between Newbold Revel and Coventry, and stole money and valuables from two of the abbot's chests. On the very next day, again with the help of Appleby and others, he allegedly repeated the assault: he broke eighteen doors, insulted the abbot, his monks, and servants, broke open three iron chests, and stole more money and valuables.

More than nine months later he was again arrested "to answer certain charges," but he was released on May 5, 1454, on bail. He promptly stole some oxen from Katherine, Lady Peyto in Northamptonshire; and, settling for a while in northern Essex, he assisted John Alleyn in cattle-stealing. Malory also supposedly gave shelter to Alleyn and plotted with him an attack on the property of William Grene of Gosfield. The attack was unsuccessful; but on October 16, Malory was again in prison, this time in Colchester. Two weeks later, on October 30, armed with various swords and daggers, he escaped from jail, only to be recaptured on November 18 and committed to the Marshalsea. In February, 1456, he was released through a royal pardon but was imprisoned again shortly afterward, this time at Ludgate, normally a prison for debtors. On October 19, 1457, he was released on bail for two months but was then returned to prison, again at the Marshalsea. Except for occasional periods of freedom, Malory apparently remained a prisoner for the next five or six years. While free he may have continued to follow the Earl of Warwick in the Wars of the Roses and may have gone with Warwick from the side of the Yorkists to that of the Lancastrians.[9] Malory's last recorded arrest was in January, 1460, when he was sent to Newgate Prison; but he was excluded in 1468 from two general pardons granted by Edward IV. He may finally have been released from prison when Henry VI was restored to the throne in October, 1470, but the fact that he was buried in a chapel at the Grey Friars near Newgate suggests that he may have died there as a prisoner.[10]

Even though further biographical material may be found, the world will probably never know the precise truth or falsehood of the charges brought against Malory. As several scholars have pointed out, the indictments against Malory were merely accusations, not evidence; and, furthermore, no record has yet been found of a trial or conviction. The matter becomes even more complicated when one realizes that indictments in the fifteenth century were often used as "a means of putting innocent but troublesome people out of the way." [11] For many readers of Malory the most obnoxious item on the list of accusations is his rape of Joan Smyth, but even this charge is ambiguous. It must be understood that accusations of *raptus* often amounted to what Edward Hicks has called "little more than a legal fiction, a formula used for good measure." [12] Moreover, if Malory had merely removed Joan from the house to keep her from interfering with the looting of Hugh's possessions, he would be guilty of *raptus*. All in all, scholars today lack the means to judge the historical record and to determine the extent of Malory's innocence or guilt. As Roger Sherman Loomis has written, it is premature to form an opinion: "Only when someone familiar with the political and social history of England during the Wars of the Roses, thoroughly acquainted with the operation of the law and its devious ways, interprets the documents will there be a real basis for judgment. . . . Even if there was some basis in fact for the charges against Malory, even if he resorted to violence on more than one occasion, the turbulent condition of England may have justified him. He himself pleaded not guilty to the gravest accusations, and the only offense he acknowledged was failure to pay a debt." [13]

To be sure, the England of the fifteenth century was neither an organized modern society nor the courtly Arthurian world described in the pages of the *Morte Darthur;* instead, it was a land "exhausted by generations of foreign enterprise and dynastic quarrels." [14] In the pages of the collection of contemporary correspondence called the *Paston Letters* one can see a vivid picture "of the complete breakdown of law and order, of the abuses of maintenance and livery and private warfare, of the corruption of officials, of the excessive taxation, of the ruin of countrysides by the enclosure of agricultural land for pasture." [15] Whatever the troubles in the twentieth-century world, it is still difficult for a scholar today to know how to interpret evidence from the world of the fifteenth century and to understand the behavior of any individual living and participating in that world.

Still, a real attempt to understand this world is found in Johann Huizinga's classic work, *The Waning of the Middle Ages*. Speaking of the violence and covetousness actually demonstrated by people and of the ideal of noble chivalry maintained by them, Huizinga points out numerous instances where the real contradicts the ideal: "In spite of the care taken on all hands to keep up the illusion of chivalry, reality perpetually gives the lie to it, and obliges it to take refuge in the domains of literature and of conversation." [16]

The possibility that the charges against Malory are valid has, nevertheless, disconcerted many readers who have felt a need to make the morals of the man square with those professed in his writing. Often this need has resulted in naïve statements about the unlikelihood that the man who wrote of the ideals of the Round Table and of the ethereal Quest of the Holy Grail could be an immoral brigand and criminal. Conversely, for such readers, if Malory were a criminal, he would then be a hypocrite whose work would have little moral, ethical, or even, through extension, literary value. A statement by R. S. Loomis is typical of this view: "To accept as proved the charges brought against Malory is to believe that he was both a hardened criminal and a hypocrite." [17] Eugène Vinaver has pointed out how ridiculous it is to feel disconcerted about Malory's apparent criminal activities when, after all, the man's biography is merely "entertaining in itself" and "an interesting sidelight of the social history of his time." Quoting Marcel Proust about writers, Vinaver states that "the more we concentrate on their *moi extérieur*, the less likely we are to understand their creative self, their *moi profond*. On this showing it seems singularly fortunate that our knowledge of Malory the man is not only limited but apparently inconsistent with the nature of his work: we are not even tempted to explain one through the other." [18]

One still might wonder what there was in Arthurian romances that would attract Malory. There is at least a possibility that his contact as a young man with the Earl of Warwick, the person whom all of Europe then recognized as embodying the knightly ideals of the age, interested him in chivalric values; and this interest may have led him to the time when knighthood was in flower and when King Arthur presided over his Order of the Round Table. A second possibility is that, since at least part of the *Morte Darthur* seems to have been written while Malory was in prison, the book may have been, in effect if not in intent, escape literature. It may have been a labor of diversion that allowed Malory to rise above the monotony of daily prison life, or even something through which he could get beyond his troubles and those of his age.

Malory's age was, in what is now a cliché, an age of transition. In the later fifteenth century, most of Europe, including England, was feeling the impact of Humanism, Classicism, and new discoveries in the natural world. In 1471, when Malory died, the Western World had already entered the Renaissance. In that year, as R. W. Chambers vividly points out, "Nicolo Machiavelli was christened in the Baptistery of Florence, and Erasmus of Rotterdam was taking such interest in the world as a child of three may do." [19] These men—along with others, such as Christopher Columbus and Leonardo da Vinci, already young men, and Nicholas Copernicus and Michaelangelo, to be born in the next few years—were of a world different from that of the Middle Ages. The incongruity of a book like the *Morte Darthur* being written at this time has been pointed out over and over. In this view, late fifteenth-century England was hardly the most fertile ground for Arthurian romance; and Malory's achievement was supposedly that, in "the eleventh hour," as it were, he "was able to go over the old ground and make it live once more." [20]

The distinct implications of this view are that the *Morte Darthur* is a freak and that part of its merit lies in its appearing in an era when the world in general was interested in other matters. What is wrong with this idea is that it fails to take into consideration the extent to which the fifteenth century, in Northern European countries at least, was marked by a desire to oversimplify or to turn away from the present. From the violence and confusion that marked the external life of the time, from the general feeling of impending calamity that was everywhere, people turned, intentionally or not, to "the good old days"—and specifically to the time when knighthood bloomed as an untainted flower. As Huizinga states, the ideal of chivalry that permeates romance served as a formula by which people could hope to comprehend "the appalling complexity of the world's way." In imagining a world ruled by chivalry, "they succeeded in explaining to themselves, as well as they could, the motives and the course of history, which thus was reduced to a spectacle of the honour of princes and the virtue of knights, to a noble game with edifying and heroic rules." Chivalry here changed from an esthetic to an ethical ideal.[21]

It is no accident that among the first books printed in English were several translations of romances and old adventure stories. These included the stories of Troy, of Jason, of the *Aeneid*, of Charlemagne, and of Godfrey of Bouillon, subtitled *The Siege and Conquest of Jerusalem*. Along with these and several others, Caxton translated and published two works on the idea of chivalry: *The Book of the Ordre of Chyualry*, from a French version of Ramón Lull's thirteenth-century *Le Libre del Ordre de Cauayleria;* and *The Book of the Fayttes of Armes and of Chyualrye*, from a French work by the early fifteenth-century writer, Christine de Pisan. These works, like Malory's *Morte Darthur*, were aimed at an audience already predisposed toward them. Nor was Malory alone as a writer of romances in the second half of the fifteenth century. Other English works composed then include the *Holy Grail* and *Merlin* of Henry Lovelich, a prose *Merlin*, and such non-Arthurian romances as *Melusine* and *Valentine and Orson*.

While King Arthur and his Knights of the Round Table may have been somewhat anachronistic in the world of the late fifteenth century, they were still very much alive in the popular imagination as part of its concern with romance and chivalry in general. The knights themselves served as models of the old ideal, and the story of their creation and ultimate destruction demonstrated the decline of the world from an age of gold to one of brass.

Concerning other reasons for Malory's retelling of the Arthurian stories, it is wholly conjectural to say, as Vinaver does, that Malory adapted the Arthurian material "to the needs of his day," by making his stories into "a record of the national past of England" and by endowing them "with the greatness and importance of a national epic." [22] A better statement about the relationship of Malory's writing to his own age is that made by Arthur B. Ferguson: "If concern for the dolorous state of English fortunes did not turn him to the Arthurian materials, once embarked on the project he found himself dealing with themes that could very readily be given timely significance." [23] Malory may have seen some similarities between Arthur and the fifteenth-century English king, Henry V; moreover, he may have been conscious of the relationship between the fratricidal struggles between the Arthurian knights that destroyed the Round Table and the Wars of the Roses that aided in the disintegration of the English monarchy. He does, it must be pointed out, tend to describe the Arthurian adventures as if they were taking place in an English world. In at least later parts of the *Morte Darthur,* Malory presents Camelot as if it were Westminster; Astolat, as what is now Guildford; the Joyous Gard (Lancelot's castle), as Almwich or Bamborough; Logres, as England; and he also emphasizes the importance of the Archbishop of Canterbury. Such relationships may be suggested by Malory's material, but they do not necessarily represent the meaning of his work.

All statements about an author's intention in a work of literature are, of course, bound to be inadequate and even irrelevant from the points of view both of the reader and of the work in its existence as a work of art. Although it is possible to note in the *Morte Darthur* references to contemporary times, it is more pertinent to see how Malory's work acts as a commentary on the problems and difficulties of human life and on the fortunes of man and society in this world, problems and difficulties that, although expressed in the terms of his particular age, go beyond that age. The explicit remarks Malory makes about the fickleness of the fifteenth-century English public (862) are interesting to note, but they should not be confused with the implicit ideas that form the overall themes of his work. These themes certainly reflect the underlying attitudes and values of Malory's time, but understanding them does not mean reading the *Morte Darthur* as merely an historical document.

Although the subject of Malory's work was the Arthurian stories that flourished in the literature of Western Europe from at least the twelfth century forward, Malory was not presenting these stories for their own sake. As Vinaver has pointed out, Malory's attitude "was essentially that of a moralist. He had none of the romantic enthusiasm for the marvellous. . . . Visions, miracles, and legends did not appeal to him by reason of their distinct poetic quality, but because they helped him to express his own moral doctrine." [24] In being a "moralist," Malory was a man of his age; he possessed an attitude toward literature different from that of today's writers and readers.

The idea that literature has a moral function is, of course, not an idea peculiar to Malory; it was not introduced to the world by him and is not necessarily best represented by him. Indeed, this concept permeated the Middle Ages, including the fifteenth century, receiving what may be regarded as its definitive statement in St. Augustine's words. In his view, some things are to be enjoyed for themselves and others are to be used; some things are ends in themselves, but others are means of reaching ends: "To enjoy something is to cling to it with love for its own sake. To use something, however, is to employ it in obtaining that which you love provided that it is worthy of love." [25] But, as Augustine continues, only those things that are eternal and immutable are to be enjoyed for themselves; everything else—everything in this transitory world—is to be used to get to the permanent. For Augustine and the medieval world the only book one can enjoy for itself is the Bible. If one delights in works of literature, works without a divine source, for their own sake, for the mere story they tell or the language they use, one is improperly responding to them. If a work itself contains only a pleasant-seeming shell but is empty inside, if it does not contain any nut of worth, then it should not exist. The medieval reader's reaction to a work of literature may be compared to the modern mathematician's response to an exciting mathematical formula. Each reacts not to the appearance of the thing—the piece of literature on the one hand, the formula on the other—but to the economy by which the outward form suggests the meaning contained within it. For the Middle Ages, the literary artist is the creator not of something of value in itself, but of something referring to what is of value. Literature should use its attractive appearance to interest the reader in getting beneath its surface and in discovering its theme, its *sententia*, that will instruct him in the basic truths of life; and these, for the Christian Middle Ages, are the truths of Christianity.

It is hardly relevant to claim, as Vinaver does, that in his handling of the Arthurian story Malory failed "to understand and sympathize with the real medieval romance." [26] What the "real" medieval romance was is moot, as is the implication that romance existed as an end in itself—to entertain, or even to teach a set of values or a code of conduct of its own unrelated to Christian ideals. [27] What is often termed Malory's "prosaic realism"—his middle-class set of values—is not something in conflict with any basic idea of romance but his expression of something already implicit in the works that were his sources.

Although one might be tempted to say that Malory's work itself is not "moral" in the sense of being explicitly didactic and that the emphasis on morality comes in with Caxton's Preface to his edition of the *Morte Darthur*, [28] this view is generally an attempt to make an after-the-fact fusion of the apparently immoral man and the work he wrote. To be sure, Caxton said that he printed the *Morte Darthur* "to the entente that noble men may see and lerne the noble actes of chyvalrye, the jentyl and vertuous dedes that somme knyghtes used in tho dayes." He hoped that all readers of the book would want to "take the good and honest actes in their remembraunce, and to folowe the same; wherin they shalle fynde many joyous and playsaunt hystoryes and noble and renomed actes of humanyté, gentylnesse, and chyvalryes." Although both good and evil are to be found in the book, Caxton admonishes his readers to "Doo after the good and leve the evyl, and it shal brynge you to good fame and renommee." Concluding his Preface, Caxton writes: "And for to passe the tyme thys book shal be plesaunte to rede in, but for to gyve fayth and byleve that al is trewe that is conteyned herin, ye be at your lyberté. But al is wryton for our doctryne, and for to beware that we falle not to vyce ne synne, but t'exersyse [to exercise] and folowe vertu, by whyche we may come and atteyne to good fame and renommé in thys lyf, and after thys shorte and transytorye lyf to come unto everlastyng blysse in heven; the whyche He graunte us that reygneth in heven, the Blessyd Trynyté. Amen" (xvii–xviii).

To think that this point of view is Caxton's alone is to fail to understand that, although written late in the fifteenth century, and during an age of transition, the *Morte Darthur* is, along with Caxton's Preface, very much a product of the Middle Ages with its ideas of the value and function of literature. Just as Chaucer could include such romances as the Knight's Tale and the Squire's Tale (not to speak of such *fabliaux* as the Miller's Tale and the Reeve's Tale) in a work containing as an ideal the Christian concept of charity, so can Malory use Arthurian adventures, stories of chivalric behavior and love, as part of a still larger context, a Christian ethic.

This is not to say that Malory's purposes were always the same as those of Caxton, for whereas one was a writer, the other was an editor. Speaking of why he wanted to print the Arthurian stories in English, Caxton writes that these stories already existed in various languages other than English; and then he says how he has printed in his book such stories of Arthur "as have late ben drawen oute bryefly into Englysshe": "I have, after the symple connynge that God hath sente to me, under the favour and correctyon of al noble lordes and gentylmen, enprysed to enprynte a book of the noble hystoryes of the sayd Kynge Arthur and of certeyn of his knyghtes, after a copye unto me delyverd, whyche copye Syr Thomas Malorye dyd take oute of certeyn bookes of Frensshe and reduced it into Englysshe" (xvii).

For centuries, the only version of the work by Malory known to the world was Caxton's 1485 edition. This edition is at present extant in two copies, one lacking eleven leaves in the John Rylands Library in Manchester, and the other complete in the Pierpont Morgan Library in New York. Because Caxton appears to have made corrections in his text after the printing had begun, there are some variations in these two copies, each representing a slightly different state of the text.[29] In 1934, however, another version of Malory's work was discovered by W. F. Oakeshott in the Fellows Library in Winchester College,[30] a version in many ways different from the edition prepared by Caxton through his "symple connynge."

This so-called Winchester manuscript is neither Malory's own copy nor the one used by Caxton as the basis of his edition, but it probably represents the closer approximation of what Malory actually wrote. Still, because each contains some elements of Malory's story not found in the other, the two versions should be considered collateral ones of a common original. More particularly, the Winchester manuscript reveals much that Caxton apparently changed in his source. As Vinaver has shown in his great 1947 edition of Malory, based primarily on the Winchester text, this manuscript represents what might be called a mechanical transcription of a source. The Winchester scribes were content merely to reproduce and seldom attempted to correct or to alter their source. Caxton's edition, on the other hand, should be viewed not as a copy but as a revised work prepared by a man who was an editor rather than a scribe and who often tried to improve on his original.

With what Caxton deceptively called his "symple connynge," he seems to have made several important changes in Malory's work, some of which are certainly inconsistent with Malory's effort as revealed in the Winchester text. The most striking changes are to be found, first, in his division of Malory's work into twenty-one books, each book further divided into chapters with rubrics prefixed to each, and, second, in his condensation of one part of the *Morte Darthur*, that called here the *Tale of Arthur and Lucius*, corresponding to Caxton's Book V. The first change is especially significant in that it affects the way in which the entire work should be viewed. In its division Caxton's edition presents a format suggesting strikingly that Malory wrote one book; but, as the Winchester manuscript reveals, Malory's work seems to exist as a series of separate tales, each with a beginning, a middle, and an end of its own. Following the section comparable to Caxton's Book IV appear these lines not in Caxton's edition:


Here endyth this tale, as the Freynshe Booke seyth, fro the maryage of kynge Uther unto [until the time of] kyng Arthure that regned aftir hym and ded many batayles.

And this booke endyth whereas sir Launcelot and sir Trystrams com to courte. Who that woll make ony more lette hym seke other bookis of kynge Arthure or of sir Launcelot or sir Trystrams; for this was drawyn by a knyght presoner, sir Thomas Malleorré, that God sende hym good recover. Amen.

Explicit.

(133)

This *explicit* reinforces the suggestion found in Caxton's edition that Malory was a knight-prisoner when he wrote at least part of his work, and it also indicates that what Caxton termed the *Morte Darthur* was really a work of several parts, this *explicit* being the end of the first part. Such *explicits* are found throughout the Winchester manuscript after what appear to be separate tales, and they provide what seem to be distinct breaks within the narrative. These apparent divisions in the Winchester text have made re-evaluation of Malory's work necessary, but this re-evaluation has led to a series of problems not anticipated by earlier readers of Malory who knew the work only as it appeared in Caxton's edition. The most important problem centers on the precise nature of the *Morte Darthur*, and about this two schools of thought exist.

The first, of which Eugène Vinaver is spokesman, feels that Malory's writing must be seen as essentially eight separate tales (although there are more than eight *explicits* indicated in the Winchester manuscript). The title of the work, the *Morte Darthur* came apparently from Caxton as part of his attempt to present the separate tales as a unified continuing romance. According to Vinaver, it is necessary to realize that Malory's writings are not one long romance and that, as title, the *Morte Darthur* (with its ungrammatical French) should be replaced by the *Works* of Malory —such, in fact, is the title of Vinaver's two editions of Malory. Vinaver's view makes it possible to see that many of the so-called inconsistencies in the various sections of the work are not inconsistencies at all but seem so only if the work is regarded as a single unit. According to Vinaver, no inconsistencies exist within the eight tales he finds in Malory. They appear only if one compares material from one tale with material from another. Vinaver realizes that in Malory's writing there is "a certain unity of manner and style," but he feels that "there is no unity of structure or design." [31]

Opposing Vinaver are the majority of contemporary Malory scholars, including D. S. Brewer, R. M. Lumiansky, Charles Moorman and Robert H. Wilson, who, whatever their own differences, maintain that Malory's work has an organic unity of its own.[32] Even though Malory may have written what might be termed a series of tales—perhaps eight, perhaps more—these are joined together by clear artistic devices such as time schemes, glimpses ahead and glances behind, indicating that the work has an existence as a whole, a structure or design that is much more than fortuitous. In Brewer's view, "It is not quite that one disagrees with the theory of the limited separateness of the tales, but that one is bound to reject what seem to be the implications of Professor Vinaver's thesis—that Malory's romances are as separate as the various novels of a modern author; that the romances may be taken in any or no particular order; and that they have no cumulative effect." [33]

Basic to the arguments of these two schools are the *explicits* found in the Winchester manuscript. To understand the full purpose of these, one must realize that they do more than separate one tale from another. Because some of them actually contain mentions of what is to come, they may also be viewed as links joining the separate tales to each other. Three *explicits* in particular show the synthesizing or connective nature of these passages. First, at the end of what Vinaver has termed the *Tale of Arthur and Lucius*, corresponding to Caxton's Book V, the *explicit* reads as follows:

> Here endyth the tale of the noble kynge Arthure that was Emperoure hymself thorow dygnyté of his hondys.
> And here folowyth afftyr many noble talys of sir Launcelot de Lake.
> Explycit the Noble Tale betwyxt
> Kynge Arthure and Lucius the Emperour of Rome.   (177)

To be sure, the *Tale of Lancelot* does follow. After the *Book of Sir Tristram* (Caxton's Books VIII–XII), the *explicit* likewise serves to join this tale with the one following. In part it reads, "But here folowyth the noble tale off the Sankegreall, whyche called ys the holy vessell and the sygnyfycacion of blyssed bloode off oure Lorde Jesu Cryste, whyche was brought into thys londe by Joseph off Aramathye" (623). Finally, following the *Book of Lancelot and Guinevere* (Caxton's Books XVIII–XIX), the *explicit* states: "And here on the othir syde folowyth *The Moste Pyteuous Tale of the Morte Arthure Saunz Gwerdon* par le Shyvalere Sir Thomas Malleorré, Knyght" (816). This is the tale that Caxton used for the name of Malory's whole composition.

Besides the unity suggested by these *explicits*, it is possible to see that the succession of romances has a cumulative effect; that the work has a "unity of tone and atmosphere," a "continual moral concern of a special kind"; that there are significant references backward and forward to important characters and events; and that the tales could have been put together in no order other than the present one, which is the same in both the Winchester text and in Caxton's edition.[34] Still another indication of unity may be found in the *explicit* at the end of the whole work. This *explicit* is the only one retained by Caxton; and, although several sheets are missing at the end of the Winchester manuscript, the *explicit* surely appeared there as well: "Here is the ende of the hoole book of kynge Arthur and of his noble knyghtes of the Rounde Table, that whan they were holé togyders there was ever an hondred and forty. And here is the ende of *The Deth of Arthur*" (883). Rather than be in apposition, the two sentences seem to be referring to two different things: the first, to the "hoole book"; the second, to the *Deth of Arthur* (the *Morte Arthure*), the final tale in Malory's composition.

In the late Middle Ages, the term "book" often suggested a compendium of volumes or different texts. As was seen earlier, the *explicit* following the section comparable to Caxton's Book IV (133) also spoke of "tale" and "booke," the former term referring to the particular work Malory had just finished writing and the latter to "the Freynshe booke," the collection of tales that apparently was his source. Malory seems to have written several tales, but for him they apparently were part of a larger work, a "hoole book." The final *explicit* of the *Morte Darthur*, with its further injunction to the reader to pray for the soul of its author, also suggests, as Vinaver realizes, an air of finality. It is not just that Malory had finished another tale; Malory seems to be "conscious that he had completed his great work with all its complex ramifications."[35]

Sometimes the question of whether the *Morte Darthur* is one book or eight tales is framed in such a way as to ask explicitly what Malory intended. Such a question is, as has been discussed earlier, irrelevant and difficult, if not impossible, to answer; and the difficulty is tremendous in the case of the *Morte Darthur*, a work based on legends and romances existing before Malory and not fully contained in any one source. As C. S. Lewis has perceptively written, the question of intention is not a proper one: "I do not for a moment believe that Malory had any intention either of writing a single 'work' or of writing many 'works' as we should understand the expressions. He was telling us about Arthur and his knights. Of course his matter was one—the same king, the same court. Of course his matter was many—they had had many adventures." [36]

Looking at Malory's writing historically, it is possible to theorize, as Vinaver has done, how Malory viewed both his own work and his sources and even to attempt a reconstruction of the way in which Malory wrote his work. Such an approach is interesting and useful in understanding what Malory apparently did to those works that were the bases of his composition; but, at the same time, probably no one will ever know whether Malory regarded his tales as eight separate compositions at the start of his writing, in the process, or at the finish. Also, no one will ever know precisely in what order he wrote his tales.[37]

Viewing the work analytically, on the other hand, it is certainly possible to show how the eight tales relate both to each other and to the whole created by them—and to understand something of the nature of this whole. As D. S. Brewer writes, Malory's form "is almost *sui generis*. It is certainly not a collection of unrelated short romances. It is certainly not a novel. It has something of the qualities of both, and something also of the quality of the old cyclic romances." [38] Malory has written what may be termed an Arthur-saga, or Arthur-cycle, in which both the individual parts and the whole work are important. The relationship of parts to whole may be compared to that in Chaucer's *Canterbury Tales* written about one hundred years before Malory's work, and to that in Spenser's *Faerie Queene*, written a little more than one hundred years after Malory. In all three works, the parts have something of an independent existence of their own. Chaucer's *Knight's Tale*, Spenser's *Legend of the Knight of the Red Cross or Holiness*, and Malory's *Tale of Arthur* (Caxton's Books I–IV), for example, may be read for and by themselves; but each is also a part and must be seen in terms of the other parts making up the whole work. Furthermore, the theme of each particular part functions in terms of the over-all themes found throughout the larger work. If a reader wants to understand the nature of any work of literature, he has an obligation to explore such relationships as these.

In relation to the question of how to look at Malory's work, it must be emphasized that Malory shows little originality in the sense of creating stories. Probably almost the entire narrative of his work existed in European vernacular literature long before he lived and wrote. Malory refers over and over to "the booke" or "the Freynshe booke" he is supposedly following, but it must not be thought that he is always referring to the same work or that he is slavishly reproducing his source. As E. Talbot Donaldson has pointed out, the phrase is one "Malory uses not infrequently when he is departing from his original—a sort of reverse confession of guilt." [39]

Malory's French sources deserve particular mention, for these works are very different from the sort of narrative now written in Western literature. Early Arthurian romances, even such twelfth-century works as those by Chrétien de Troyes, are in general simple affairs when compared to thirteenth-century French prose romances. These lengthy compositions, such as the Prose *Tristan* and the romances making up what is ordinarily called the Vulgate Cycle—the *Estoire del Saint Graal;* a prose version of the *Merlin* of Robert de Boron, with a lengthy sequel; the Prose *Lancelot;* the *Queste del Saint Graal;* and the *Mort Artu*—are constructed along several lines of episodes in which adventures tend to pile on adventures in apparently indiscriminate ways and in which innumerable personages, mostly anonymous, appear in a wild succession. As Vinaver says, the main object in these romances seems to be "to relate on an every-increasing scale the miscellaneous experiences of a group of fearless knights spurred to action by their indefatigable king."

To a twentieth-century reader, such romances may seem to be unformed, but they do have "an architectural design so unlike our own conception of a story that we inevitably fail to perceive it." [40] They may be likened to tightly woven tapestries so extensive that they cannot be taken in by the spectator in one glance. In them, many threads are started and interwoven, and even though it is difficult to follow one thread through or to see the connection between various threads, these strands, taken together, make up the whole work. When the tapestry maker decides to stop, "he simply cuts the threads at arbitrarily chosen points, and anyone who chooses to pick them up and interweave them in a similar fashion can continue the work indefinitely." [41] The interweaving, or *entrelacement*, is usually done by breaking off a still-incompleted episode, by bringing in another episode that may deal with another group of characters, and by stopping that one and perhaps bringing in another new episode or even returning to the first one. Such *entrelacement* can create suspense or relieve monotony, and it also allows the work to show as parallel several actions occurring ostensibly at the same time. [42]

In using these French prose romances, Malory apparently tried both to reduce the bulk of the stories and to arrange the narratives in some kind of simple or direct order. To do so, he seems to have used three main methods: one, simple mechanical reduction; two, telescoping, that is, making two different scenes or characters into one; and three, separation, that is, substituting for the *entrelacement* found in the French sources a method of detaching a particular story from the plethora of digressions associated with it and telling it in a short sequence. [43] Related to this third method, insofar as it clarifies the narrative, is Malory's tendency to give names to many characters that were anonymous in his sources. [44]

Although Malory may have used several sources, his achievement was thus based not on taking many separated stories and unifying them but rather on "breaking up the complicated structure of earlier fiction and in using its fragments for smaller narrative patterns." [45] Malory, apparently not interested in the "indiscriminate exaltation of adventure" found in the French sources, did not "delight in lingering over episodic details" but slowly cut "a road through a jungle of interwoven digressions." [46] It must not be thought, however, that the whole of Malory's artistry consisted in reducing and simplifying the French prose romances; for, along with these works, he used other sources, including two native English verse romances that were constructed according to what might be termed a simple narrative.

Because of the prior existence of the Arthurian material found in Malory, there exists a critical position which asserts that, to understand Malory's achievement, it is primarily necessary to see what Malory has done with and to his sources. In this view, what should be emphasized are the changes Malory makes. Such a critical position cannot help but fail to give an over-all view of the work itself. Although it is certainly desirable to understand how Malory changed or even just worked with material that existed before his composition, such study cannot exist as an end in itself; for the changes he makes are only part of his total effort. Along with what an author changes or omits, it is necessary to consider what he retains. C. S. Lewis has made a relevant statement about the study of sources: "It is possible for our reading of an author to become what we may call 'source-ridden,' so that we no longer see his book as it is in itself, but only as it contrasts with its sources. This is clearly an injustice to the author, for we are preserving in their original form elements which he has transmuted, and even elements which he rejected. It is as though we ate all the raw ingredients of a pudding along with the pudding itself; such an eating is emphatically not the pudding's proof." [47] And, speaking of Malory's *Tale of the Sankgreal* in particular, Lewis continues: "If we wish to know how far Malory's Grail is a success, we must sooner or later read it as if we knew nothing about its sources." [48]

It is, in fact, only when we understand the nature of Malory's achievement that we can make relevant statements about his handling of sources. If one looks at Malory's work primarily in relation to his sources, one is apt to make the sort of statement Vinaver does when he says that Malory extracted from his sources "with varying degrees of success"; he often failed though "his successes redeemed most of his failures." [49] The implication is that the worth of Malory is directly related to his handling of his sources. It is debatable whether or not Malory was a "good" translator and adapter: whether he understood what his sources were doing and what he himself wanted to do with them. But, even if Vinaver's statement is true, it still does not mean that Malory should not be considered a good writer or that his tales of Arthur and the Round Table should not be called great works of literary art.

Malory's composition, which for the sake of convenience we may still call the *Morte Darthur*, is something that is the result of many artists' hands. It is an organic growth that was nourished by Malory, by his specific sources—the French romances and the English poems—and by all the early Arthurian tales and legends ultimately affecting these works. The *Morte Darthur* contains within itself the early chronicles, culminating in Geoffrey of Monmouth's *Historia Regum Britanniae*, which present the "historical" Arthur; the romances, best illustrated by those of Chrétien de Troyes, which show the courtly Arthur; and even the Celtic legends, such as the *Culhwch and Olwen* and the *Spoils of Annwn*, which show what may be termed the mythological or supernatural Arthur.[50] To be sure, Malory is in many ways the most important nourisher in the growth of the *Morte Darthur*. It is he who, in desiring "crisp and compact construction," [51] reworked the French prose romances; it is he who substituted dialogue for narrative, who cut away excrescences from his sources to make his story direct, and who "steered clear of both coarseness and artificiality." [52] Although the *Morte Darthur* is written in many styles and reflects the various styles of Malory's sources, one can see in some passages that are undoubtedly by Malory, derivatives and doublets that may be considered a mark of Malory's own prose style. But, as Vinaver has said, Malory's "fundamental merit is not so much his Latin fluency and facility as his art of combining pathos and simplicity, romance and epic straightforwardness. His language has all the strength of an oration, all the ease of a popular tale." [53] Nevertheless, the greatness of the *Morte Darthur* is not merely in how Malory changed his sources or in how he expressed himself. Although Vinaver describes Malory's style as the "one important and unchallengeable quality" of the *Morte Darthur*,[54] P. E. Tucker speaks of Malory as "at times a wayward and even a careless writer." [55]

What must be realized is that there exists in the *Morte Darthur* a totality larger than the content and style of Malory and his sources. The other writers who used the legends before Malory, however, cannot be viewed as merely his predecessors and then dismissed. As D. S. Brewer remarks, "Sometimes the effect of the book is due primarily to Malory's source, and sometimes it is due primarily to Malory's own personal contribution," but distinguishing "between what is derived and what is personal . . . cannot affect our final judgment on the total work of art." [56] A useful analogy has been drawn by an anonymous reviewer of Vinaver's 1947 edition in the *Times Literary Supplement*. We should approach Malory's work, the reviewer writes, "not as we approach Liverpool Cathedral but as we approach Wells Cathedral. At Liverpool we see what a particular artist invented. At Wells we see something on which many generations laboured, which no man foresaw or intended as it now is." [57]

But not only must Malory's work be seen as formed by many hands. It must furthermore be remembered that, just as the work stands apart from its author, though it passed through Malory in order to be what it is, so does it exist apart from all other works in the Arthurian tradition that may have exerted both direct and indirect influences on Malory. Although in a sense it is possible to see two umbilical cords nourishing the work, one linking it to Malory and a second joining it to other Arthurian writings, it is necessary at some point to view the *Morte Darthur* as a work from which these cords have been cut. No matter what went into the work, it has to be seen as a whole in its own right and as doing something on its own terms. To approach the problem in another way, it may even be said that Malory's work and all its sources, both direct and indirect, have become indissolubly united; and there exists from the union "the hoole book" that must be discussed for itself.

Consequently, although many of the points in the commentary that follows may be seen as valid interpretations of episodes found, for example, in one of the romances in the Vulgate Cycle, such a fact does not mean that these points should not be regarded as valid interpretations of Malory's *Morte Darthur*, as it has existed from the late fifteenth century, in both Caxton's edition and the Winchester manuscript.

# CHAPTER 2

## *The Birth of the Ideal*

### I  *The Ambiguous Beginning*

THE first section of the *Morte Darthur*, which Eugène Vinaver
has termed the *Tale of Arthur*, corresponds to Caxton's Books
I–IV. Malory's source was the French prose romance known as
the *Suite du Merlin*, a romantic continuation of the material
found in the prose redaction of Robert de Boron's *Merlin*. This
work, dating from the thirteenth century, contains a miscellany of
Arthurian material organized in terms of three main episodes: the
life and death of the enchanter Merlin; the wars of Arthur against
those knights who oppose his rule; and the treacherous machina-
tions of Arthur's half sister, Morgan le Fay. Although the actual
version of the *Suite* used by Malory is unknown, it is still possible
to compare his version to that found in extant French manuscripts
—especially the Huth manuscript and the so-called Cambridge
manuscript, both in the British Museum—to get an idea of how he
handled his sources.[1] It appears that, in general, Malory first of all
omitted what was superfluous to showing the origin of the world
of the Round Table, its initial difficulties, and its subsequent successes under Arthur; and, second, he related the story so as to
make the action of the three main episodes appear in strict sequence, thus reducing the *entrelacement* that marks the French.
In effect, as Thomas L. Wright says, he used the French work "as
a sourcebook to implement, rather than to determine, his Arthurian scheme." [2]

The *Suite du Merlin* begins with the history of Arthur's predecessors, specifically with a detailed account of the supernatural
events surrounding the birth of Merlin and with a history of the
reigns of Pendragon, Arthur's uncle, and Uther, Arthur's father.
Malory, however, omits all this early material, which occupies
about one-fifth of the *Suite;* and, beginning, as it were, *in medias
res,* he starts with the details of Arthur's conception: "Hit befel in

the dayes of Uther Pendragon, when he was kynge of all Englond and so regned, that there was a myghty duke in Cornewaill that helde warre ageynst hym long tyme, and the duke was called the duke of Tyntagil" (2). The reader is immediately taken into a world different from the present (different from that even in Malory's time). It is unimportant how the reader got there, and it does not matter whether or not he is even familiar with the characters he finds in this world. The change becomes a *fait accompli* before the reader is even aware, and he accepts as realities the people and the action in this world in which he now finds himself. There is no need for Malory to introduce his characters to the reader, for what they had been doing before the story opened is irrelevant to his purpose. He does not have to explain either the character of Uther or the earlier fights between this king and the usurping Saxons. Here Uther is a powerful king of Britain, a titanic figure who becomes Arthur's father. Nor is Merlin seen as having a past. Sought by one of Uther's knights, he appears as the aged and ageless wise man, always at hand to help. He needs no introduction, for his function in the *Tale of Arthur* soon becomes clearly defined.

In this tale the initial section—called by Vinaver "Merlin"—may be regarded as falling into two parts: the first shows the coming of Arthur and the assertion of his right to be king; the second, the sins and troubles that menace Arthur and his realm and that will ultimately be instrumental in causing the destruction of his new order. It is almost as if this initial chapter of Malory's Arthur-saga is an overture containing two great themes—prosperity and happiness on the one hand, and misfortune and trouble on the other—with each theme apparently juxtaposed against the other. Throughout the chapter, the figure guiding the movement and acting as the obvious unifying principle is Merlin, the supernatural figure who gives meaning to everything that happens and is to happen. It is Merlin who enables Uther to sleep with Igrayne and so conceive Arthur, who foretells the birth of Arthur, who—far more than in the French—guides Arthur, who interprets the future significance of the adventures, and who generally gives this initial section the stamp of magic it possesses.

After the conception and birth of Arthur and the death of Uther (2-7), the emphasis in the first part of the "Merlin" is on Arthur's asserting his right to be king. The action is centered around a magical sword that can be removed from a rock only by the chosen king (7–14). The sword in the rock first appears to Uther's knights on Christmas Day; and, although all try to pull it out, all fail. Arthur, unknown son of Uther, first removes it on New Year's Day but is subsequently called upon by the disgruntled noblemen to repeat this act on Epiphany, Candlemas, Easter, and Pentecost. The act seems to have a significance that is almost ritualistic and that definitely links the coming of Arthur and his new Order of Knights of the Round Table with Christ and the coming to earth of the Christian Church. In particular, the book's beginning with the coming of Arthur corresponds to the Christian year's beginning with Advent, the celebration of the Coming of the Hero, the Savior. In Christianity, the time of Advent, traditionally a preparation for Christmas, also corresponds to the period of darkness between the fall of man and the birth of Christ. In Malory's work, this period of darkness is suggested by the barren time following the death of Uther Pendragon; for, as Malory writes, "Thenne stood the reame in grete jeopardy long whyle" (7).

It is not necessary to make a Christian allegory out of the *Morte Darthur* to see that Arthur is presented initially as the savior of the world. After the death of Uther when the land is, as it were, in darkness, Merlin tells the Archbishop of Canterbury to call together all the lords of the land at Christmas time "for this cause, that Jesu, that was borne on that nyghte, that He wold of His grete mercy shewe some myracle, as He was come to be Kynge of mankynde, for to shewe somme myracle who shold be rightwys kynge of this reame" (7). The miracle Christ shows is the sword in the rock, and his choice as "rightwys kynge" is Arthur, who has been living apart from the court under the protection of the supernatural being, Merlin.

At Christmas, then, a divine sign in the form of the sword in the rock is given to the world. On New Year's Day—in Christianity, the Feast of the Circumcision—Arthur is revealed to the world by being able to pull out the sword. The Circumcision symbolically signifies the coming of the new man, the *novus homo;* and it also typifies the submission of the Incarnate God to the ordinances of the flesh—to the law of nature. Although Arthur has lived before this New Year's Day, he has been merely a man; in fact, he has been something of a rustic churl, simple, even naïve, serving his foster father, Ector, and his foster brother, Kay. On New Year's Day, however, Arthur leaves his old life, that of the *vetus homo*, and lives entirely in his new role of Christ's chosen king.

At the Feast of the Epiphany on January 6—traditionally the holy day celebrating the Manifestation of Christ's glory—Arthur repeats the significant act that reveals his presence in the world. Again he is called upon to remove the sword at Candlemas, February 2—the Feast of the Purification and the climax of the rites celebrating the Incarnation of Christ—and again at Easter—the holy day celebrating the Resurrection and the beginning of a new and glorious life.

The last time Arthur performs the feat that identifies him as the true king is at the Feast of Pentecost, fifty days after Easter and ten days after the Feast of the Ascension of Christ. Pentecost, celebrating the great awakening that came to the world after Christ ascended into Heaven, refers specifically to the descent to the world of the Holy Spirit, an act enabling the new order—represented by the Church—to come about. In Malory, Arthur's success with the sword on Pentecost is immediately followed by cries from the commons: "We wille have Arthur unto our kyng! We wille put hym no more in delay, for we all see that it is Goddes wille that he shalle be our kynge, and who that holdeth ageynst it we wille slee hym" (11). The new order is thus made possible; in Malory it is the Order of the Round Table, the fellowship of chivalry, that comes to the world with and through Arthur.

Symbolically, then, the most important event in the first part of the *Tale of Arthur* is not the coming of Arthur—as a savior or Christ figure—but rather the beginning of a new society, one that is seen in Christian terms. Were the coming of Arthur to be what was emphasized, it would have been more appropriate for the realm to accept him as king on Christmas, or Easter, or perhaps on Ascension Day—a day not even mentioned in the tale. To have him be successful on Pentecost is to emphasize the new world to exist because of Arthur. It is to be a world uniting church and state, and Arthur is to be lord of this order; he is, in effect, to be Emperor of the Holy Roman Empire, a role clearly seen in Malory's next tale. Pentecost, which occurs generally around the time of the summer solstice, is the last great holy day in the Christian year before Advent the next winter. The half of the year following Pentecost is mostly occupied by a series of vaguely defined Sundays after Pentecost, during which time the Church rehearses the ministry and miracles of Christ; but, more important, this part of the Christian year is concerned with the waning of the sun. At the time of greatest darkness, the winter solstice, Christianity again celebrates the birth of Christ; and the cycle begins again.

With Arthur and his order there also come to earth gradual imperfection and disintegration corresponding to the coming of darkness after Pentecost. In the *Morte Darthur* this disintegration reaches a climax in Malory's last tale, in Arthur's final battle with Mordred, which takes place on the day following Trinity Sunday, the first Sunday after Pentecost. Everything that appears in Malory's book, including the Quest of the Holy Grail and the love stories of Tristram and Isode and Lancelot and Guinevere, may thus be seen as happening immediately after the acceptance of Arthur. All the actions in the long narrative are symbolically pushed together to occupy, as it were, one moment in time, one week in the Christian year, and to give the most encompassing sequence of time seen in the *Morte Darthur*. As the Christian year is part of a cycle, so is the life in this Arthur-saga. Joy and sorrow are inextricably joined together, and each follows the other. Just as Christ dies and symbolically returns, so does Arthur after his death in the final battle with Mordred: "Yet som men say in many partys of Inglonde that kynge Arthur ys nat dede, but had by the wyll of oure Lorde Jesu into another place; and men say that he shall com agayne, and he shalle wynne the Holy Crosse. Yet I woll nat say that hit shall be so, but rather I wolde sey: here in thys worlde he chaunged hys lyff. And many men say that there ys wrytten uppon the tumbe thys: HIC IACET ARTHURUS, REX QUONDAM REXQUE FUTURUS" (873). Arthur, like Christ, is the once-and-future king; like Christ, he died but will return to the world. Interestingly, the last knights mentioned in the *Morte Darthur*—Sir Bors, Sir Ector, Sir Blamour, and Sir Bleoberis—go into the Holy Land "thereas Jesu Cryst was quycke and deed"; and there, fighting the Saracens, they die "upon a Good Fryday for Goddes sake" (883).

As the great cycle of life continues, what occurs in the Christian year after Good Friday is the Feast of Easter when the dead hero lives once again.

The encompassing framework of the Christian year is pertinent not only to the *Tale of Arthur* but also to the whole of the *Morte Darthur*. To read Malory as if one were reading a continuous narrative is to bring a false premise to the work. Along with straightening out and simplifying his French sources, Malory, as several critics have realized, used an internal time scheme that resulted in what R. M. Lumiansky has termed "retrospective narrative." This retrospective narrative enabled Malory, as Charles Moorman has pointed out, "to present clearly and with great emphasis his total concept of the meaning of the traditional Arthurian story without at the same time diffusing the force of that concept in the maze of chronological sequence." This is "a method of presentation which blocks out its episodes in structural and thematic units." [3] While retrospective narrative is doubtless present in the *Morte Darthur*, the movement in terms of themes containing chronological sequence may also be seen as part of a larger movement that makes the actions of the knights and the entire existence of the Order of the Round Table part of the Christian year and that causes the existence of this new Order to be symbolically meaningful.

The second part of the "Merlin" suggests what the fate of Arthur's new Order will be. In two subdivisions, it first shows in detail Arthur's fights with the nobles and kings, the old order that will not accept him or his rule. Although Arthur defeats these kings in several battles, he is unable at this time to achieve total victory. Merlin predicts that Arthur will ultimately win, but his victory is to be in the future. Here Malory is more concerned with revealing something of the trouble that has been in the land and that is to be in the future of Arthur and the realm than with showing the end of this trouble.

Although the battles are not in themselves important in deciding anything, they are significant insofar as they present concrete proof of the worth of Arthur and his new Order. Arthur is the new king; and with his new allies, King Bors and King Ban, he stands up against the old order, the titanic figures belonging to the older generation. The battles, taken as a whole, play an obvious thematic role in this first section of the *Tale of Arthur;* but they, nevertheless, give the impression of being too long or too detailed, or of being generally out of proportion to the other events in the chapter. One may know that in comparison with the battles of interminable length detailed in the *Suite du Merlin,* those in Malory are strikingly abridged, but such a fact does not justify or show a reason for the extensive account of battles in the *Tale of Arthur.* In them Malory does not give merely an indication of the trouble to come to the land. Nor does he present only a panoramic picture of the fighting, telling what goes on here, there, and then somewhere else. Rather, he is like a camera that gives a wide-angle view followed by a series of close-up pictures. His wide-angle view is sufficient to suggest trouble; his close-up pictures, on the other hand, show the actions of individual knights, such as Sir Kay and Sir Lucas, and reveal in striking detail the prowess and valor of these representative warriors. These initial battles may be seen as the first tests of the knights making up Arthur's new Order, and the close-ups seem designed to reveal the fine showing the men make. At the same time, Malory praises the leaders of Arthur's enemy. Although these warriors, such as King Lot and King Uriens, are here Arthur's foes, they had been allies of his father, and some are later to be his own allies. Consequently, their prowess is emphasized here at the beginning of the *Morte Darthur.*

Still another reason for the detailed picture Malory gives of the fighting is to show the comradeship and courtesy of the warriors. Over and over, acts of courtesy go hand in hand with acts of valor, and at times the combat almost seems to be one in which the victor will be he who is most courteous and gentle:

Whan sir Kay saw sir Gryfflet on foote, he rode unto kynge Nentres and smote hym downe, and ledde his horse unto sir Gryfflette and horsed hym agayne. Also sir Kay with the same spere smote downe kynge Lotte and hurte hym passynge sore. That saw the Kynge with the Hondred Knyghtes and ran unto sir Kay and smote hym downe, and toke hys horse and gaff hym kynge Lotte, whereof he seyde gramercy. Whan sir Gryfflet saw sir Kay and sir Lucas de Butler on foote, he with a sherpe spere grete and square rode to Pynnel, a good man of armys, and smote horse and man downe, and than he toke hys horse and gaff hym unto sir Kay.

Than kynge Lotte saw kynge Nentres on foote, he ran unto Meliot de la Roche and smote hym downe horse and man, and gaff hym (to kynge Nentres) the horse and horsed hym agayne. Also the Kynge with the Hondred Knyghtes saw kynge Idres on foote, he ran unto Gwyniarte de Bloy and smote hym downe horse and man, and gaff kynge Idres the horse and horsed hym agayne. Than kynge Lotte smote downe Clarinaus de la Foreyste Saveage and gaff the horse unto duke Estans.

(21–22)

Such courtesy, which to a modern reader may appear rather absurd, is very important both to Malory and to the knights of the world of chivalry. To them, it is more important to save a friend than to kill an enemy. Also, although the fighting is fierce, the knights on each side respect those on the other and do not refrain from voicing their admiration. When King Lot sees Arthur's ally, King Bors, he exclaims: "Jesu defende us from dethe and horryble maymes, for I se well we be in grete perell of dethe; for I se yondir a kynge, one of the moste worshipfullyst men, and the best knyghtes of the worlde be inclyned unto his felyship" (24). In like manner Bors' brother, King Ban, refers to his foes as "the beste fyghtynge men and knyghtes of moste prouesse that ever y saw other [or] herde off speke" (27). To summarize, these battles so detailed in the "Merlin" have at least two important functions: first, they reveal something of the trouble and unrest that Arthur must face and that his Order must correct; and, second, they reveal the worthiness—the prowess and courtesy—of the warriors that will later sit at the Round Table.

The second division of the "Merlin" (30–44) may seem at first reading to be merely a series of unconnected adventures that have neither unity nor direction. On close analysis, however, one sees that various kinds of sorrows and sins are revealed and that Arthur is presented as responsible for them. The initial sins shown are those of the flesh, and the one emphasized is lechery. Arthur first copulates with Lyonors, "a passynge fayre damesell," conceiving Borre; he then casts his eye on Guinevere, "and ever afftir he loved hir"; but the greatest act of lechery is his copulating with Margawse, who is not only wife of King Lot and mother of Gawain, Gaherys, Agravain, and Gareth, but also, though unknown to Arthur, his own sister. The product of this incestuous union is Mordred, who later usurps both Arthur's kingdom and his wife,

Guinevere, thereby fulfilling the prophecy Merlin utters to Arthur: "ye have done a thynge late that God ys displesed with you, for ye have lyene by youre syster and on hir ye have gotyn a childe that shall destroy you and all the knyghtes of youre realme" (35). The trouble revealed in this second section of the "Merlin" is integrally linked to the carnal sin committed by Arthur. Also the wondrous happenings that follow ostensibly occur because of his sins and are in themselves symbolic of future events.

The episode immediately following Arthur's union with Margawse tells of a "mervaylous dreme" Arthur had, one "whereof he was sore adrad. . . . hym thought [it seemed to him] there was com into hys londe gryffens and serpentes, and hym thought they brente and slowghe all the people in the londe; and than he thought he fought with them and they dud hym grete harme and wounded hym full sore, but at the laste he slew hem" (32–33). After this obviously prophetic dream, Arthur sees a "grete harte" which he chases. The stag hunt is traditionally the prelude to a supernatural event. To follow this magical animal is, in effect, to go deep into the world of faerie; and Arthur sees next "the strongeste [strangest] beste that ever he saw or herde of" (33). Again he falls asleep and soon sees approaching a knight on foot who takes his horse so as to follow the strange beast, identified parenthetically by Malory as the "questynge beste." Arthur then sits as "in a study" (34).

In these scenes it is difficult to distinguish when Arthur is asleep from when he is awake. It is almost as if time has ceased, and all that appears is a shadowy play of figures, a play that is more a symbolic comment on the action of the story than a part of the actual narrative itself. The knight that appears to Arthur is King Pellinore, a figure seen several times in the *Tale of Arthur*. It is surely he who fights and wounds the young knight Gryflet (38); it is likewise he who fights with Arthur, defeats him, and would have killed him had not Merlin interceded. Pellinore is also identified by Merlin as one of the best knights in the world and—in words not in the French—as the future father of Sir Perceval and Sir Lamorak. He is also supposed to be the man who will reveal to Arthur the name of Arthur's illegitimate son, who "shall be the destruccion of all thys realme" (41). Pellinore's presence seems to be an indication of the future trouble in store for Arthur's realm.

At the same time, his quest—the search for the questing beast—seems to stand as a forecast of the later one that will occupy Palomides in the *Book of Tristram*, and of the final, greatest one of all, the Quest of the Holy Grail that will be attempted by all the Knights of the Round Table and that will be achieved by only a few select knights, including Pellinore's son, Perceval.

Other episodes in this section of the "Merlin" reveal other sins in Arthur and in his realm. It cannot be accidental that in this section troubles come in many forms, such as envoys from Rome demanding tribute from Arthur and messengers from King Royns demanding both Arthur's homage and his beard. These episodes are not symbolic, or at least are not in the sense that the scenes centering around Pellinore are. Nor are these troubles concluded within this *Tale of Arthur*. Like the fights with the rebelling kings, they continue on—the second tale in Malory's Arthur-saga is, for example, the account of the trouble Arthur has with Rome and, in fact, describes the coming of the messengers as if it were a new event. These episodes seem to be included in the *Tale of Arthur,* specifically in the "Merlin," to reveal other kinds of trouble in the land and other sins in Arthur, especially the sin of pride. Not only are the demands from Rome and from Royns made out of pride, but also each demand requires Arthur to be humble and to give homage. Arthur's refusal and his defiance of the demands make him likewise a prey to pride. In response to King Royns' demand, for example, Arthur says it is "the moste orgulus [proud] and lewdiste [ill-mannered] message that evir man had isente unto a kynge." Continuing, Arthur says of Royns, "or hit be longe to, he shall do me omage on bothe his knees, other ellis he shall lese hys hede" (43). Although Arthur's refusal to submit is in one sense good—it reveals him as a resolute, courageous king—in another it is bad in that its expression reveals a pride in Arthur that makes him imperfect as a Christian hero.

The imperfection in Arthur caused by the presence of lechery and pride—sins of the flesh and of the spirit—shows up clearly in a strange scene that is the final episode in the "Merlin." Merlin tells Arthur that the man who will ultimately destroy the realm has been born on May Day, a traditional day for kings to be challenged for both their realms and their queens.[4] Arthur then gathers together all the children born on this day, puts them in a ship, and sets them adrift at sea. When the ship is wrecked, all the children are killed but Mordred, who, as the summary states, is rescued and brought up by a foster father. Later, Mordred comes to Arthur's court where, ironically, he is made a knight of the Round Table. In this final episode Arthur assumes more the role of Herod than of Christ, and Mordred seems more the young, persecuted hero than the arch-villain. The ambiguity suggested here marks the rest of the tale. Although the lords of Arthur's land were "displeased" with Arthur's action of killing the children, "many putte the wyght [blame] on Merlion more than of Arthure. So what for drede and for love, they helde their pece" (44). Fear and love are inextricably intertwined and remain so throughout the tale. The good is joined with the bad, and the rest of the *Tale of Arthur* likewise reveals the workings of this mixture.

## II  *The Force of Destiny*

The forecasts and prophecies of the "Merlin" also serve to suggest how important a role fate plays in the Arthurian world described by Malory. This emphasis on fate, which reveals man's actions as parts in a great play, parts from which man cannot escape even though he might try, continues and is heightened in the second section of the *Tale of Arthur,* "Balin, or the Knight with the Two Swords" (Caxton's Book II). In this story, which could easily exist by itself, Malory shows in detail the workings out of fate. Again the source is the *Suite du Merlin,* and again Malory strikingly reduces the original. It is curious, however, that in shortening his original, Malory seems to have omitted most of the references to fate. But, contrary to Eugène Vinaver's view, such omission does not represent "Malory's failure to understand the basic significance of the story";[5] for Malory's changes result in something of an understatement that is very dramatic. Specifically, as Laura Hibbard writes, the sense of fate in Malory "depends not upon an outward word, but upon an inner mood and atmosphere." In fact, as she continues, it is Malory alone "who releases the tragic primary episodes of the story from trivial and unrelated things, who has focussed all the interest on the figure of Balin, and who has enhanced . . . the sense of mystery and of 'swift oncoming doom.' " [6]

The story of Balin also has a symbolic function, for it may be

seen as presenting an analogy to Arthur's fortunes. In this sense
what happens to Balin, the rash man, acts as a forecast of what
will happen to Arthur. Fate appears, however, not as a force
against which the hero must fight but as a power holding sway over
individual actions and over the world of man. Just as Balin cannot
escape the future laid out for him because of his rashness, so, it
will be found, neither can Arthur. It is not that everything is pre-
determined, for the story emphasizes over and over the consequences of human actions, both the rash and the well thought out.
From the beginning Balin is shown as the unfortunate, and his
achievements are mixed with misfortunes. The story tells how he
achieves a sword brought to court by a damsel of Lady Lyle of
Avalon and how in full view of Arthur and his court he uses the
sword to cut off the head of the Lady of the Lake, who had been
responsible for the death of Balin's mother. After being exiled by
Arthur for his rash act, Balin wins back his favor by capturing Arthur's foe, King Royns. He has many adventures that invariably
turn out disastrously, until finally he fights an anonymous conflict
with his brother, Balan, in which both are killed.

In one sense, Balin chooses his fate; in another, he is chosen by
fate for his adventures. The damsel from Lady Lyle brings a
sword that can be drawn only by a knight who "muste be a passynge good man of hys hondys and of his dedis, and withoute
velony other [or] trechory and withoute treson" (45). No one in
Arthur's court including Arthur himself, who has been shown as
sinful, can draw the sword except the poor knight Balin. It is significant that Balin is chosen as hero in much the same way that
Arthur is recognized as king. Both are picked almost in spite of
their outward circumstances. But the chosen man in this instance
is not just a hero; as the episode shows, he is also a scapegoat.
When asked to return the sword he has gained, Balin refuses; and
the damsel informs him that, as a consequence, "ye shall sle with
that swerde the beste frende that ye have and the man that ye
moste love in the worlde, and that swerde shall be youre destruccion." Not daunted by this fearful prophecy, Balin answers: "I
shall take the aventure . . . that God woll ordayne for me"
(47). From this point on, everything that happens to Balin is rendered explicitly ambiguous.

At the beginning of the chapter he had been a poor knight in

Arthur's disfavor. Now, noticed by the king, he has apparently every chance of recouping his fortunes. But when the Lady of the Lake rides in and demands the head of either Balin or the damsel, only to have Balin cut off *her* head, he again falls out of favor with the king. Balin's violent action, which may in itself be justified since the Lady of the Lake had killed Balin's mother, is rash because committed in the presence of the king. Although of excellent character, Balin "gropes in a world of no established standards, where the finest purpose and the truest instincts of untutored honor do but lead a man into ever worse blunders and failures." [7] To maintain his family's honor as well as his own, Balin not only violates the honor of Arthur's court and attacks a person to whom Arthur is indebted but also kills a lady. The rashness and insensitivity seen in this action might be called Balin's tragic flaws; in a sense, they act as the cause of what happens to him.

The ambiguity continues, first, in the form of evaluations of the actions. Merlin calls the damsel who had brought the sword the "falsist damesell that lyveth" and at the same time praises Balin, now in Arthur's disfavor, saying, "there lyvith nat a knyght of more prouesse than he ys" (50–51). Also, the ambiguity is to be seen in incidents that occur after Balin's exile from Arthur's court. Challenged by Launceor, an angry knight from Arthur's court, Balin kills him in fair combat. But then a lady rushes forward, sees Launceor lying dead, and immediately kills herself. Merlin appears and blames Balin for not preventing the death of the lady. He predicts that, because of her death, Balin will "stryke a stroke moste dolerous that ever man stroke, excepte the stroke of oure Lorde Jesu Cryste. . . . and thorow that stroke, three kyngdomys shall be brought into grete poverté, miseri and wrecchednesse twelve yere." In response Balin says that, if he believed this prophecy, he would kill himself: "I wolde sle myself to make the a lyer" (54). At this point there is what may be regarded as a pause in the troubles of Balin. He and his brother, Balan, capture King Royns and deliver him to Arthur, then stay on to help Arthur fight and defeat Royns' brother, King Nero, and his ally, King Lot. But after these fights, when the two brothers separate, Balin's misfortunes continue.

While a woeful knight rides in the protection of Balin, the

knight is killed by Garlon, a false knight able to make himself invisible. After another companion of Balin is killed by Garlon, Balin rides searching for this false knight. He finds him in the castle of King Pellam—later called King Pelles (632)—and again Balin is well-intentioned but rash. He kills Garlon in the presence of his brother, King Pellam. To escape the wrath of the king, Balin retreats until he sees "a mervaylous spere strangely wrought" (64); and with this he gives Pellam "the dolorouse stroke," thereby fulfilling Merlin's prediction. The castle falls around him; three countries are destroyed; and Balin rides out of the land fleeing both the destruction around him and the cries of people who encounter him: "A, Balyne! Thou hast done and caused grete dommage in thys contreyes! . . . And doute nat but the vengeaunce woll falle on the at the laste!" (65).

After fleeing the Waste Land he has unintentionally created, Balin becomes "passynge fayne," but his contentment is soon changed to more grief. He meets a knight who is sad because his lady will not see him. Trying to help, Balin goes to talk to the lady, but finds her lying "with the fowlest knyghte that ever he sawe." He tells what he saw to the sad knight, who kills the two lovers and then stabs himself. Balin immediately leaves "lest folke wold say he had slayne them" (66). In his way, Balin is something of a Midas: almost everything he touches is destroyed, and he must justly be called the slayer. Death is with him, all around him, and is even to be identified with him. Baleful are the fortunes of Balin, and the terrible fate in store for him is now made immediate by a succession of omens and supernatural events.

Balin approaches a castle and sees a cross on which is written, "it is not for no knyght alone to ryde toward this castel" (67). An old man, who speaks and then vanishes, tells him to turn and depart; but Balin, who accepts whatever comes his way, will not turn back: "And soo he herd an horne blowe as it had ben the dethe of a best. 'That blast,' said Balyn, 'is blowen for me, for I am the pryse, and yet am I not dede' " (67). Speaking of this scene, Vinaver has no sympathy for Malory's handling of his source; for Malory has apparently discarded many elements of the magical or supernatural that Vinaver feels are important to the understanding of the tale.[8] Nevertheless, as C. S. Lewis has cogently pointed out, "Two enchanters, two ghosts, two ferlies are always half as impressive as one." [9] In reducing his story and its wonders, Malory may, in fact, have heightened its mystery and its suspense. At this point in the story of Balin, the reader knows that Balin's death is imminent. The developing story follows a single, uncomplicated thread; and, whereas actions of only related interest are omitted, dread and anxiety increase.

Balin meets lords and ladies who require him to fight a knight on an island. Before the fight, however, he is persuaded to exchange his shield for a larger one; consequently he makes another error in judgment, as he discovers when he reaches the island. There he encounters a damsel who says, "O, knyght Balyn, why have ye lefte your owne sheld? Allas! ye have put yourself in grete daunger, for by your sheld ye shold have ben knowen" (67). Balin answers, repeating his earlier acceptance of life and the working of fate: "Me repenteth . . . that ever I cam within this countrey; but I maye not torne now ageyne for shame, and what aventure shalle falle to me, be it lyf or dethe, I wille take the adventure that shalle come to me" (67). The adventure is the fight with Balan in which both brothers die.

The story of Balin is in its own right a tragedy comparable to those in the Greek drama. Balin, the rash man, may be viewed as learning how significant all human actions are. From confidently accepting whatever comes his way, Balin proceeds until he learns that there is a web joining together everything he does as well as everything that happens to him. Still, even at the end, Balin does not despair. He continues to live his life facing whatever he encounters. In terms of the medieval idea of tragedy, the tale shows the omnipresence of Fortune in the world and, in this sense, the insignificance of the human will as a determinant of the future. Fortune raises a man up on her wheel, then hurls him down. Prosperity and adversity are inextricably joined together, and every man feels both. In terms of Malory's Arthur-saga, Balin is an insensitive sinner against both the laws of God and the honor of man—he not only kills the lady, but does so in Arthur's presence —and the tale shows how he pays for his sins. Furthermore, Balin's story acts as a comment on Arthur's future. Just as Balin sinned and paid for it, so, it is implied, will Arthur. Also, just as Balin brought in a Waste Land that is ambiguous, so will Arthur's

Order, that of the Round Table, bring back life to the world. It will be an ambiguous sort of life, however, since the highest action of the Round Table, the Quest of the Holy Grail, acts in itself as something removing men from concern for this world. Also, the fight between Balin and his brother, Balan, may be seen as a symbolic prelude to the chaos ultimately coming to the land: specifically, the final fight of the *Morte Darthur*, that between Arthur and his son, Mordred.

There are many other ways in which the story of Balin is linked to the action of both the *Tale of Arthur* and the whole of the *Morte Darthur*. Such events already mentioned—such as Arthur's fight to be ruler of the British Isles and, in particular, his conflict with King Royns—appear in this second section and serve to tie the adventures of Balin to the adventures of Arthur himself. Balin's adventures are thus linked to the past, and they are also joined to events of the future. Human actions, far from being complete in themselves, exist in an unfinished state. Even with Malory's process of episodic simplification, one action is again and again shown to be related to another and another. Everything is joined to everything else, and the joining is revealed through the device of forecast. Following three burials, there are three prophecies strikingly linking past and future, death, and that which, because of death, comes to life.

After Balin kills Launceor, and his lady kills herself, the double death is rendered significant by King Mark of Cornwall, uncle to Sir Tristram, who comes forward to commemorate the love of Launceor and the lady and to lament their deaths. Also, Merlin prophesies that the spot on which the lovers died will be the site of a great fight between two knights to be known as "the trewyst lovers"—that is, Sir Lancelot and Sir Tristram (54). Not only are the great loves of the Round Table forecast but so, indirectly, is the Quest of the Holy Grail, which may in one sense be regarded as the central adventure of the *Morte Darthur*. Merlin says explicitly that, because Balin did not prevent Launceor's lady from killing herself, Balin should give the Dolorous Stroke causing the Waste Land. In the French *Suite du Merlin* the Dolorous Stroke has no connection with the death of Launceor's lady. There it seems to be the punishment for Balin's entering the Grail chamber and touching the sacred lance. Also, although in the French this

[ 50 ]

Dolorous Stroke, along with the Balin story itself, acts as a prelude to the Grail Quest, in Malory the Stroke may be viewed primarily as a punishment for Balin's rash actions.[10] But even though Malory's main concern here is with rash actions, and even though he later gives another source for the Dolorous Stroke (708), he would still seem to be using it to tie the tale of Balin to the themes and motifs of the story of Arthur.

The second major prophecy occurs after Balin and his brother help Arthur in his fight against Nero and Lot. During the fight Lot is killed by "the Knyght with the Strange Beste" (58), Pellinore. Because of this action, says Malory, Pellinore will later be killed by Lot's son, Gawain. Arthur buries Lot in a magnificent tomb on which Merlin places twelve candles. These burn day and night and, as Merlin tells Arthur, will go out only "aftir the adventures of the Sankgreall that shall com amonge you and be encheved." He also tells Arthur again of the Dolorous Stroke that Balin will give, and, continuing his forecast, he warns Arthur always to keep the scabbard of Excalibur, his magic sword, "for ye shall lose no bloode whyle ye have the scawberde uppon you" (59). Here, in place of what exists in the *Suite du Merlin* as a long digression, Malory inserts an account of how Morgan le Fay, Arthur's treacherous sister, will take the scabbard from Arthur and trick him into fighting his knight, Accolon, and of how Arthur will fight with Mordred.

Forecasts of the Grail adventure are interspersed throughout the story of Balin in general and throughout this part of it in particular. A damsel accompanying Balin is seized in a castle to be bled because, as Balin is told, only a silver dish full of blood from "a clene mayde and a kynges doughter" can cure the lady of the castle (62). Malory then states that it will be the sister of Perceval, offspring of Pellinore, who will, during the Grail Quest, finally give her life to cure the lady. Also after Balin gives King Pellam the Dolorous Stroke, Malory summarizes—in a passage not in the French—what will happen and particularly suggests the importance and meaning of the Holy Grail:

And kynge Pellam lay so many yerys sore wounded, and myght never be hole tylle that Galaad the Hawte Prynce heled hym in the queste of the Sankgreall. For in that place was parte of the bloode of oure Lorde

Jesu Cryste, which Joseph off Aramathy brought into thys londe. And there hymselff lay in that ryche bedde. And that was the spere whych Longeus smote oure Lorde with to the herte. And kynge Pellam was nyghe of Joseph his kynne, and that was the moste worshipfullist man on lyve in tho dayes, and grete pité hit was of hys hurte, for thorow that stroke hit turned to grete dole, tray and tene [pain and sorrow]. (64–65)

The final episode of the Balin story, as well as the third great prophecy, takes place after the deaths of the two brothers. On the spot of their battle, Merlin "lete make there a bedde, that ther shold never man lye therin but he wente oute of his wytte. Yet Launcelot de Lake fordyd [destroyed] that bed thorow his noblesse" (70). Merlin also takes Balin's special sword that he had received from the messenger of Lady Lyle of Avalon and puts on it a new pommel that renders it unwieldy. He says the sword will not be handled until it is used by "the beste knyght of the worlde, and that shall be sir Launcelot other ellis Galahad, hys sonne. And Launcelot with hys swerde shall sle the man in the worlde that he lovith beste: that shall be sir Gawayne" (70). The fight between Balin and Balan is therefore linked to another great fight as well as to the final combat between Arthur and Mordred; and Balin may be linked by analogy to Lancelot who, though in many ways more fortunate than Balin, is most directly responsible for the final destruction of the realm. Next, after building a magic bridge, Merlin leaves the scabbard on the island so that "Galaad sholde fynde hit," and he causes Balin's sword to be placed in a marble stone that floats on the water. As Malory says, this is the sword that years later floats down to Camelot to be found by the greatest knight, Sir Galahad, "as hit ys rehersed in THE BOOKE OF THE SANK-GREALL" (70), perhaps a reference to Malory's sixth tale.

Contained in the account of Balin are thus the germs of the great themes of the *Morte Darthur:* the loves of Lancelot and Guinevere and Tristram and Isode, and the Quest of the Holy Grail. Revealing the ultimate causes of these adventures, the "Balin" may be viewed as joined to the "Merlin," which details another great theme: the ultimate destruction of Arthur's realm and his Order of the Round Table. The fate of Balin shows by analogy this same ultimate destruction. Both the "Merlin" and the "Balin" may consequently be regarded as part of a prologue to the main action. In these sections, the main events of the *Morte Darthur* are suggested, and the machinery that causes the main events to come about is put into motion. The reader can believe in the machinery and in the force of destiny behind it because he is able to see how strikingly and violently fate has worked in the case of Balin.

### III  *Stating the Ideals*

Whereas the story of Balin may be regarded as showing in striking fashion the need in the land for ideals and order, the next section of the *Tale of Arthur* (Caxton's Book III), called by Vinaver "Torre and Pellinore," emphasizes the coming about of the Round Table and its ideals of chivalry, loyalty, mercy, and prowess. In "Merlin" the emphasis had been on courtesy among the knights, especially those on Arthur's side. Also revealed there was the great comradeship and courtesy found even between foes. In "Torre and Pellinore," on the other hand, the direction of the courtesy changes; now the knights become aware of the need to be merciful to the defeated and courteous to the helpless. This section thus turns from the masculine world of comradeship to what might be called the feminine world outside the fellowship. The knights must protect and control this world, and, because its inhabitants are weaker than they, they must learn not to take advantage of or to hurt them. This change of direction is described by Malory through parallelling quests made by three of Arthur's knights, but these stories do not stand alone. They are held firmly within a frame that is the Arthur-saga; specifically, they are related to the bringing of the actual Round Table to Arthur's realm and to the explicit creation of the Order of the Round Table, the Order that has been suggested and even imminent since the coming of Arthur as king.

The section begins with a brief summary of Arthur's fight to be recognized as king, telling how he was chosen "by adventure and by grace" (71)—by a combination of chance and divine will, the same combination revealed as controlling what happened to Balin. There then follows Arthur's decision to take a wife. He tells Merlin that he loves Guinevere. Merlin's reply, in Malory's clarification of the French, is that Arthur would be better off with someone else, that "Gwenyver was nat holsom for hym to take to wyff. For he warned hym that Launcelot scholde love hir, and sche hym agayne, and so he turned his tale to the aventures of the Sankegreal" (71). Nothing more is revealed here about these future events; Merlin tells Arthur he will be cuckolded and then abruptly, as it were, changes the subject, and describes the Quest of the Grail. But this Grail Quest represents a new kind of love, one directed at an object beyond this world. In a sense, the Quest may be further viewed as the adventure that ostensibly redeems the sins of the court, as well as the event that is the *raison d' être* of the Round Table.

Along with his daughter, Guinevere, King Lodegraunce presents Arthur with the Round Table, seating one hundred and fifty knights, which Uther Pendragon had previously given to him. The Table, an ancestral possession of Arthur's family, must wait apparently for the special ruler who can bring into existence the order to be associated with it. Arthur is this ruler, and the story now shows him and his adviser, Merlin, searching for the best knights in the land to sit at it and make up the order. In the French *Suite*, the account is somewhat different: Arthur's one wish is to have the Round Table and its knights, and the subsequent power these will give him; he has no feelings about Guinevere. In the *Morte Darthur*, on the other hand, Malory has made Arthur's motives seem noble. He shows Arthur desiring first of all Guinevere, whom he has loved for a long time; but Malory's emphasis still is on the Table and on the search for knights to sit at it.

Young Gawain, Arthur's nephew, asks to be knighted; but, before the ceremony can take place, a poor cowherd enters, bringing with him the youth Torre, who also wants to become a knight. Torre is supposedly the cowherd's son; but, as Merlin reveals, he is really the offspring of King Pellinore. Torre is knighted before Gawain, and Pellinore is seated at a special seat of the Round Table, a seat in which only men "moste of worship" should sit. This seat is next to the "Sege Perelous there shall nevir man sitte but one, and yf there be ony so hardy to do hit he shall be destroyed, and he that shall sitte therein shall have no felowe" (75). Gawain, full of envy because Pellinore and his kin are so honored and full of hatred because Pellinore had slain his father, Lot, wants to kill Pellinore immediately but is restrained by his brother, Gaherys, who gives Gawain good advice throughout the tale. Here Gaherys points that "hit ys beste to suffir tyll another tyme, that we may have hym oute of courte, for and [if] we dud so we shall trouble thys hyghe feste" (75–76). Gaherys's caution and sense of propriety contrast with Gawain's propensity to violence and also with the innocent rashness earlier seen in Balin.

The preliminaries are now finished, and the real narrative contained in the section begins. At the wedding feast of Arthur and Guinevere, Merlin announces that everyone will see "a straunge and a mervailous adventure" (76). A white hart then runs into the hall, chased by a white "brachet" and by sixty black dogs that follow close behind. A knight, knocked over by the hart, picks up the white dog and leaves the hall. Then a lady on a white palfrey enters and asks for the white dog. She is immediately followed by an armed knight who abducts her in spite of her cries for help. Here again appears the magical stag hunt, and every event related to it has some supernatural significance. But Arthur's only response to the events is to be glad they are finished, for the lady had "made such a noyse" (76). Merlin, however, says Arthur must see that the adventure is completed lest he bring "disworshyp" to himself and his feast. Consequently, Merlin calls on Gawain to bring back the white hart, Torre to get the white dog and the knight that had taken it, and Pellinore to find the lady and the armed knight that had abducted her. Before these quests are over, says Merlin, the three knights will experience "mervayles adventures."

The first quest, Gawain's, is in the French a prelude to the Grail Quest and is thus like the Dolorous Stroke incident of the "Balin." But for Malory, who apparently removed the Grail relationship, the quest exists primarily to show improper behavior. Gawain's endeavor is unsuccessful because he lacks knightly virtue. This lack may be seen when, after two preliminary adventures, Gawain, accompanied by Gaherys, sets his greyhounds on the track of the white hart. They follow the animal into a castle and there kill it. A knight then comes out of a chamber and chases the dogs away, killing two of them. Gawain and the knight subsequently fight; the knight asks for mercy; but Gawain, angered because the knight had killed two of his dogs, will not grant it. Just as Gawain raises his sword to kill the knight, a lady rushes in and throws herself on the knight. Unable to hold back his blow, Gawain unintentionally strikes off her head.

Gaherys immediately reprimands Gawain, saying, "ye sholde gyff mercy unto them that aske mercy, for a knyght withoute mercy ys withoute worship" (79). With these words the first great theme of the "Torre and Pellinore" section is stated. Four knights who then ride in accuse Gawain of shaming his knighthood. They repeat Gaherys's reprimand, saying that "a knyght withoute mercy ys dishonoured," and also that Gawain's killing the lady will be to his "grete shame unto the worldys ende" (80). The four knights then fight Gawain and Gaherys and are on the verge of killing the two brothers when four ladies, acting as a court of love, appear and ask for the two shamed knights. The four victorious knights grant their request, consequently showing how different their behavior is from that of Gawain. Although the ladies hold the knights prisoner for a time, they finally release Gawain because he is King Lot's son and King Arthur's nephew. In releasing him, the ladies ironically grant mercy to Gawain and furthermore highlight his shame: they release him not because of his own worth but because of that of his relatives. Gawain is still delinquent, and as penance he must, like the Ancient Mariner with the albatross, "bere the dede lady with hym on thys maner: the hede of her was hanged aboute hys necke, and the hole body of hir before hym on hys horse mane" (81).

Gawain then returns to Arthur's court, bearing the body of a lady rather than the body of the hart. His shame is immeasurable, and an actual court of ladies judges that Gawain, "for ever whyle he lyved to be with all ladyes and to fyght for hir quarels; and ever that he sholde be curteyse, and never to refuse mercy to hym that askith mercy" (81). This episode differs in emphasis from that in the *Suite*, which shows Gawain praised by Merlin and which omits the stress on courtesy. In Malory the chivalric ideal is again stated, this time definitively by a court and by ladies. Although Malory does not explicitly make use of Gawain as a protector of ladies, he, nevertheless, reveals him as such in the final episodes of the *Morte Darthur* when, after his death, Gawain is seen in paradise surrounded by all the women he had helped in his lifetime (865).

The second quest, that of Torre, appears in direct contrast to that of Gawain in which the Arthurian knight's relationship to the outside world was inadequate. Torre, who, as is emphasized, always takes simple hospitality and hears Mass every morning, is an ideal knight. But just as Gawain had been put to what in reality turned out to be a test, so is Torre examined. After several preliminary adventures, he comes to a white pavilion, which he enters and there takes the white dog from a sleeping lady. The lady awakens and says that, if Torre takes the dog, he "woll be mette with and greved." Torre's answer is like Balin's earlier one, "I shall abyde what adventure that commyth by the grace of God" (83). Soon Torre meets a knight who demands the dog. When Torre has vanquished the knight, he asks him to yield, but the knight refuses. Immediately a damsel rides forward and requests a gift from Torre. Torre agrees, and the damsel asks for the head of the vanquished knight and denounces him as the "falsyste" and the "moste outerageous [vicious] knyght that lyvith" (84). Torre says that, rather than have the knight killed, the damsel should allow him to make amends. The damsel, however, replies that reparations are impossible, for the knight killed her brother after she had begged him to be merciful. Torre is consequently faced with the difficult problem of deciding whether he should grant mercy to a man who has refused it to others. The implications are significant, for here the virtue of mercy is shown to have ambiguities. The problem is further complicated when the knight himself asks Torre to grant him mercy. Torre's decision is to fulfil his promise to the damsel, and he consequently cuts off the knight's head. The episode shows that not only is mercy important but so too is a sense of justice. A knight must be able to choose between two alternatives, especially when the morally and ethically correct choice is not obvious.

When Torre returns to Arthur's court, he is praised by all as a man of prowess and courtesy. Merlin predicts that Torre "shall preve a noble knyght of proues as few lyvynge, and jantyl and curteyse and of good tacchys [qualities], and passyng trew of hys promyse, and never shall he outerage [commit excesses]" (85). Torre is thus extolled as a man of moderation, as possessing the invaluable virtue of *mesure*, of not being violent and rash, as was Gawain on his quest.

A third element of chivalry is manifested in Pellinore's quest;

and Pellinore, in terms of his success, occupies a place between Gawain and his son, Torre. As Pellinore rides out, he comes upon a damsel holding a wounded knight in her arms. The damsel begs Pellinore to help; but, as Malory writes, "kynge Pellynore wolde nat tarry, he was so egir in hys queste." When the damsel sees that he will not stop, she prays to God "to sende hym as much nede of helpe as she had, and that he myght feele hit or he deyed" (86). After Pellinore rides off, the wounded knight dies, and the damsel kills herself.

Pellinore soon achieves the lady, the object of his quest; but, before he returns to Arthur's court, he again sees the damsel who had asked him for help. She and the knight with her have been "etyn with lyons othir with wylde bestis, all save the hede" (89–90). Pellinore repents not having stopped to help her; and on the advice of the lady, Nyneve, he takes the damsel's head back with him to court. There, all—but the queen especially in Malory's version—blame him for being too "ferse" in his quest; and Merlin informs him that the damsel was his own daughter. He also repeats the damsel's curse, making it more concrete: "because ye wolde nat abyde and helpe hir, ye shall se youre beste frende fayle you whan ye be in the grettist distresse that ever ye were othir shall be" (91). Pellinore regrets that this should happen but is confident that "God may well fordo desteny" (91). He thus appeals to the Christian idea that Fortune is a servant of God, not a force existing apart from divine will—an idea that is quite different from the view in the French that what fate decrees must come about. Pellinore's flaw is that he lacks the sense of proportion, of *mesure*, found in Torre. Pellinore is *outerageous*, though in a different way from Gawain; and the consequences are vividly seen. Also *outerageous* in a different sense is the lady who killed herself, and Pellinore is right to assert that he is not to blame for her suicide. Although he had a duty to save her, she also had a duty to preserve her own life. Such a point, which seems to be part of Malory's addition to his text, represents a significant advance over the similar situation in the story of Balin, where Balin is blamed for not saving Launceor's lady.

It is likewise vividly seen that the objects of these three quests are insignificant and that the quests act mainly as tests of the knights, tests specifically of the ideals of the Round Table, and as demonstrations of the real need for a code of behavior that all may know. The Order of the Round Table must have what Vida Scudder calls "a standard through which the confused instincts of nascent chivalry may be focused and preserved." [11] Following the three quests, the Order of the Round Table is firmly and finally set up. Now it is more than a group of knights who are valiant and courteous to each other. Because of the "mervayles" that Merlin has shown to the assembled lords, all understand something more of chivalric values and conduct in the outside world. More particularly, the knights now recognize their duty to this world existing outside them, and the chapter ends with a kind of ritualistic oath spoken for all by Arthur:

Than the kynge stablysshed all the knyghtes and gaff them rychesse and londys; and charged them never to do outerage nothir morthir, and allwayes to fle treson, and to gyff mercy unto hym that askith mercy, uppon payne of forfiture of their worship and lordship of kynge Arthure for evirmore; and allwayes to do ladyes, damesels, and jantilwomen and wydowes socour: strengthe hem in hir ryghtes, and never to enforce them, uppon payne of dethe. Also, that no man take no batayles in a wrongefull quarell for no love ne for no worldis goodis. So unto thys were all knyghtis sworne of the Table Rounde, both olde and yonge, and every yere so were they sworne at the hygh feste of Pentecoste.

(91)

This oath has no real equivalent in the *Suite*. There the Round Table ceremony is different in spirit and, also, coming as it does at Arthur's feast before the various quests, different in positon. In Malory the oath is seen as the fulfilment of what was begun at the feast and developed through the quests.[12] Just as Arthur's final assertion of himself as king, heralding the new Order, came at Pentecost, so does the Round Table explicitly come into being at the same feast. Furthermore, the Round Table may be likened to the Christian Church, which also came into existence at the Feast of Pentecost. Like priests of the new way, the Knights of the Round Table now understand what is expected of them as they journey into the world. The new ideal, which is more fully stated here than anywhere else in the *Morte Darthur*, is now firmly manifested; the rest of Malory's book will show what happens to it.

"Torre and Pellinore" is thus of great significance in establishing attitudes and ways of behavior that will act as guides for future actions and episodes. As Thomas L. Wright says, contrasting Malory and the *Suite,* "Where his source wanders in a profusion of incidents mysteriously associated with the Grail, Malory supplies his own theme of emerging order in Camelot." [13] Furthermore, the section suggests more of the trouble to come: specifically, the enmity that will arise among the knights of the Order. The innate hostility between factions, in particular between the families of Lot and Pellinore, will ultimately help cause the disintegration of the realm and the destruction of the new ideals. Just as the great foe of chivalry and its standards is here hinted to be *outerage* or violence—the opposite of *mesure* or proportion—so will personal emotions resulting in inordinate love and inordinate hate, and setting individual against individual, friend against friend, and father against son, be responsible for the end of the Order of the Round Table and of the new world that comes into existence with it. At the same time, treachery toward Arthur is hinted at in a strange scene in the chapter. When Pellinore and Nyneve are returning at night to Arthur's court, they hear two passing knights talking. One speaks of Arthur's court as "such a felyshyp that they may never be brokyn," and the other reveals that he carries with him "the grettist poysen that ever ye herde speke off." He plans to take it to the court, for there "we have a frende ryght nyghe the kynge, well cheryshed, that shall poysen kynge Arthur" (89). The knights then ride off in the darkness, and nothing more is said about the treason. Such a hint serves, however, to show other dangers to the new Order.

## IV   *The Testing of the Order*

Although this short section, corresponding to the first five parts of Caxton's Book IV, has been called by Vinaver "The Death of Merlin and the War with the Five Kings," indicating two divisions, structurally, the section is really formed in three parts with the first (91–93) centering around Merlin again. Throughout the first three sections of the *Tale of Arthur,* Merlin has been not only the prophet and adviser of the king but also the guiding force behind virtually everything that happened. In the first part of this fourth section, he is shown as knowing everything that will occur but as being powerless to control the future. No matter how Merlin may have appeared earlier in relation to the action of the *Tale*, he does not control destiny. Rather he, like the merest mortal, is subject to it. In particular, Merlin, unable to control himself, falls so much in love with Nyneve, the damsel brought to court by Pellinore, that he is, as it were, "in dotage." Nyneve learns Merlin's magical skills, but then, being weary of him and fearing him as "a devyls son," she uses one of his magical spells to trap him in a pit under a great stone, where he remains forever. In being so "assoted" (infatuated) with Nyneve, Merlin shows strikingly the excessive kind of passion that the knights must avoid.

It is necessary that Merlin be removed from the action, for the real function of this section in the *Tale of Arthur* is to show the Order of the Round Table existing as a human order in its own right, not as one receiving continual and direct supernatural guidance from someone associated with the old order before Arthur. If the Order is to succeed, it must succeed on its own; and it must depend primarily on the strength, courtesy, *mesure*, and general worth of its knights. Now that the Order has been established, and its aims and ideals propounded, it must be tested. "The War with the Five Kings" shows this testing and also its result: the Order is on the whole strong and healthy and, consequently, worthy of receiving divine help.

The second part of the section (93–96), the actual war with the five kings, thus functions as the first real test of the Round Table in general and of certain knights in particular. Sir Kay here stands out as a noble warrior. When Arthur and his small group of knights are in camp, Kay recommends that they remain armed; but Gawain and Gryflet counsel disarming. At that moment the great army of the five kings attacks the camp; and Arthur, Guinevere, Kay, Gawain, and Gryflet are forced to flee. As they escape, they encounter the five kings themselves, and it is Kay alone who wants to fight them. To persuade Gawain and Gryflet, Kay says he himself will take on two of the kings and kill them. This he does and consequently acts as a model for the other men, each of whom kills a king. The tide of battle is turned, Arthur's small band of knights is victorious, and Kay is singled out by Guinevere for praise. The first test is thus nobly passed. Against great odds, the Order of the Round Table has won victory and has held together; but there is again the hint of internal disunity. The bad advice and lack of courage of Gawain and Gryflet could have caused everything to be lost.

The third part of the section (96–98) follows directly from the second part. Because eight Knights of the Round Table have been killed in the battle with the five kings, Arthur must replace them. Following the advice of Pellinore, who acts here as Merlin's human surrogate, Arthur agrees to add to the order four older and four younger knights. Among the older warriors is King Uriens, husband of Morgan le Fay and former foe of Arthur, whose presence now shows the emphasis on unity within the Order. For the younger knights Pellinore recommends Gawain, Gryflet, Kay, and either Bagdemagus or Pellinore's son, Torre. Arthur decides to honor Torre at that time, consequently angering Bagdemagus, who then rides away from court. Malory mentions that he has many great adventures but describes in particular only two of them. First, he writes that Bagdemagus "founde a braunche of holy herbe that was the signe of the Sancgreall, and no knyght founde no suche tokyns but [unless] he were a good lyver and a man of prouesse" (98). Second, Bagdemagus is the only man to speak with Merlin while the necromancer is in his pit under the stone. Malory concludes the chapter by saying that Bagdemagus is to be proved a good knight and later is to be given a seat at the Round Table.

Although Bagdemagus's anger may indicate the continuous presence of internal trouble in the new Order, the hints of his adventures are important in linking the present events to future happenings, much as the prophecies of Merlin did in former chapters. The only forecasting occurs before Merlin is imprisoned. With Nyneve he goes to the land of King Ban, Arthur's old ally, where the two see Ban's wife, Elayne, and their young son, Lancelot. While there, Merlin predicts that Lancelot will be "the moste man of worship of the worlde" (92), thus providing a basis for Lancelot's future appearance as the greatest knight of the Order and as the central character of the *Morte Darthur*. Aside from this prophecy, forecasts and suggestions of future action are now not extensive and not emphasized. Of greater immediate importance is the fact that Arthur and his knights—the young ones like Kay and the old like Pellinore—are capable of valor and wisdom. This capability, along with the prediction about Lancelot, is a good sign for the fortunes of the Round Table.

## V  *The Presence of Evil*

The fifth section of the *Tale of Arthur*, corresponding to the first part of Caxton's Book IV (chapters 6–mid 15), is called by Vinaver "Arthur and Accolon." Just as the action in the "Merlin" was followed by the supernatural—the battles followed by a magical stag hunt—so here, after the battle of "The War with the Five Kings," comes magic—and again in the form of a stag hunt. The hunt, as before, acts as a clear sign that supernatural adventures, actions beyond the sphere of ordinary human understanding and control, will follow.

Arthur, Uriens, and Accolon follow a "grete harte" so long and so fast that they ride their horses to death. While on foot they see the hart being attacked by dogs at the side of a "grete watir" (99). Arthur kills the hart, and with this action the knights cross the threshold between the natural and the supernatural and at once find themselves involved in something beyond rational comprehension. They see an ornately decorated ship sailing across the water to them. After going aboard and meeting twelve fair damsels who salute Arthur and welcome him by name, the knights dine and then go to sleep in the royal chambers. On waking, they are conscious that they have been in the power of the supernatural. Uriens discovers that he is back in Camelot in bed with his wife, Morgan le Fay. Arthur finds himself in a dark prison with twenty woeful knights, all prisoners of the false knight, Sir Damas, who is searching for a champion to fight in his place against his good brother, Sir Oughtlake. Rather than help such an evil man, the knights prefer to remain in prison. This decision is a change from Malory's source, for the knights in the French are all willing to fight to escape starvation. In the *Morte Darthur*, however, only Arthur is willing to act as Damas's champion; for, as he puts it, he would rather "fyght with a knyght than to dey in preson" (101). Practical man that he is, Arthur realizes that by fighting he may free himself and the other prisoners.

By singling out Arthur as the only man willing to fight, Malory has made the scene thematically meaningful in terms of the chivalric ideals emphasized throughout the *Tale of Arthur*. The question in fact arises whether Arthur has followed the proper course of action or whether he has violated the chivalric code of conduct. At the end of the "Torre and Pellinore" section all the Knights of the Round Table promise as part of their oath, which is repeated yearly at Pentecost, to "take no batayles in a wrongefull quarell for no love ne for no worldis goodis" (91). Arthur, by fighting for Damas, *is* taking part in a "wrongefull quarell"; but he is not doing so out of avarice or wrath. His sin may be viewed as similar to that of Sir Gawain in the great fourteenth-century English romance, *Sir Gawain and the Green Knight*. Both men are overly concerned with preserving themselves—Arthur also with preserving others—and both knights falter in their conduct. When faced with death or terrible imprisonment, they both reveal an attachment to the self that is perhaps not the sin of *cupiditas* or covetousness, in the usual sense of the word; but it is, nevertheless, excessive in that it makes the characters do what they should know is wrong. Although in both cases there are obvious complicating and alleviating circumstances, Arthur has, without a doubt, succumbed to a temptation; and, because of this failing, he almost dies.

Accolon, the third of the adventuring knights, awakens to find himself "by a depe welles syde within half a foote, in grete perell of deth" (101). Realizing that he, Arthur, and Uriens had been tricked by "fendis" on the ship, he vows to avenge himself on them. But just then a dwarf comes to him from Morgan le Fay, Arthur's sister; presents him with both Arthur's sword, Excalibur, and its magical, life-preserving scabbard; and asks him to fight a knight "lyke as ye promysed hir whan ye spoke laste togedir in prevyté" (102).

At this point the reader might remember Malory's interjected remarks in the Balin story. Merlin had at that point warned Arthur to "kepe well the scawberd of Excaleber," and there then followed a summary of what would happen in the future: "So aftir for grete trust Arthure betoke [entrusted] the scawberde unto Morgan le Fay, hys sister. And she loved another knyght bettir than hir husbande, kynge Uriens, othir Arthure. And she wolde have had Arthure hir brother slayne, and therefore she lete make anothir scawberd for Excaliber lyke it by enchauntement, and gaf the scawberd Excaliber to her lover. And the knyghtes name was called Accolon, that aftir had nere slayne kynge Arthure" (59).

The "Arthur and Accolon" section is the working out of these prophetic words. It is the story of what was summarized in these few lines: but, unless the reader remembers these words, he will find here only vague hints of the underlying treachery. Malory interjects, for example, a remark showing that things are not as they seem. Arthur, thinking he has recognized one of the damsels he sees in Damas's court, tries to place her; but the damsel says she is a stranger to him. At this point Malory comments, "Yet was she false, for she was one of the damesels of Morgan le Fay" (101), a distinct suggestion that a plot exists, behind which is Arthur's cruel sister.

Morgan le Fay plays a significant role in this section and throughout the *Morte Darthur*. As representative of evil she is several times the cause of malevolent happenings. As is seen here in particular, she constantly attempts both to shame Arthur and his knights so as to make them fall from their chivalric ideals and even to kill them, if possible, while they are in a state of sin. As R. M. Lumanisky says, Morgan is for Malory more than "a captious supernatural being who places minor annoyances in the way of Arthur"; rather, in her betrayals of Arthur she reveals "that all is not well in the ideal society, and that the seeds of its tragic downfall are inherent from its inception."[14]

The central episode in "Arthur and Accolon" reveals explicitly Morgan's character and her aims; but, at the point when the dwarf asks Accolon to fight, the reader has no real knowledge of Morgan's plans. He does not know of all that is to happen; he knows only that internal turmoil and treachery are at hand. Such vagueness serves to give the chapter suspense. The reader knows that something dire is about to happen, but he does not know what or how.

Accolon follows Morgan's wishes and proceeds to fight for Sir Oughtlake, Sir Damas's good brother. Although his opponent is Arthur, Accolon does not as yet know this. Using Arthur's sword and scabbard, he slowly but steadily weakens the king until Arthur, fighting with an inferior weapon made to look like Excalibur, is severely wounded. When Arthur's weapon finally breaks,

Accolon asks the king to yield; but Arthur replies that he cannot since "I promysed by the feythe of my body to do this batayle to the uttermuste whyle my lyff lastith, and therefore I had levir [rather] to dye with honour than to lyve with shame" (104–5). With these words Arthur redeems himself. Now he no longer prefers shameful life to death, no longer is he controlled by *amor sui* (love of self). Now honor and the chivalric code are everything to him, and he would rather die, even though enlisted in a wrong cause, than surrender and break a promise he had made.

Arthur also says to Accolon that, if the knight slays him while he is without a weapon, Accolon will be shamed. But Accolon replies, "as for that shame I woll nat spare" (105). This reply contrasts with Arthur's previous words; Accolon, unlike Arthur, does not care for courtesy and honor. While identified with the cause of the good knight, Sir Oughtlake, Accolon has been successful in his fight; but now that he has revealed himself as unworthy, his fortunes change. There is also a corresponding shift in Arthur's fortunes. Arthur could not win the fight while he was in a state of sin; Accolon cannot win the fight now that he has likewise fallen. At the same time, Arthur's fighting on the wrong side makes the predicament even more ambiguous. For either to win, justice will of necessity be perverted. The solution comes through supernatural intervention.

Nyneve, the "Damesell of the Lake," has been watching Arthur fight; and when she sees "how full of prouesse his body was, and the false treson that was wrought for hym," she causes an enchantment that makes Accolon lose Excalibur and Arthur recover the sword (105). Nyneve apparently has now replaced Merlin in the story. Having learned Merlin's magic, she is now the supernatural force in Arthur's realm; but she is somewhat different from Merlin, for, rather than be of the old order, she is in Malory identified with the new.

When Arthur in turn has Accolon at his feet and is ready to kill him, he asks the man's identity. Accolon reveals himself and, still not realizing that he has been fighting Arthur, explains that Morgan le Fay intended that he kill Arthur with Excalibur. The reason he gives for Morgan's plot is that "Arthur ys the man in the worlde that she hatyth moste, because he is moste of worship and of prouesse of ony of hir bloode." Accolon further explains that he

[ 66 ]

himself is Morgan's lover: "And if she myght bryng hit aboute to sle Arthure by hir crauftis, she wolde sle hir husbonde kynge Uryence lyghtly. And than had she devysed to have me kynge in this londe and so to reigne, and she to be my quene" (106). Such words may call to mind the earlier scene in "Torre and Pellinore" when Pellinore overhears a plot to poison Arthur. Here is a similar kind of plot, but one that has been put fully into motion and one that has almost worked. Arthur and his new Order have never been more in danger than at this time.

It is noteworthy that Arthur comes through this ordeal successfully, not primarily because of Nyneve's interceding, but more because of what is termed his *prouesse*. This term is repeated several times here in association with Arthur and later in reference to other valiant knights. It describes not only Arthur's ability at fighting and his courage as a warrior but also his character as a knight of chivalry: his preference for keeping a promise and dying with honor to living with shame. Because of his *prouesse*, Nyneve, representative of the supernatural, wants, and is able, to intercede. Had Arthur lacked *prouesse*, had he been a man still overcome by sin and shame, there would doubtless have been no help for him. Miraculous assistance is consequently available but only for those who merit it, and the Order of the Round Table is still seen to be, as it were, on its own. In the French *Suite du Merlin*, on the other hand, Nyneve does not watch the fight but arrives only at the moment of Arthur's greatest danger. In that version of the story she saves Arthur because Merlin had foretold the danger the king was in. Malory has apparently taken the act of rescue and given it a different motive, one that again emphasizes the qualities of honor and worth that he presents throughout the *Tale of Arthur*.

After Arthur has heard Accolon's confession, he reveals himself, and Accolon asks for mercy. Arthur's reply is significant in showing to what extent the code of chivalry now governs his thoughts and actions: " 'A, sir Accolon,' seyde kynge Arthur, 'mercy thou shalt have because I fele be thy wordis at this time thou knewest me nat, but I fele by thy wordis that thou haste agreed to the deth of my person, and therefore thou art a traytoure; but I wyte [blame] the the less for my sistir Morgan le Fay by hir false crauftis made the to agré to hir fals lustes' " (107). As was earlier exemplified in "Torre and Pellinore," justice and mercy go hand in hand; and here these two prime qualities are fused together in Arthur himself. Afterward, in a scene that apparently is largely of Malory's own invention, Accolon praises Arthur and identifies him to the spectators, who fall down and beg mercy. Again Arthur is merciful, but again he judges, giving the lands of the false knight, Damas, to his good brother, Oughtlake.

In his treatment of Arthur's fight with Accolon, Malory shifts the emphasis from "magic wrought by a supernatural influence," as is found in his source, to a "human conflict between a noble monarch and a traitor." [15] This shift is in line with the over-all change he makes in this section of the *Tale of Arthur* from Merlin the great magician to Arthur the great king. At the same time, however, it must be noted that Arthur functions as more than a king: he is shown as possessing the qualities associated with his new Order. The episode is highly significant as a test for Arthur, but the king is to be viewed less as an individual than as the representative and leader of the Order of the Round Table.

A postscript to this scene may be seen in what happens to Accolon. Although forgiven by Arthur, the knight never recovers from his wounds, in contrast to Arthur who, as Malory stresses, recovers easily. The courteous man, shown to be the victor again, thrives even though not possessing the magical, life-preserving scabbard of Excalibur. This idea is developed in the final episode of the section (109–12) in which the action centers on Arthur's judgment of his sister, Morgan le Fay. Thinking Arthur has been killed, Morgan plans to slay her husband, Uriens, while he is asleep; but a maiden warns their son, Ywain, who saves his father just as Morgan has raised a sword over him. Ywain, interestingly, identifies his mother as a "fende" and contrasts her with Merlin, who was supposedly begotten of a devil. Morgan, who lies to disguise her actions, promises never to try to kill her husband again (109–10).

When she finds out that it is Accolon, not Arthur, who has been killed, Morgan leaves and rides to where Arthur is asleep on his return to Camelot. There she steals his scabbard—Arthur sleeps with the sword in his hand—but, when chased by Arthur, she throws the scabbard into the deepest part of the lake and escapes from her brother by turning herself and her attendants into great stones. Although it is not clear whether Arthur knows that Morgan and her men have turned to stone—the Winchester manuscript implies that he does not know, Caxton that he does—the king exclaims, "here may ye se the vengeaunce of God" (111). Vinaver takes this statement to mean that Arthur sees human forms in the stone—as in the French—and thinks that Morgan and her men were changed into stone by God as punishment for their evil.[16] Although such a reading is likely, yet, when Arthur later receives a messenger from Morgan, he shows no surprise to find that his sister is still alive. Arthur's exclamation about the "vengeaunce of God" may consequently refer to God's vengeance on Arthur, who had not taken sufficient care of his precious scabbard. The exclamation is, in fact, followed in Malory by a passage describing the king's looking in vain for his scabbard.

The good magic that can save Arthur is now lessened. The scabbard, one of the magic talismans, is gone; and from now on, Arthur, like all men, is subject to the loss of blood. But the talisman is no longer really necessary, for now Arthur, by leading a good life and by following the chivalric code, has the power of heaven on his side. Also, an opposing kind of magic is revealed in Morgan. She is an evil force, specifically representing the opposite of all courtly virtues held and prized by Arthur and by his Order of the Round Table. The episode ends with a scene showing Morgan's viciousness and lack of courtesy.

Meeting a knight leading a prisoner he plans to drown, since the prisoner and the knight's wife had been unfaithful to him, Morgan reverses the two knights and causes the cuckolded one to be drowned by the other. The false knight happens to be Accolon's cousin, and Morgan saves him, as she says, in memory of Accolon. Here is the reverse of justice. Everything is so twisted around that the virtuous is confused with the vicious. Also, Accolon's cousin is a knight of Arthur's court; and, bound by the chivalric code, he should not be copulating with another knight's wife. Arthur's Order is still impure in many ways, and Morgan intends to do everything she can to add to the impurity. To dishonor Arthur and his knights becomes her *raison d'être,* and her presence is felt throughout Malory's work. Fleeing from her brother into "the contrey of Gore," she builds strong castles and towns; she constructs in effect a realm hostile to and rivaling that of Arthur. Her realm, a land of evil, contrasts with the lands protected by the Order of the Round Table and guided by the chivalric code.

## VI  *Restating the Values*

The final section of the *Tale of Arthur*, called by Vinaver "Gawain, Ywain, and Marhalt," corresponds to the last part of Caxton's Book IV (Chapters mid-15–29).[17] Following immediately on the adventures ending the previous section, this new one begins with a transition from Arthur's conflict with Accolon, along with a development of an earlier theme. Returning to Camelot after his fight with Accolon and his chase of Morgan, Arthur "founde his quene and his barownes ryght glad of his commyng" (112). Treachery is thus contrasted with loyalty. Accolon's actions in the previous section are contrasted with those of the knights who here welcome Arthur, and Morgan's faithlessness to Arthur, her king, and to Uriens, her husband, is contrasted with Guinevere's loyalty to Arthur. Moreover, Morgan's falseness is relevant in still another way: it may be regarded as a foreshadowing of the later infidelity of Guinevere when she deceives the king by taking Lancelot as her lover.

The first episode of "Gawain, Ywain, and Marhalt" likewise stresses Morgan's treachery, reinforcing both her role as villainess and the danger she represents to Arthur and his realm. Arthur says he will be avenged on Morgan, whom he describes as a "kynde" sister, a natural one, ironically emphasizing the unnaturalness of her behavior. Before he does anything, however, a damsel comes to court bearing the king a gift from Morgan, "the rycheste mantell that ever was sene in the courte, for hit was sette all full of precious stonys" (113). The damsel says that Morgan sends the present to beg Arthur's forgiveness. Arthur, unsuspecting, is pleased; but, before he puts on the mantle, he is warned by Nyneve to make the damsel wear it first. After she is forced to put it on, "forthwithall she fell downe deede and never spoke worde after, and brente to colys" (113). This episode is one popular in folklore, and the burning mantle is a universal motif that goes back in classical mythology to the rich garment the "sorceress" Medea presented to Jason's new wife. Morgan is likewise a sorceress, and her black magic cannot be discounted. Arthur and his court see that it is both potent and terrible.

The prologue to the section now finished, the real narrative begins. Deciding that Morgan's son, the young knight Ywain, is in league with his mother, Arthur unfairly and rashly banishes him from court. In the *Suite du Merlin* the banishment of Ywain does not occur until later in the story. By linking it in his version with the magic mantle, Malory, as Vinaver points out, gives his narrative "more coherence and unity" than was in the French and allows the quest of Ywain, Gawain, and Marhalt to be "a natural outcome of one of the main themes of the *Tale of Arthur*—the story of Morgan's treachery." [18]

Along with Ywain goes voluntarily his cousin, Gawain, who shows in this action a loyalty of sorts but one that is, nevertheless, misplaced. Gawain joins Ywain in his exile not because he thinks the man has been unjustly treated but because Ywain is his "cosyn jarmayne," his first cousin. For Gawain, family bonds are again shown to be more compelling and important than loyalty to king and court. Gawain's action, therefore, represents a pride of sorts (an *armor sui*) and gives another indication of the internal strife everpresent in Arthur's realm. In the French version, Gawain is innocent, for he accompanies Ywain at his request.

The initial adventure of the two knights, resulting in their meeting Marhalt, seems at first strangely out of place; for it presents Gawain in a light different from the one in which he usually is seen. When the knights come upon damsels spitting and throwing mire upon a white shield, they ask the reason for this outrage and are told that the shield belongs to a knight who, although "a passyng good man of his hondis," nevertheless "hatyth all ladyes and jantylwomen" (114). Gawain, unusually cautious, seeks to understand more and to explain the knight's behavior. After Marhalt rides up and defeats two knights accompanying the damsels, he fights with Ywain and Gawain. First he defeats the young Ywain, who had not seen any reason to fight him at all; then he engages in a long battle with Gawain, who had desired to test the knight's prowess. At one point in the battle, when Gawain is on foot and Marhalt on horseback, Gawain demands that he dismount. Marhalt replies, "Gramercy . . . of your jentylnesse! Ye teche me curtesy, for hit is nat commendable one knyght to be on horsebak and the other on foote" (116). The role of instructor in chivalry is an unusual one for Gawain to play, but in this scene Gawain exists not so much a debased knight as a heroic, even mythic, figure. In fact, the contest between Gawain and Marhalt hints strongly at an earlier cosmic struggle presented in symbolic terms: "Gawayne, fro hit was nine of the clok, wexed ever strenger and strenger, for by than hit cam to the howre of noone he had three tymes his myght encresed. And all this aspyed sir Marhaus and had grete wondir how his myght encreced. And so they wounded eyther other passyng sore. So whan hit was past noone, and whan it drewe toward evynsonge, sir Gawayns strength fyebled and woxe passyng faynte, that unnethe he myght dure no lenger, and sir Marhaus was than bygger and bygger" (116).

At this point, however, Marhalt stops the fight out of courtesy. He says to Gawain, "oure quarellys ar nat grete, and therefore hit were pyté to do you hurte, for a fele [I feel] ye ar passynge fyeble." The two knights remove their helmets, kiss each other, and swear "togedyrs eythir to love other as brethirne" (116–117). With these words the action descends from the realm of the cosmic to that of the human. Marhalt is now portrayed as the epitome of courtesy, and Gawain soon returns to his old position of sinner against the ideals of chivalry. Before the episode is concluded, Marhalt defends himself against the accusations made by the damsels that defiled his shield by explaining that they were "sorsseres and inchaunters" who tried to make knights become cowards. Of "good ladyes and jantyllwomen," he adds, "I owghe them my servyse as a knyght ought to do" (117).

So far, the story of "Gawain, Ywain, and Marhalt" may be seen as largely reinforcing ideas and themes permeating the whole of the *Tale of Arthur*. The rest of the section likewise gives parallels to themes and methods seen earlier, but it emphasizes explicitly courtesy in matters of love for the first time in the *Morte Darthur*. This new theme is combined with the older one of mercy and prowess and is revealed through the device of individual quests by Gawain, Ywain, and Marhalt.

After their meeting, the three knights go off together and enter a great forest, which Marhalt says is a place of "strange adventures" (117) for all knights that enter it. This hint of the supernatural soon becomes a certainty when the knights see three damsels sitting by a fountain at the head of a stream, a significant place since the fountain may be viewed as the source of the waters of life. The damsels reflect this meaning. The first is age sixty; the second, thirty; and the third, fifteen. Representing man in his three ages—old age, middle age, and youth—they say they are there to show wandering knights strange adventures. Ywain, the youngest of the three knights, chooses the oldest damsel to accompany him; Marhalt, the middle one; and Gawain is delighted to be left with "the yongyst and the fayryste" (118). The knights and damsels promise to meet at the fountain in a year, and then they go their own way, each knight with a damsel.

Gawain's adventure is the first related; and, as in the third section of the *Tale of Arthur* where in his quest Gawain fell sadly short of Torre and Pellinore, Gawain again is shown shaming the chivalric code and the Order of the Round Table. His adventure, by far the longest of the three, is unified in that every episode in it seems designed to reveal Gawain's inadequacy and to prepare the reader for his shame.

First, Gawain sees a knight who is "the fayreste knyght and the semelyest man" but one making "the grettyst dole [lamentation]" (119). Such incongruity marks the other actions of this knight, identified as Pelleas, and likewise permeates the episodes of Gawain's quest. With a "grete spere" Pelleas defeats ten knights but then allows himself to be captured, bound hand and foot, and ignominiously tied under his horse's belly. Such actions are without a rational basis, and Gawain's damsel says he should correct the situation by helping the knight. Gawain, however, replies that the knight does not appear to want any help and that he could prevent being made prisoner if he desired. A perversion from the courtly way of life is certainly apparent here; and, because Gawain in a sense encourages the perversion, he is recreant in his duty as a knight. He too, within his own actions and character, shows a perversion from the courtly ideal, as the damsel states in lines not in the French source.

In the next episode Gawain and his damsel meet a knight fighting a grotesque dwarf for a lady. The opponents ask Gawain to settle their dispute, and in his new role of judge, Gawain refrains from making any decision at all. He avoids the issue by allowing the lady herself to choose whom she prefers. When she chooses the dwarf, who has "a grete mowthe and a shorte nose" (120), and rides off with him, another perversion is seen. Though in a modern view, it may not appear that Gawaín has been lax, the ignobility of his behavior is made manifest by his damsel's criticism of his conduct and becomes explicit when she chooses to leave with another knight rather than to stay with Gawain. Furthermore, the falseness and lack of courtesy of the knight are clearly revealed in the next, the central, episode of his quest.

Gawain discovers that Pelleas acts as he does out of love for a lady, Ettarde. For Pelleas, Ettarde is "his soveraygne lady," and he will never "love other but her." Ettarde, however, is "so prowde that she had scorne of hym and seyde she wolde never love hym thoughe he wolde dye for hir" (121). This perversion gives meaning to the former ones of the chapter, which are all to be regarded as related to love. It is here possible to see that the idea of love that Malory is presenting is directly related to his concept of the chivalric code, specifically to that part of the code revealing the ideals of mercy and justice. These two qualities are based on, and reveal in themselves, a sense of *mesure,* of proportion; and, when they are warped or perverted, *mesure* is replaced by *outerage*—as has been seen in the "Torre and Pellinore" section of the *Tale of Arthur.* The lady who preferred the dwarf to the knight demonstrated in her conduct an excess—in the French, she chooses the dwarf because the knight has been false to her—a perversion, perhaps because of the presence of lust or some other sinful emotion; what is most important, however, is that her behavior is unreasonable.

Likewise excessive is the incongruous behavior of Pelleas, who allows himself to be mistreated. This behavior is also unreasonable; but, as Pelleas is presented, he is not to be blamed for the excesses. Instead, Ettarde is the one at fault, for her unreasonable behavior in scorning the meritorious Pelleas is the cause of his excesses. Every week Pelleas fights Ettarde's knights, defeats them, but then allows himself to be taken prisoner only so as to have a glimpse of his love, even though she constantly shames him and "doth hym grete dispyte" (121). Pelleas realizes how he is treated and knows the incongruity of his behavior, but he also knows that "love causyth many a good knyght to suffir to have his entente" (122). Love, not Pelleas, is to be blamed, and love is a culprit only because it is denied through the pride of Ettarde. Her sin against the Christian God is pride, and her sin against the god of Love is what is often called *daunger*, offishness and unreasonable holding back. Pelleas, a worthy knight, deserves to have the love of Ettarde; she is unjust and sinful to scorn the man and not have *pyté* on him. In the French, on the other hand, Ettarde's excuse for scorning Pelleas is that he is of low birth. By making Pelleas "lord of many isles," Malory takes away Ettarde's excuse.

The sinful nature of the woman, suggested by her unreasonableness, is revealed clearly as the episode develops. Gawain, offering to help Pelleas achieve his love, says he will go to Ettarde and talk to her. He does so; but, instead of persuading Ettarde to love Pelleas, he seduces her. The fact that Ettarde is so easily persuaded to have Gawain as her lover, as well as the fact that she prefers the false Gawain to the virtuous Pelleas, emphasizes both how perverted she is as a woman and how perverted love is in her. Likewise, Gawain's perfidy represents his crowning falseness. Only Morgan is more vicious in the *Tale of Arthur;* and later in the *Morte Darthur,* only the treachery of Mordred can compare with the falseness of Gawain. In Gawain's negating of love and honor, all courtly virtues in general are in danger of being destroyed.

Pelleas waits three days for Gawain's return although Gawain had promised "by the feythe of his body" to return with news after a day and a night. Going to see what has happened, Pelleas discovers Gawain and Ettarde lying together in bed. In sorrow Pelleas laments, "Alas, that ever a knyght sholde be founde so false!" (124). His regret of this perversion in Gawain is even greater than his personal sorrow of knowing that his love, Ettarde, has been false to him. His further reactions emphasize even more the difference between Gawain and Pelleas. After riding away disconsolate, Pelleas thinks to kill Gawain and Ettarde, returns, but says, significantly, "Though this knyght be never so false, I woll never sle hym slepynge, for I woll never dystroy the hyghe Ordir of Knyghthode" (124). Malory's "hyghe Ordir of Knyghthode" has no counterpart in the French. There Pelleas refrains from killing Gawain because it would be *desloyouté* to kill a man who is son of a king and a good knight. The French emphasizes

Pelleas's sense of sinning, but Malory stresses the necessity of preserving the Order.

Although Gawain's falseness puts chivalry in danger of destruction, Pelleas redeems it through his virtue. He leaves, but again vacillates and returns. Again, however, "he thought shame to sle hem" (125), and he merely lays his bare sword over their throats. In the French, no physical threat is involved; for in it Pelleas places his sword on the head of the bed, an action going back to the Tristan legend where King Mark, after finding Tristan and Iseult asleep in the forest, is first angry but then willing to spare them. Before he leaves, Mark lays his sword beside them as a sign that he no longer thinks of avenging himself on the lovers. As Vinaver points out, in the French source, "as in the Tristan romances, the sword is a symbol of forbearance"; in Malory, on the other hand, "it is a token of an unfulfilled desire for vengeance." [19]

When the two false lovers awaken, Ettarde knows how treacherous Gawain has been and says to him that, had Pelleas "bene so uncurteyse unto you as ye have bene to hym, ye had bene a dede knyght. But ye have dissayved [deceived] me, that all ladyes and damesels may beware be you and me" (125). Gawain then departs in shame. The ending of this scene is quite different from that in the French, for, as F. Whitehead writes, "A gracious and high-bred charm lingers over the pages of the French: the courtly protagonists are prepared to forgive and forget with the utmost readiness." [20] There Gawain, filled with contrition at the sight of Pelleas's sword, regrets his falseness. Nor does the lady blame Gawain; she tries to comfort him; and finally she agrees to go back to Pelleas, who then forgives Gawain and rides off happily with his love. In Malory, the emphasis is, as Vinaver says, on punishing Ettarde for her falseness and on rewarding Pelleas by giving him a more worthy love. [21]

The rest of this adventure in Malory consequently shows how the tables are turned—how Pelleas is rewarded for his virtue and how Ettarde is punished for her sin. Nyneve, the Damsel of the Lake, prevents Pelleas from dying for love. Just as earlier she had saved Arthur after the king's noble character was revealed, so here she objects to "a proude lady that woll nat have no mercy of suche a valyaunte knyght" (125) and saves Pelleas. By enchantments she makes Ettarde fall in love with Pelleas—explaining her action as "the ryghteuouse jugemente of God"—and, at the same time, she causes Pelleas to hate Ettarde. Ettarde's punishment is completed when she later dies of sorrow, but Pelleas lives on happily; for, as Malory writes, he and Nyneve "loved togedyrs duryng their lyfe" (126).

Although Malory's changes might be said to be the result of a dislike or misunderstanding of "the French tradition of courtly sentiment," [22] they are more than this. For Malory, just as loyalty and mercy are to be prized in the world of the warrior, so are the same qualities to be valued in the world of the lover. Thus, he cannot overlook Ettarde's sin or provide a happy ending that exonerates Gawain as the French can. Malory is aware of the courtly love of his sources; he knows that it is the origin of many of the best features of chivalry, but he also recognizes that it is illicit and based on passion. Malory uses the essentially paradoxical nature of love to distinguish between two kinds of love. The first, marked by impetuosity, excessive passion, and sensuality has been seen from the beginning of the *Tale of Arthur* as responsible for much of the trouble in Arthur's realm; it is also to be instrumental in the destruction of the Round Table. The second kind, characterized by stability, reason, and loyalty, is later termed "vertuouse love" and is for Malory the ideal kind of earthly love. This love has an ennobling effect and, as is later seen in detail, is necessary in noble knights. In the "Gawain, Ywain, and Marhalt" section, Pelleas attains a nobility through rising above his lust and anger. On the verge of committing acts of *outerage,* he finally proves his worthiness and is then rewarded by Nyneve, just as Arthur was earlier rewarded in his fight with Accolon when he chose the right course of action.

In the final pages of the section the falseness of Gawain continues to be emphasized as Malory relates the adventures of Marhalt and Ywain. These adventures are completely different from those appearing in the *Suite du Merlin* and, according to Vinaver, have "little in common with any known French romances." [23] Their function seems to be to contrast these noble knights with the false Gawain; the adventures reveal the knights as eminently successful men who, like Pelleas, demonstrate those virtues which should be associated with ideal knights. Marhalt defends the honor of Arthur's court by fighting against and by achieving the friendship of a man who hates Arthur and his knights because Gawain had slain one of his sons. Marhalt also fights in a tournament, winning it and "grete honoure," and fights a giant, defeating him and rescuing several knights from his prison. Ywain likewise achieves honors by winning a tournament but instead of fighting a giant, he rescues the lands of a lady from two false and vicious knights and subsequently is praised for his *jantylnesse*. Not only does the behavior of both Marhalt and Ywain contrast with that of Gawain but also these two successful knights, along with Pelleas, serve to act as *exempla* of ideal knighthood. Back at Arthur's court, at the significant feast of Pentecost, both Pelleas and Marhalt are made Knights of the Round Table and continue to excel as virtuous knights. The section ends with a description of Pelleas's subsequent treatment of Gawain. Although Pelleas has no love for this false knight, and although he defeats him often in tournaments, he nevertheless spares his life "for the love of the kynge" (133).

As in the other sections of the *Tale of Arthur,* there appear in this one several general forecasts of future action. Marhalt, for example, is said to be one of only six knights able to stand up to Gawain in battle. The other five are Lancelot, Tristram, Bors, Perceval, and Pelleas. Pelleas is also related to future events; for, although Malory does not present the story, Pelleas is said to be "one of the four that encheved the Sankgreal" (133). Also it is here stated that Nyneve always prevented him from fighting with her other favorite knight, Lancelot. The greater part of the forecasts in this chapter, however, serve to tie the story of the *Tale of Arthur* to that of Sir Tristram, an appropriate linking because of the extent to which love appears in both stories. Marhalt is said to meet Earl Fergus "that aftir was sir Trystrams knyght" (129); the giant Marhalt fights has a brother said to be killed later by Tristram; and Marhalt himself is described as falling under Tristram's sword after he gives Tristram the famous wound that can be healed only by Isode of Ireland.

The main themes of the *Tale of Arthur* thus involve the setting up of the guiding principles and ideals of life. Over and over these principles are stated in a variety of ways, and each restatement adds to the principle and to the reader's understanding of it. The concepts of prowess, loyalty, mercy, and justice are all developed, not only through various situations, but also in themselves; and they should, by the end of the tale, be meaningful to the reader. What is confusing about the tale is that the various episodes contained in it do not have any apparent chronological order. Rather, they seem to derive from the concepts to be examined and may even be described as present not to provide a narrative as such but to give an illustration of the various chivalric ideals held by Malory. The form or development of the tale, though perhaps not to be labeled organic, gives the impression of growing out of its themes and not out of the story it tells. The story is important but only as a concrete manifestation of the ideas that are behind it and that are its reason for being.

# CHAPTER 3

## Prowess, Courtesy, and Love

### I  The Universal Order

THE *Tale of Arthur and Lucius* (Caxton's Book V) is noticeably different in style from both the preceding *Tale of Arthur* and the other tales making up the *Morte Darthur*. This difference is due to its source, which is not a French romance but a
native English poem, the fourteenth-century, alliterative *Morte
Arthure*.[1] In his treatment of this poem, Malory shortened "by
summary, by free paraphrase, by a kind of précis in which the
more significant words and phrases of a passage are linked in a
briefer restatement, and by the omission or drastic shortening of
some scenes and lengthy descriptions." In omitting everything not
essential to the progress of his narrative, Malory reduced his
source to about half its original size.[2] Still, because so much of
this alliterative poem appears verbatim in Malory's romance, that
is, in the version found in the Winchester manuscript—Caxton
apparently edited the tale, condensing it by one-half—and because the piece is not in the same courtly tradition as the French
works used as the basis of other tales, this story stands out strikingly as something of an anomaly. In many respects it does not
seem to fit into the over-all structure of the Arthur-saga Malory
composed—its tone may be described as heroic rather than
courtly; its language is alliterative and archaic; its characters are
noticeably different in many ways from the figures of the same
names in the previous *Tale of Arthur;* and its broad humor contrasts with the delicate sentiments found elsewhere in Malory's
work.

*Arthur and Lucius* presents the "historical" Arthur of the chronicle tradition. Arthur, termed again and again "the Conquerrour,"
appears as a Germanic warrior and not as a Latinate courtier.
Also, Arthur's knights, especially Gawain and Lancelot, are seen
more as fierce warriors than as gallant courtly gentlemen. These

two knights are presented as the epitomes of knightly prowess: Gawain is the valiant warrior, not a debased figure; and Lancelot is his fierce brother in arms, not Guinevere's lover, a knight of the boudoir. In place of sentimentality, languishing lovers, and woeful knights, the heroes are fierce, strong, and valiant; and the reader is taken back to the masculine world of the warrior briefly revealed in the early battles at the beginning of the *Tale of Arthur*.

In spite of the many differences between this romance and those around it, however, the *Arthur and Lucius* does function significantly in the whole of Malory's *Morte Darthur*. Arthur has already become ruler of the British Isles and neighboring lands; the new Order of the Round Table has been created, and its ideals have been codified. But Arthur's Order still is not universal in scope; it becomes so in this second tale. Just as Arthur had earlier fought to be recognized as king and as Uther's successor, here he struggles to become conqueror of the whole Western world, emperor of the Holy Roman Empire, and, most important, defender of Christendom. The Knights of the Round Table are again in the world outside themselves, but their environment is revealed not as one of magic, quests, and love but as a masculine one of warfare. This world, however, is not one of the intramural war of tournaments, or even of civil war, as when Arthur fought the dissenting kings. Now, war itself is taken outside the knights and the realm. Also, the Order is shown still to be responsible for what it does and for what happens to it, as is indicated in the full title of the tale in the Winchester manuscript: *The Tale of the Noble King Arthur That Was Emperor Himself Through Dignity of His Hands*. Arthur succeeds in making his Order and its ideals universal "through dignity of his hands," not only through his personal worth and merit, but also through his physical prowess. The qualities of *curtesie* are important, but *prowesse* is emphasized in *Arthur and Lucius*.

The tale may be regarded as divided into four distinct parts, each revealing something about the king and the Order, and each being necessary to the narrative of the tale. The first part (136–41) begins with a transition giving the action of the tale a place in Malory's Arthur-saga. The action occurs after Arthur's marriage to Guinevere, after the establishment of the Round

Table, and also after both Sir Lancelot and Sir Tristram have come to court. The first tale had ended, as Malory wrote, just before the arrival of these two knights; now the second tale begins sometime afterward. In the order seen in the first five tales of the *Morte Darthur*, one proceeding from the encompassing and general down to the specific and individual, the adventures of Lancelot and the related exploits of Tristram are properly told in detail after the story of all the knights and their Order.

Following this introduction, one that is both a transition from the first tale and a means of anchoring the present action, Malory begins his story, omitting the first seventy-seven lines of his source. Rather than speak of Arthur's victories, the foundation of Carlion, Arthur's capital, and a feast at Carlisle, Malory again jumps into his story *in medias res* and shows messengers coming from Lucius, Emperor of Rome, to demand tribute from Arthur. This event had already been seen at the beginning of the *Tale of Arthur* (38) where it was used to suggest the troubles that were coming to the realm. Here, however, it is not presented as trouble; rather, the knights welcome the hostilities. They are delighted at the challenge from Rome, for, in Sir Cador's words, "now shall we have warre and worshyp" (137). All the knights are anxious to prove themselves and their Order to the world, and all are anxious to attain the honors that prowess in battle can give them. In this tale the key descriptive terms are "warre and worshyp"; these are what the tale is about, and these form the rallying cry of the knights. Passive courtesy is not here a trait of Arthur and his knights. Rather, as seen initially, the warriors are filled with an eagerness resembling ferocity. When their eagerness is directed against Lucius, it is used properly; and Malory can refer to them as "oure noble knyghtes of mery Ingelonde" (150).

When the messengers from Rome appear and see Arthur's "grymme countenance" (136), they can barely speak. Their fear is well founded; for, when Arthur's knights hear the messengers, they can hardly be restrained from killing them. Arthur, however, still shown as generous and merciful, forbids his knights "upon payne of dethe to myssaye [insult] them ne doo them ony harme" (137). Although courtesy is still present, it is a sterner kind than before, as is clearly seen when Arthur permits the messengers to leave under his protection but grants them only seven days to get

out of the country. In the alliterative *Morte Arthure,* the emphasis
is on Arthur's brutality. There the king is explicitly a man of excess, a ruthless conqueror, who, as William Matthews has recently
shown in detail, falls at the end because of his excesses.[3] Malory,
however, has throughout his tale tempered Arthur's violence with
self-control and his passion with restraint; he has presented prowess and warlike qualities not as marks of excess but as virtues.
Arthur consequently appears in this tale as "the true embodiment
of heroic chivalry."[4]

Arthur's answer to the messengers further reveals his sternness
and determination. Giving a history of the British claim to the
Roman throne, Arthur states how Rome had formerly been conquered by his relatives, Belin and Bryne, and later by Constantine, who "recoverde the Crosse that Cryste dyed uppon" (137).
The king thus demonstrates not only that he has a claim to the
Roman throne but also that he is not a "rebelle" against the established order, as Lucius has accused him of being (136). Instead,
Arthur suggests that Lucius himself is the usurper; he rules "with
grete wronge" (140). By presenting himself as a descendant of
Constantine, Arthur also emphasizes that he, not Lucius, is the
proper defender and preserver of the Cross and, consequently, of
the Christian Church. Lucius, like Lucifer, is a false ruler, perhaps
even an anti-Christ; and Arthur and his knights are determined to
fight against him.

The original conflict found in the tale has thus been transformed. Beginning merely as some trouble between a sovereign
and an underlord who would not pay homage, it develops until
Arthur is no longer on the defensive. He challenges the position of
Lucius, and now the trouble between them is more than a local
fight. Now it is comparable to a crusade against the idolaters; and,
as Arthur's answer to the messengers clearly indicates, the king
and his knights are confident of the rightness of their cause and of
their ultimate success: "Now sey ye to youre Emperour that I
shall in all haste me redy make with my keene knyghtes, and by
the rever of Rome holde my Rounde Table. And I woll brynge
with me the beste peple of fyftene realmys, and with hem ryde on
the mountaynes in the maynelondis, and myne [destroy] doune
the wallys of Myllayne the proude, and syth [then] ryde unto
Roome with my royalyst knyghtes" (139).

When the messengers return to Lucius and describe Arthur and his court, their words imply that there is a striking difference between the Order of the Round Table and Lucius's court: "And of all the soveraynes that we sawe ever he is the royallyst kynge that lyvyth on erthe, for we sawe on Newerys day at his Rounde Table nine kyngis, and the fayryst felyship of knyghtes ar with hym that durys [exists] on lyve, and thereto of wysedome and of fayre speeche and all royalté and rychesse they fayle [lack] of none" (140). The contrast between the two monarchs is made clear when Lucius, instead of gathering together "the fayryst felyship of knyghtes" and "the beste peple of fyftene realmys," as did Arthur, enlists the aid of the heathen Saracens and "many gyauntys of Geene," specifically fifty giants of the kin of Cain, "that were engendirde with [by] fendis" (140–41). These heathens and monsters negate the value of the Christian forces under Lucius's command and cause the conflict between the two kings to become one between the forces of right and those of wrong, specifically between Christianity and paganism. Arthur is no longer a mere British monarch; he, like Charlemagne in the *Song of Roland,* is the champion of Christ who will, in a war similar to that related in the French *chanson de geste,* rid the land of evildoers and wrong believers.

The first part of *Arthur and Lucius* thus gives the proper dimensions to the imminent conflict that represents more than the adventures and exploits of a few knights, even of a few kings. Two ways of life are opposed and the battle lines are in the process of being drawn up.

In the second part of the tale (141–48), Arthur prepares to leave Britain with his army. Instead of following the story in the alliterative *Morte Arthure* and having Arthur leaving Mordred as his viceroy, Malory changes the text and shows Arthur leaving Sir Baldwin and Sir Constantine as rulers. Malory, who obviously did not intend to end this tale with the rebellion of Mordred and the death of Arthur—as in the alliterative poem—concludes by describing the crowning of Arthur as Emperor of the Roman Empire and the peaceful return of the king and his knights to Britain. Such a change indicates strongly that Malory's theme in *Arthur and Lucius* concerns the glory of the new Order and not its destruction and, furthermore, that there is an over-all unity to the eight tales making up Malory's Arthur-saga.

Before the king and his knights leave Britain to fight Lucius, Malory makes several remarks, ones not in the alliterative poem, that become more meaningful in later tales. He writes, for example, that "sir Trystrams at that tyme beleft [remained] with kynge Marke of Cornuayle for the love of La Beale Isode, wherefore sir Launcelot was passyng wrothe." When Malory follows this statement with a description of Guinevere in "grete sorow that the kynge and all the lordys sholde so be departed" (142), it is apparent not only that Tristram and Isode are together but also that Lancelot and Guinevere seem already to be in love with each other. This love and lamenting, replaced here by a concern for prowess as the army prepares to leave, are presented in detail in later tales.

Following this scene occurs the main action of the second part: the fight with the giant at the top of Saint Michael's Mount. When, before the action, Arthur dreams of a brilliant, shining, "dredfull" dragon from the West fighting a "grymly" black bear from the East, "the fowlyst beste that ever ony man sye [saw]" (143), the supernatural quality that marked the *Tale of Arthur* is shown to be still present. Here, however, it appears in the more likely form of a dream-vision rather than in the prophecies of Merlin or in the magical enchantments of Nyneve. In place of these two guides, Arthur now relies on "a philozopher" who interprets the dream to mean that Arthur will soon fight and defeat a giant. Immediately following this interpretation, Arthur receives news of "a grete gyaunte of Gene" (143) that is tormenting the people of the land. In the past seven years this giant has destroyed more than five hundred children, "Crysten chyldern" (146); he has killed boys and raped girls and women. Arthur is summoned, for the giant has just abducted the wife of Sir Howel, Arthur's cousin, and, as is later discovered, raped and killed her.

Such a creature, along with such destruction, challenges Arthur in his roles of both warrior of prowess and protector of the lands under his rule. The giant, like Lucius, is more than a local threat. Harassing many lands and threatening Arthur—even shown, in lines not in Malory's source, as desiring Guinevere—he has "a coote full of precious stonys, and the bordoures thereof is the berdis of fyftene kynges, and they were of the grettyst blood that dured on erthe" (145). This coat is like that of King Royns in the *Tale of Arthur* (43); and, like Royns, the giant of Saint Michael's Mount threatens both the person and the rule of Arthur. Also this giant is no mere ogre; he is a demon, a representative of primitive wildness—the opposite of civilized chivalry—that Arthur is struggling to control. Not only does the giant exhibit all the Christian Deadly Sins, but he is described explicitly as "the foulyst wyghte [creature] that ever man sye [saw], and there was never suche one fourmed on erthe, for there was never devil in helle more horryblyer made" (146). If Arthur is a rightful and a righteous king, he should be concerned with putting an end to the atrocities committed by this giant; and he should have the power of heaven behind him in his fight with this representative of evil. Indeed, the knight who brings the news of the giant says, "Now, as thou arte oure ryghtwos kynge, rewe on this lady and on thy lyege peple, and revenge us as a noble conquerroure sholde" (144).

In effect, the entire episode of the giant seems to function as a prelude to or as practice for the main action of the tale, the fight with Lucius. Also, the episode shows Arthur squarely facing evil and horror and able to win on his own. If, it may be implied, Arthur cannot subdue this creature, he can hardly hope to achieve victory over Lucius's force with its fifty giants and countless heathens, followers of the demon Mahoun. In the giant, human sins—those of the flesh in particular—are seen in full horror; and in Arthur's victory over him, it is possible to see that Arthur has been cleansed of the sins that earlier stained him, including those stemming from his own act of killing Christian children. As in his fight with Accolon, he succeeds, first, because he has proved himself worthy and, second, because he has right on his side.

The fight itself is short and even easy although the giant at the end, like a bear, "caughte the kynge in his armys and handeled the kynge so harde that he crusshed his rybbes" (147). But Arthur extricates himself and rises as victor. The king is here not merely an empty allegorical symbol of virtue. He is a leader, conscious of his responsibility for the well-being of the people in his realm; but, as the many realistic and humorous details indicate, he is a man of flesh and blood and not a two-dimensional shadow shape.

Immediately after the fight, Arthur refers to the giant of Saint Michael's Mount as a "corseynte," or body of a saint; and Sir Bedevere remarks: "In fayth . . . this is a foule carle. . . . I have mykyll wondir, and [if] Mychael be of suche a makyng, that ever God wolde suffir hym to abyde in hevyn. And if seyntis be suche that servys Jesu, I woll never seke for none, be the fayth of my body!" (147). Although these warriors exhibit grim and rough humor, they are not blasphemous. By making light of his fight, Arthur shows a modesty of sorts. Also, when faced with the immense treasure the giant has hoarded, Arthur is interested in taking only "the curtyll [coat] and the clubbe" (148). Everything else he offers to his knights and to the people of the land. Likewise, Arthur's modesty and sense of *mesure* are revealed when the people of the land praise him and God for destroying the giant; for Arthur replies, "All thanke ye God . . . and no man ellys" (148). As a real token of his thanks to God and of his own sense of humility, Arthur commands that a church in honor of St. Michael be built on top of the Mount. With this action, stressing more than ever Arthur's role as champion of Christ and as protector of the oppressed and innocent, the second part of *Arthur and Lucius* ends.[5]

In part three (148–63), the actual fight with Lucius takes place; and this section has three subdivisions. In the first, showing a preliminary fight that Gawain, Bors, Lionel, and Bedevere have with the Romans, the center of attention shifts from Arthur to his knights, who now reveal their individual prowess and worth just as Arthur himself did in his fight with the giant. Gawain, in particular, here becomes the center of the action. With Galantyne, his sword, he does "many wondyrs" (151). Even when "wounded wondirly sore," for example, he does not stop fighting until he rescues his friends that had been captured. The Gawain seen here is strikingly different from the Gawain of the *Tale of Arthur*. Now, nobility personified, he even instructs Arthur in matters of chivalry as when he moralizes that "hit were shame to sle knyghtes whan they be yolden [have surrendered]" (152). This Gawain is the heroic one found in the early chronicles of Geoffrey of Monmouth, Wace, and Layamon. Here is the valiant nephew of Arthur, a heroic British knight, and the pride of the realm.

In the second subdivision, which centers on an attack on some of Arthur's knights while they are leading their Roman prisoners to Paris, Lancelot, Cador, and Bors are singled out for praise. When told that they are riding into an ambush and that they are outnumbered, these knights have the choice of fighting or retreating. Their response is unanimous and immediate. Lancelot says fight, so as not to lose *worshyp;* Cador expresses the same idea in another fashion, "I had lever [rather] dye this day than onys [once] to turne my bak"; and Bors, who echoes the two knights, anticipates the honors they can receive, the "lordshyppis and landys" Arthur will give them for their "noble dedys" (154). Honor, praise, and tangible awards, as well as the real desire for battle, are the driving motives. Even when the fight itself is over, and the knights return in victory to hear Arthur say that they did not have to stay and fight against large numbers, Lancelot disagrees, saying that, had they fled, "the shame sholde ever have bene oures." Other knights echo him, pointing out that "knyghtes ons [once] shamed recoverys hit [nobility] never" (157). A knight cannot relax; to keep honor and avoid shame, to be worthy of *worshyp,* he must constantly show his prowess and defend right causes.

In this subdivision, Lancelot especially is praised. In his prowess he rivals, even supersedes, Gawain, who is used primarily as a means of emphasizing Lancelot's worth. Of Lancelot it is said, "nother knyght that day myght stonde hym ony buffette. Therefore was he honoured dayes of his lyff." Also, as Cador tells Arthur, "of wyse wytte and of grete strengthe of his ayge sir Launcelot hath no felowe" (156–57). In this section of the *Morte Darthur,* Lancelot appears for the first time in English literature as one of the chief figures in Arthur's entourage. Although Lancelot had been a main character in Continental Arthurian romances from the twelfth century, when Chrétien de Troyes wrote his *Lancelot,* this knight had been relatively insignificant in English literature before the time of Malory. In fact, in Malory's source, the alliterative *Morte Arthure,* Lancelot is mentioned only six times in the more than four thousand lines of the poem; and, on three of the six occasions, his name appears merely in an enumeration of several knights. In emphasizing Lancelot and in giving him a place equal to Gawain, Arthur's nephew, and second only to the king, Malory, as Mary Dichmann says, "sets the pattern that he uses throughout the eight romances—the pattern of Lancelot's supremacy." [6] In the *Tale of Arthur*, the infant Lancelot had been singled out for prophetic mention by Merlin, who said he would be "the moste man of worship of the worlde" (92); earlier in the *Arthur and Lucius* he had appeared as a young, eager, lighthearted knight—in his response to the words of Lucius's messengers, Lancelot "leepe in . . . with a lyght herte" (138), a passage not in Malory's source. Now, as warrior, Lancelot is the acknowledged champion of all the warriors on the battlefield; moreover, in Malory's next tale he emerges as the central character of the *Morte Darthur*.

The final subdivision of part three of *Arthur and Lucius* contains the main battle with Lucius. In it Arthur and his knights, all of whom have now proved themselves, do the greatest of deeds, killing the giants and driving back the Saracens. In fact, their fighting might be justly called the greatest ever done, not only by these knights, but also by knights anywhere in the world: "Was never kyng nother [nor] knyghtes dud bettir syn [since] God made the worlde" (160). As the champions of Christ defeat the false rulers, the false believers, and the monsters, both Arthur and Christianity have their greatest day.

But the forces of good are not impervious to hurt. Sir Kay and Sir Bedevere, in particular, are mortally wounded—though the knights later appear in other tales—and these deaths spur on Arthur and his forces. After Lancelot wounds Lucius and Arthur kills him, the fight continues; for Arthur orders that, to avenge Kay and Bedevere, not one of the enemy is to be spared, "none for golde nothir for sylver" (161). This revenge is not to be taken as a human sin, for Arthur is acting as the instrument of divine wrath. Also, his enemies are foes of God—even the Christians in Lucius's forces who have wilfully associated with the unbelievers and monsters. Arthur is to be regarded as wholly justified, therefore, in his slaughter. Finally, when the fighting ceases, the king sends the corpses of Lucius and his senators back to Rome as a grim, ironic payment of the tribute demanded of him.

After the battle, the fourth part of the tale begins (163–77) and summarizes how Arthur, on his way to Milan and Rome, conquers Flanders, Lorraine, Germany, Lombardy, and Tuscany. In these lands he destroys tyrants and, by proclaiming "lawys . . . that dured longe aftir" (164), sets up his new Order. While this step-by-step conquering occupies the background of the narrative, the foreground is composed of specific, valorous acts of various knights. Of special importance is an encounter of Gawain with Priamus, a heathen knight. After a great fight, which ends in a draw, Priamus is converted to Christianity, and a new emphasis comes into the tale. Now Arthur's knights are shown as fighting explicitly heathen forces and not merely those of false rule and misrule. The scope of the fighting has steadily increased, and now Christianity is clearly set against paganism. Christian virtues and powers are portrayed through the action: Priamus is, for example, rewarded for becoming a Christian—after being baptized, he is made a duke and a Knight of the Round Table—but those who remain in darkness are killed. It is significant that Priamus is descended from some of the noblest heroes of history: Alexander the Great, Hector of Troy, Judas Maccabeus, and Joshua. These legendary and Biblical figures were eminent in the Middle Ages as four of the Nine Worthies of the World, a group of heroes including three Jews, three pagans, and three Christians, among whom is Arthur himself. By relating Priamus to the Old Testament and pagan Worthies, Malory presents strikingly his innate merit; but he also implies that the merit is wasted unless the man becomes a Christian.

At the end of the tale, Arthur, whose fairness continues to be emphasized, receives tribute from Milan and enters Rome where he is "crowned Emperour by the Poopys hondis, with all the royalté in the worlde to welde for ever" (175). This scene is the reason for the existence not only of everything that happens after the death and defeat of Lucius but also of the whole tale of *Arthur and Lucius* in Malory's work. In the alliterative *Morte Arthure* Arthur, a victim of his pride, falls on the wheel of Fortune. Moreover, before he can be crowned emperor, news comes to him of Mordred's rebellion; and he is forced to return home to defend his realm. Malory, who apparently removes the irony and explicit moral lesson of his source, has Arthur and his Order receive the blessing of the Church and the crown of the Western world.[7]

Such a change may indicate that Malory, as early as this tale, was thinking of his tales as part of a series or cycle. Contrary to

Vinaver's idea that the *Arthur and Lucius* represents Malory's first work,[8] Malory seems to have been familiar with the kind of romances constituting the French Vulgate Cycle and may already have adapted some of them.[9] The crowning in Rome is not at odds with what is still to come in the *Morte Darthur;* in fact, it is the key event that makes the tale of *Arthur and Lucius* fit into the over-all pattern of the work.

Arthur is now truly defender of the faith, and both his fortunes and those of the Round Table have reached another summit. The way of life of the Round Table is now universal; and its aims, ideals, and methods are in conjunction with those of Christianity. All that remains is for Arthur to reward his faithful knights, disband his army, and return home. The king and the Order can go no further in this world; they can continue only as they turn from this world, as they later do in the Quest of the Holy Grail. But, before the knights turn, it is necessary to see them in the fulness of their halcyon days, to witness their individual prowesses and virtues, their adventures, and their loves.

## II   *The Perfect Worldly Knight*

Consequently, from emphasizing the fortunes of Arthur and his knights as world conquerors and defenders of Christianity, Malory next turns to individual heroic adventures and to chivalric love. Since the Order of the Round Table is as established in this world as it can ever be, Malory now illustrates and emphasizes the prosperity that results. He shows the secular glory of Arthur's realm, the glory that is later transformed by the Quest of the Holy Grail into a concern for the afterlife. To demonstrate how the Order fares in this world, Malory must place Arthur in the background of his story and emphasize his knights and their affairs. As D. S. Brewer says, "Arthur is the point of departure and return for all the knights, and their glory is his." [10]

To reveal the greatness of the Order and its ideals, Malory must also show it attaining more than universal acceptance; now it must demonstrate perfection. There must, consequently, be a perfect knight—or rather, a knight that can be as perfect as this world allows—and he must be perfect in all the terms of the courtly code. He must contain prowess, courtesy, and the qualities that come from being in love; to be the chivalric hero, he must fuse together the states of the warrior, the man of courtesy, and the lover. In the third tale of the *Morte Darthur*, the *Tale of Sir Lancelot du Lake,* Lancelot is presented as this perfect knight.[11]

Along with being the briefest of the eight tales Malory wrote, the *Tale of Lancelot* (Caxton's Book VI) is in many ways the least dramatic; for its narrative is not concerned with the development of a character, a way of life, or a perilous and significant situation. Instead, a series of episodes—two major ones from the long prose romance in the thirteenth-century French Vulgate Cycle called the Prose *Lancelot*[12] and one from either the *Perlesvaus* or, more likely, a version of the *Suite du Merlin*—reveal, by repetition of one victory after another, how Lancelot is without doubt the noblest and most perfect of all men on earth. Everything in the tale may be viewed as designed to this end and, consequently, though Malory has strikingly abbreviated his source, there seems to be a surfeit of adventures. Lancelot had excelled in the fight with Lucius, but now his merit is without limit. A warrior of prowess and knight of honor, he evinces mercy and justice; he is loyal to his king and queen; and, though his future relationship with Guinevere is merely suggested, he is faithful to love. As Vida Scudder says, the incidents in this tale seem to have been chosen "to illustrate as many aspects of Lancelot's perfection as possible." [13]

Using a style and manner in many ways similar to that of the first tale, the *Tale of Arthur,* Malory makes a transition from Rome to Britain and points out that, although many knights in Arthur's realm excel in "armys and worshyp" and in "prouesse and noble dedys," the knight that stands out above all others is Lancelot; "for in all turnementes, justys, and dedys of armys, both for lyff and deth, he passed all other knyghtes, and at no tyme was he ovircom but yf [unless] hit were by treson other [or] inchauntement" (180). Treason and enchantment in a variety of forms—against the king and against courtly ideals—are the foes of Arthur and his Order; and in this tale the actions of every villain fall into one category or the other.

At the same time that Malory tells of the worthiness of Lancelot, he also suggests the relationship between the knight and Guinevere. Because of Lancelot's "worship and honoure," Guinevere held him "in grete favoure aboven all other knyghtis, and so he loved the quene agayne aboven all other ladyes dayes of his

lyff, and for hir he dud many dedys of armys and saved her from
the fyre thorow his noble chevalry" (180). Although this statement hints of future development, in this tale the love is kept on
an exalted spiritual plane. Guinevere's love is interpreted—by
Lancelot at least—as a proper admiration, one that may be compared to the affection she showed toward Sir Kay when, during
the war with the five kings described in the *Tale of Arthur,* he was
largely responsible for saving her, the king, and the realm. Likewise, Lancelot's love of Guinevere is depicted as the proper sort
all worthy knights should exhibit toward their queen. It is a love
of courtesy and honor; here it is not physical, not in the least sensual; everything Lancelot does for the queen is "thorow his noble
chevalry." Guinevere may be regarded as the prime mover of his
actions—as, in fact, the reason for his "noble chevalry." It should
not be thought, however, that Malory has platonized a pre-
existing sensual love. Rather, to the sole obscure reference in the
French describing Lancelot's feeling for Guinevere, Malory has
added four other references that emphasize Lancelot's character
as a lover.[14]

The actual narrative of the tale begins with Lancelot, who had
"rested hym longe with play and game," feeling the need "hymself
to preve in straunge adventures" (180). Even if the "play and
game" have not been with Guinevere, Lancelot, as his actions indicate, has not been so concerned with the world of the warrior as
he should have been. Consequently, with Sir Lionel accompanying him, he leaves the court for the "depe foreste" to "seke adventures" befitting the warrior. Such adventures, however, will also
prepare Lancelot for the world of the lover and thus function as
means by which he may win the approval of Guinevere. This
point is strengthened when Lancelot tells all whom he defeats
that they must yield themselves to the queen.[15]

The first adventure occurs when Lancelot falls asleep, saying,
"for this seven yere I was not so slepy as I am nowe" (180). As
this line, not in the French, indicates, there seems to be something
strange about the sleep; and, although it may act initially as a
device creating a drawn-out episode holding together other adventures, it may also be regarded as indicative of the laxness
Lancelot is trying to overcome through seeking adventures. While
perhaps not signifying sloth per se in Lancelot, the sleep is, never-

theless, the actual cause of his being captured. While Lancelot is
asleep, forces of treachery and enchantment are able to exist unchecked. Such an interpretation suggests that not only does the
tale show Lancelot as a perfect knight, it also makes his perfection
functional by presenting it as a specific force destroying and holding down the imperfect, the evil, in the realm.

While Lancelot lies asleep, a knight, Sir Tarquin, appears and
defeats several knights, including Sir Lionel who has challenged
him. After making these knights his prisoners, Tarquin strips
them, beats them with thorns, and throws them into a dungeon
where many other knights are already imprisoned. The only hope
for these prisoners who have been mistreated by Tarquin is
Lancelot who is sleeping. As they themselves say, "but yf [unless]
sir Launcelot helpe us we shall never be delyverde [set free]"
(182). As is later shown, however, Lancelot is ironically the man
indirectly responsible for their imprisonment—not here because
he is asleep, but rather because he had earlier killed Tarquin's
brother, thus causing Tarquin to insult and injure Arthur's knights
as a means of meeting Lancelot. Just as Ettarde had caused an
excess of love in Pelleas, Lancelot has caused an excess of hate in
Tarquin. Although Tarquin is wrong to hurt others in his hatred
of Lancelot, part of the responsibility is surely Lancelot's.

At this point, a pause occurs in the action, and the scene shifts
from Tarquin's prison back to the sleeping Lancelot. Four queens
ride up and, being in love with the knight, they cast an enchantment on him and take him to a castle where he must choose one of
them to be his love "unto peramour" (183). In the French, the
queens apparently fail to recognize Lancelot but marvel at his
great beauty. Malory significantly emphasizes that the queens are
attracted to Lancelot because they know of his "worthynesse," his
interior beauty. Like Tarquin, these queens are evil; all are sorceresses, and their leader is the arch-sorceress, Morgan le Fay.
Against their excessive desire for him and their malicious words
about Guinevere, Lancelot stands firm: he maintains his and, most
important, the queen's honor. He answers that he will choose
none of the sorceresses: "Yet had I lever [rather] dye in this preson with worshyp than to have one of you to [as] my peramoure."
And concerning Guinevere, he says that "she is the treweste lady
unto hir lorde lyvynge" (184). The details of the episode all tend

to glorify Lancelot as the ideal lover. He is the man all women desire, but he loves only one woman, the most illustrious of all, the chief queen of Christendom. Furthermore, he will never be unfaithful to his love and will always defend her honor.[16]

In spite of the magic of the sorceress-queens, Lancelot is able to escape because he promises a damsel that he will help her father, King Bagdemagus, fight against three false knights from Arthur's court, one of whom is Sir Mordred. This connection between Lancelot's escape and the fight for Bagdemagus is not in the French and may be seen as part of Malory's attempt to link episodes together in a unified, direct narrative. The connection enables Malory to imply that Lancelot's escape is due primarily to his knightly courtesy and prowess and also to illustrate his role as "the invincible and generous champion of the weak and oppressed." [17]

On his way to fight for Bagdemagus, Lancelot has an adventure that demonstrates vividly how Malory is using episodes from his source. Coming to an empty pavilion, Lancelot decides to spend the night. As he is lying in bed, a knight arrives and, thinking that his lady is in the bed, begins to kiss Lancelot. As soon as the knights realize the error, they fight, and Lancelot wounds the intruder. The strange knight, however, then explains that the pavilion is his; and Lancelot, sorry for the mistake, heals him and promises that he will try to help him become a Knight of the Round Table (185–86). In the French, the scene is completely different, for Lancelot, feeling someone in bed with him and thinking it is a damsel, takes the intruder in his arms. When he realizes his error, Lancelot not only defeats the strange knight but kills him. Malory's change is apparently to emphasize the purity and courtesy of Lancelot, and it may also stress the fact that Lancelot honors love and will not hinder true lovers.

After defeating the foes of Bagdemagus, Lancelot finally meets Tarquin, who, he discovers, has in his prison sixty-four knights. Coming upon Tarquin after he has just taken Sir Gaherys prisoner, Lancelot engages him in a fierce and bloody fight and finally cuts off his head. After Lancelot sends Gaherys to free the prisoners, he rides off into a forest in search of more adventures; and the first episode, that centering around Lancelot's sleep, comes to an end.

This end is also that of the first fragment Malory took from the Prose *Lancelot*. For transition between the sections of his tale, Malory uses the device of Lancelot's riding off into forests and valleys. His whole handling of the Prose *Lancelot* shows an organization that is what Vinaver calls "a new principle of composition" through which he has created a work "more palatable to the modern reader than any part of the original *Lancelot-Graal*." [18] For example, in Malory's source, after Lancelot defeats the enemies of Bagdemagus, there appears a digression equal in length to five hundred pages of Vinaver's edition of the *Morte Darthur*. Malory, by omitting this digression, brings the first adventure of Lancelot to a quick conclusion and then goes on to a new action.

Many of the adventures to follow, also taken from the Prose *Lancelot*, seem present merely to reinforce the chivalric qualities that have already been revealed in Lancelot. Rather than add any new qualities of perfection to the knight, most of these episodes serve to give a quantitative justification to the claims of Lancelot's perfection. It is almost as though saying something five times makes the statement more effective than it would be if said only once. This reinforcing may be seen after Lancelot's adventures with Tarquin when he continues his exploits by killing a false knight "that dystressis all ladyes and jantylwomen, and at the leste he robbyth them other lyeth by hem" (193). As is stated, this knight is comparable to Tarquin; but, whereas Tarquin had mistreated knights, this knight mistreats ladies. After his victory, Lancelot is praised as "the curteyst knyght . . . and mekyste unto all ladyes and jantylwomen" (194). He also defeats two giants; rescues their prisoners, "three score of ladyes and damesels"; and again receives praise, this time for having done "the moste worshyp that ever ded knyght in this worlde" (196). Furthermore, he saves Sir Kay and, wearing his armor, defeats several knights who, recognizing Kay's shield, think they can easily conquer him.

In these adventures, which continue to emphasize Lancelot's victories over the uncourteous and proud, the only doubt cast upon his perfection concerns his relationship with Guinevere. In a speech that has no counterpart in any known French romance of Lancelot, the knight replies to the accusations that, by being "a knyght wyveles," he is at fault and that, because of an enchantment placed on him by Guinevere, he loves only the queen:

I may nat warne [forbid] peple to speke of me what hit pleasyth hem. But for to be a weddyd man, I thynke hit nat, for than I muste couche with hir and leve armys and turnamentis, batellys and adventures. And as for to sey to take my pleasaunce with peramours, that woll I refuse: in prencipall for drede of God, for knyghtes that bene adventures sholde nat be advoutrers [adulterers] nothir lecherous, for than they be nat happy nother fortunate unto the werrys; for other they shall be over-com with [by] a sympler knyght than they be hemself, other ellys they shall sle by unhappe [ill fortune] and hir cursednesse bettir men than they be hemself. And so who that usyth peramours shall be unhappy, and all thynge unhappy that is aboute them.

(194–95)

Such words represent, in effect, a statement of the courtly code of the *Morte Darthur* and also indicate how aware Lancelot is of the fact that, to be a worthy knight, one must fuse within himself the roles of lover and warrior. There can be no excess, no *desmesure;* and anything which would lead to it, no matter how attractive, must be avoided. Although Lancelot omits responding directly to the charge that Guinevere has enchanted him, he answers the accusation by moralizing and by describing his conduct as being on a level above the worldly and the familiar, a conduct not nec-essarily to be understood by all.[19]

The final section of the *Tale of Lancelot* has no agreement with any extant version of the Prose *Lancelot*. In this section appears what may be regarded as, after the sleep and fight with Tarquin, the most dramatic and significant adventure in the tale—that of the Chapel Perelous. The source of this adventure may have been a version of the French romance called the *Perlesvaus,* but the re-cently discovered though still unpublished Cambridge manuscript of the *Suite du Merlin* likewise contains the Chapel-Perelous epi-sode and may prove to be closer to Malory than is the *Perlesvaus.*[20] In the Chapel-Perelous adventure in Malory's *Tale of Lancelot,* the tone is completely different from that of the rest of the tale. The supernatural is present—not the supernatural of en-chantments and sorceresses but that of a force wholly above the human and worldly. In a hazy, mysterious atmosphere, anticipat-ing that found in the Quest of the Holy Grail, Lancelot faces, in fact challenges, the supernatural. To save Sir Melyot, a fellow knight of the Round Table, Lancelot must enter the Chapel Perelous and take the sword he finds there, as well as a piece of the bloody cloth covering the body of Sir Gilbert, who has recently been killed by Melyot. Although the Chapel Perelous is not identified or explained, the episode is doubtless a major one that is most revealing of Lancelot's true worth.

Being concerned with more than a demonstration of prowess or courtesy—though the presence of these qualities is a prerequisite to success in the Chapel—the adventure may be regarded as the one most actually testing Lancelot. For him to fail would truly be disastrous. There can be no weakness or imperfection in the knight, but at the same time victory cannot come about through any direct effort he makes. As a damsel says, if Lancelot cannot obtain the sword and cloth, no one can: "I know no knyght lyvynge that may encheve that adventure" (203). One must have the qualities before one is allowed to accept the challenge that pertains to what is beyond worldly reality.

As Lancelot comes to the Chapel, thirty huge knights, who glower and gnash their teeth, oppose him; but then, as he dauntlessly approaches, they step aside and make a path for him. Inside, he cuts a piece of the winding sheet; and, as he does, the earth shakes under his feet. Although afraid, he takes this cloth and also "a fayre swerde" he sees, and then hurries out of the chapel. Again he is opposed by the huge knights who demand that he leave the sword or die; but again, as Lancelot prepares to fight them, they scatter before him. Lancelot has courageously and loyally helped a fellow knight. His testing, however, is not yet finished; he is now challenged by a damsel who demands that he leave the sword. Again Lancelot refuses, and the significance of his courage is revealed in terms that are probably Malory's addition to his source. As the damsel says, had he feared enough to leave the sword, he would never have seen Guinevere again. Likewise, after Lancelot refuses to kiss the damsel, she says, if he had kissed her, his "lyff dayes had be done" (204). Consequently, it appears that Malory's primary, immediate reason for including the Chapel-Perelous story has been to give a final test of Lancelot's loyalty to the queen. He has thus transformed the story so that the knight's refusal to kiss the damsel is as significant as his refusal to leave the sword.[21]

Unlike the unfortunate knight, Balin, in the *Tale of Arthur*,

Lancelot succeeds in doing everything right, although he does not fare so well later on the Grail Quest. He is undoubtedly the chosen hero and is praised as such. The episode concludes with Lancelot saving Melyot's life and with the damsel admitting she is a sorceress who, because of her inordinate love for Lancelot, planned to kill him, embalm him, and keep him with her forever.

Other adventures of Lancelot are now briefly delineated. Betrayed by a false knight, Phelot, and his wife, Lancelot is attacked while without arms; and later, while a lady is under his protection, a knight, Pedyvere, cuts off her head. These actions are perversions of both chivalric behavior and love; and each knight illustrates a fault that Lancelot, in a sense, redeems through his nobility. Furthermore, both Phelot and Pedyvere treat their ladies in ways that are perversions of love—Phelot, by making his wife aid him in an *outerageous* action; and Pedyvere, by showing his wife hatred and no mercy. Finally, having proven himself in "straunge adventures" and thus having done all he set out to do, Lancelot returns to Arthur's court and receives universal praise. As Malory writes, ending the tale, "at that tyme sir Launcelot had the grettyste name of ony knyght of the worlde, and moste he was honoured of hyghe and lowe" (209). Lancelot is, however, not only the best knight but a representative of the new chivalry that is now the norm in Arthur's realm. As Charles Moorman has discussed in detail, this chivalry, centering on the proper attitude of knights to women and of victors to vanquished, contrasts strikingly with that presented in the initial *Tale of Arthur,* in which such older knights as Gawain, Marhalt and Pellinore typify an earlier, more brutal civilization.[22]

In the concluding scene, one not in the French, Malory unifies his tale by bringing together all those for whom and with whom Lancelot has fought during the tale. Those who have been defeated by Lancelot come, as the knight had directed, and yield to Guinevere. This scene, with its references to Guinevere, also functions, as R. M. Lumiansky has written, to show Lancelot and Guinevere "drawing more closely together in preparation for the adultery, which comes to be a matter of almost common knowledge by the time we reach the fifth tale, that of Tristram."[23]

### III  *The Fair Unknown*

The *Tale of Sir Gareth of Orkeney* (Caxton's Book VII) may be viewed as essentially a continuation of Malory's presentation of the ideal knight. A basic difference between this tale and that of Sir Lancelot, however, is that Gareth, the central figure, is not already known for his excellence. The tale acts, therefore, not as a testing of any previously known worth but as the actual development of the man. The revelation of prowess and courtesy is neither after the fact, as it was in the *Tale of Lancelot,* nor in any way superfluous; for the reader does not know how valiant Gareth is. In fact, at the beginning of the tale the reader does not even know the identity of the main character. He exists for all as Beaumains, a name at first apparently meaning "Great Hands," and one contemptuously given him by Sir Kay.[24]

Even though the reader, along with Lancelot, soon finds out that this unknown man is of noble heritage—youngest son of King Lot and brother of Sir Gawain—he still exists throughout much of the romance as Beaumains, an unproven figure. Through his adventures his innate virtues are revealed both to the reader and to the character himself. Nor can these adventures be considered as mere demonstrations of pre-existing valor. Gareth's nobility cannot be regarded as mainly an inherited possession, since Gawain, his brother, is lacking in courtly virtues. While Gawain may be a gallant warrior, he is not a courteous knight. In fact, throughout the tale, Lancelot, rather than Gawain, acts as Gareth's ideal.

A problem that seems to be suggested in this tale is the late medieval conflict between the higher and the lower nobility, the problem of whether true nobility is passively inherited or actively achieved. Knightly qualities can theoretically be held by anyone; but, as Maurice Valency states, they "would sit badly on a churl since he would normally be lacking in the qualities requisite to a noble way of life." [25] Gareth has inherited nobility, but he keeps this fact hidden so as to prove himself and to be accepted for himself as knight in his own right and not as son of Lot and brother of Gawain. Here nobility of birth, shown supplementing nobility based on personal merit, makes meaningful the idea that the two must go together: just as the hero must be ideal warrior and lover, so must he combine within himself all facets of nobility.[26]

The *Tale of Gareth* consequently acts also as a dynamic demonstration of the personal merit of its main character. As such it demonstrates the "new principle of nobility, individualistic in character, which could be deduced solely from a man's bearing and behavior." Nobility is "an aptitude and a process" with self-perfection as its end.[27] Only after the hero is proved as Beaumains can he become Gareth; the nobility is really the identity, and it cannot be taken for granted. Also the tale shows Gareth fighting and defeating knights who are quite different from the evil figures found in the *Tale of Lancelot*. What is mainly wrong with these knights is that they are inadequate: although excelling in prowess, they, like Gawain, are lacking in courtesy. The story of Gareth functions furthermore as a demonstration that the perfect knight must combine prowess with courtesy. Lancelot and Gareth show this combination in themselves; they excel and are unbeatable.

Of Malory's romances, the *Tale of Gareth* is unique in not having a known source. Although Malory refers to a "Freynsh boke" as his source (272), this French romance is unknown. Nevertheless, the story probably goes back to a French source, perhaps to one that may have been "a French non-cyclic prose romance" in which Malory "introduced a few episodes of his own."[28] At the same time, as Vinaver notes, "practically each important episode of the story has a parallel in medieval French romance."[29] Still, as Vinaver also states, whether or not the story in Malory's source was a self-contained narrative, it was "the type of work which Malory himself endeavoured, with varying degrees of success, to shape out of his long-winded cyclic sources, and for this reason alone it must have been much after his own heart."[30]

In particular, the romance is related to the popular kind centering around the figure of some *bel inconnu,* some fair unknown. This man, seeming to be of humble origin, excels as a knight and, as is later discovered, really comes from a noble family. Sometimes the hero is the son of a famous figure, as in a version of the *bel inconnu* story represented, for example, by the English *Libeaus Desconus,* in which the main figure turns out to be the natural son of Gawain. At other times the hero does not know who he is, and his *enfances* are revealed as a kind of comedy, as in, for example, stories centering around the young Perceval. Malory also used a story of the *bel inconnu* kind in the *Book of Tristram* in the section called "La Cote Male Tayle," one which may have some connection with the Gareth story.[31] In the *Tale of Gareth* the hero knows who he is but cloaks his ancestry on purpose. Gareth, perhaps like Prince Hal in Shakespeare's *1 Henry IV*, wants to hide his light so that, when he is finally known, "he may be more wond'red at." So too do Hal and Gareth experience all sides of life, and the excellence of both must certainly be based partly on their full experience.

The *Tale of Gareth* begins (212–18) with Arthur preparing to dine at the Feast of Pentecost, but demanding first to witness a "grete mervayle" (212). It comes in the form of Gareth, shown here as a tall man who, not able to walk by himself, must lean on other knights. Gareth presents himself to Arthur as hungry and lacking in strength. Although this helplessness seems strange and may, as Vida Scudder thinks, be merely sham,[32] there may also be a fuller meaning that is not completely brought out by Malory. Symbolically, Gareth's weakness may be an indication that he is not as yet whole or fully developed, for he must still prove himself. His lack of perfection is thus revealed in terms of physical weakness. Still, even in his unformed state, Gareth stands out as, in Arthur's words, "one of the goodlyest yonge men that ever I saw"; and he also appears to be a man who will, in Arthur's estimation, "preve a man of ryght grete worshyp" (213). But, before Gareth can become such a man and before he can be complete, he must experience adversity.

It is traditional in stories showing the development of heroes that good fortune be preceded by misfortune: the hero must experience some sort of lowering or humiliation that may function as an initial purging or preparation.[33] In the *Tale of Lancelot* that knight experiences a lowering because of his inadvertent sleep but Gareth brings about his misfortune himself. Like any common churl and like a man overly concerned with the gross and earthly, Gareth asks Arthur to give him "mete and drynke" for a year, even though Arthur tells him to "aske bettyr," and even though the knights wonder at his boorishness. Kay, in particular, regards Gareth as merely "a vylayne borne" (213), who belongs only in the kitchen, and continually mocks the man. This derision that Kay levels at Gareth supplies in detail the lowering and humiliation that is symbolically Gareth's first test. Through the insults thrown at him, his humility and patience are being tested. Should he give way to his feelings and reveal himself, he will not be strong. It is not then the "mete and drynke" that will build up Gareth and give him strength to stand by himself; it is the humility and patience he must show in the face of the scorn directed at what seems to be his inordinate concern for food. Also, as Gareth later explains (229), his own conscious humiliation acts as a test for the Knights of the Round Table; for Gareth in his lowly position is able to see who his real friends are. He can, in particular, differentiate between those who value him for himself and those who do so only for his inherited rank.

Along with the development of Gareth, Malory also continues to emphasize the nobility of Lancelot, who appears principally as the courteous benefactor of the young man. Although Gawain too would like to help Gareth, Malory discounts his courtesy as one based on kinship. Even though Gawain is consciously unaware that any relationship exists between him and Gareth, he is still Gareth's brother, and his response to him is an instinctive one. Lancelot's actions, on the other hand, are presented as coming completely from "his grete jantylnesse and curtesy" (214).

After a year of preparation, Gareth moves from his humiliation and servitude to ask permission to go with a damsel who has come to Arthur's court requesting aid for her lady. Because the damsel will not reveal her lady's name but says only that she needs help against a "tirraunte," the Red Knight of the Red Lands, Arthur refuses to give her a champion from his Knights of the Round Table. When Gareth, however, is allowed to follow this adventure, the damsel is angry that she should get only a "kychyn knave." But Gareth now changes. As if by magic, rich armor appears for him; he fights and easily defeats Kay, who had wanted to know whether Gareth would recognize him "for his bettir" (216); and, concluding his preliminary preparation at Arthur's court, he fights to a draw and is knighted by Lancelot, the greatest knight in the world.[34]

The first part of Gareth's story ends with the hero rising from his position of "kychyn knave" and redeeming himself in the eyes of Arthur and his knights. In the second part of his tale (218–32) Gareth proves himself both to the damsel he accompanies and to the world outside Arthur's court. Although in this section Gareth shows great prowess, he also continues to reveal courtesy. His humility and patience are again put to the test, for the damsel continually berates, insults, and scorns him. For example, when Gareth overtakes her, she asks, "What doste thou here? Thou stynkyst all of the kychyn, thy clothis bene bawdy of the grece and talow. . . . What art thou but a luske [sluggard], and a turner of brochis [spits], and a ladyll-waysher?" (218). In her scorn, the damsel appears similar to Kay; but her taunts are harder for Gareth to bear. He cannot be revenged on her as he was on Kay; with the damsel, he experiences a real test of his innate courtesy, his *gentilesse*. Even after Gareth rescues a knight bound by "six theffis," kills two knights at a ford, slays the Black Knight, and defeats and receives homage from the Green Knight [35] and the Red Knight, the damsel still treats him with scorn. She states that his victories must have been accidental: "evir thou doste is by mysseadventure and nat by preues [prowess] of thy hondys." Throughout his adventures she condemns him with statements that he succeeds only through "myshappe" and "myssefortune" (220).

There is a kind of paradox in Gareth's situation. Unless the man be noble and worthy, his strength and prowess are in vain. It is, for example, like the strength of giants; and, in fact, when Gareth was earlier fighting Lancelot, Malory described him as fighting "more lyker a gyaunte than a knyght" (217). At the same time, unless the man be an able and strong fighter, he cannot be noble. There is truly a narrow path here, and only the best can walk along it.

It is not Gareth's prowess that makes the damsel recognize his worth and inherent nobility but his patience and endurance. The damsel and her words test him, but the test is not finished even after she acknowledges his nobility. When they come to the Blue Knight, the damsel admits that Gareth has done valorous deeds and acted and spoken well with her. Because he has proved himself, and because he and his horse are tired, she advises him to save himself and not fight the Blue Knight. Gareth, however, replies that he will still fight the man and thus refuses to feel that perfection is something one attains momentarily and then forgets. At this point the damsel, who is truly sorry about her previous scorn, says to Gareth, "so fowle and so shamfully dud never woman revyle a knight as I have done you, and ever curteysly ye have suffyrde me." Gareth modestly replies that "a knyght may lytyll do that may nat suffir a jantyllwoman" (229), and he consequently retains his humility.

While acting symbolically as a test for Gareth, the damsel also exists as a real flesh-and-blood person; she is not merely a creature of the supernatural or of magic evoked to prove him. In her treatment of Gareth she has been rash, too outspoken, and too full of *desmesure*. Gareth's humility shames her, and she develops into a more moderate, tolerant person.

The second part of the tale ends with Gareth's defeating the Blue Knight and receiving homage from him. Gareth has, in effect, proved himself as the hero—specifically, as the man of prowess and the gallant man of courtesy—and he is now allowed to know of his future test: the adventure that is the reason for his being with the damsel and that is the heart of the tale (232–41). It is revealed that the damsel is Lynet and that she is taking him to the Castel Daungerous to fight for her sister, Dame Lyones, who is besieged by the Red Knight of the Red Lands. This fight, however, is to be seen as more than a local fight and as more than a proving of Gareth's prowess. This Red Knight has kept up the siege of Lyones in hopes of fighting the noblest knights of the world: Lancelot, Tristram, Lamorak, or Gawain. By fighting for Lyoness, Gareth may be regarded as joining these warriors in prestige. Also Gareth fights not as an individual knight but as champion of Arthur's court and of knighthood in general.

The Red Knight of the Red Lands, Sir Ironsyde, is in one sense "a full noble knyght"—Gawain had earlier described him as "one of the perelest knyghtes of the worlde" (215)—but he is also lacking: "he is nother of curtesy, bounté, nother jantylnesse; for he attendyth unto nothyng but to murther" (234). In particular, this knight—like Tarquin in the *Tale of Lancelot* —makes "shamfull warre uppon noble knyghtes"; and, after he defeats them, he hangs them "by the necke, and their shyldis about their neckys with their swerdis and gylte sporys uppon their helys" (235). In other words, although this knight is "a full lykly man and a noble knyght of proues, and a lorde of grete londis and of grete possessions," he is imperfect because "in hym is no curtesy" (236).[36]

The conflicts in the *Tale of Gareth* may so far be seen in terms of three stages of development. First, Gareth himself acts as an *exemplum* of the conflict between hereditary nobility and achieved nobility. Then, when Gareth is in the company of the damsel, the first conflict is resolved; but a new one, a conflict between the man of prowess and the man of courtesy, is revealed and begins to be developed. Third, there appears the necessity of the hero's possessing both prowess and courtesy—the fusion of the two is lacking in the Red Knight of the Red Lands; and the fight between him and Gareth is symbolically a fight between imperfection and perfection, at least perfection as it exists so far in Gareth.

A variety of qualities not emphasized in the preceding *Tale of Lancelot* is brought out in the *Tale of Gareth*. The adventures, moreover, do not exist for their own sake but illustrate various imperfections and perfections and are, furthermore, steps along the way in the development of Gareth from Beaumains, the kitchen boy. Like the damsel Lynet, the Red Knight functions as a test for Gareth. He is, in fact, something of a supernatural creature whose strength, like Gawain's, increases till noon and then decreases. Gareth is told by Lynet that he should wait until afternoon to summon the Red Knight to battle, but Gareth characteristically refuses; and his response shows clearly the extent of his courtesy: "A! fy for shame, fayre damesell! Sey ye nevir so more to me, for and he were as good a knyght as ever was ony I shall never fayle hym in his moste myght, for other I wylll wynne worshyp worshypfully othir dye knyghtly in the felde" (236). Gareth would not be a true knight, a noble man, if he did not fight when his opponent had his full strength.

Also, a new development now appears: Gareth's prowess and valor are not wholly for the world of knighthood but are also for the Lady Lyones, with whom he falls in love. When Gareth falters during the fight, he is revived by Lynet's words: "A, sir Bewmaynes! Where is thy corrayge becom? Alas! my lady my sister beholdyth the, and she shrekys and wepys so that hit makyth myne herte hevy" (239). Gareth's renewed strength enables him to defeat the Red Knight, who then begs for mercy. Gareth says he cannot with *worship* spare him because of the shameful way he has treated his former opponents, but the Red Knight explains that he "putte hem to so shameful a deth" because of a promise to a lady and that she is responsible for his doing "vylany unto Arthurs knyghtes" (240). Unlike the evil Sir Tarquin of the *Tale of Lancelot*, the Red Knight has acted unchivalrously only because he has kept his word to someone else; he is not the one seeking revenge. Like Pelleas in the *Tale of Arthur*, the Red Knight is driven to an excess through the evil of someone else. When Gareth hears the arguments of "many erlys and barowns and noble knyghtes" who come forward to beg the life of the Red Knight and say that, if he is killed, "his myssededys that he done may not be undone" (240), Gareth agrees to spare the man. This victory ends the third section of the tale.

The fourth section (241–50) centers around Gareth's love of the Lady Lyones. When, after defeating the Red Knight, he goes to see her, he finds his way blocked; and the lady tells him that he will not enjoy her love until he is "one of the numbir of the worthy knyghtes." He is therefore supposed to "go and laboure in worshyp this twelve-monthe" (242). This assignment is the fourth step in Gareth's development, his ascent to earthly perfection. To be perfect in combat and in the world of the warrior is not necessarily to be so for love. The warrior and the lover represent not only two different ways of life, but the demands of each are different. One requires an external perfection, while the other insists on an internal worth. One would think that Gareth's courtesy would be enough to show that he is not only a man of prowess, but his courtesy must be demonstrated explicitly in terms of love. Although Gareth says to Lyones that he has already "bought" her love with the blood of his body, the lady adamantly insists that he prove himself further.

There is, however, confusion in the story; for no sooner does Gareth sorrowfully go his way than the lady sends her brother, Sir Gryngamour, after him to abduct Gareth's dwarf whom the lady plans to ask "of what kynrede" Gareth is come (243). Consequently, notwithstanding her earlier words to Gareth, it seems that what the Lady demands from Gareth is proof not only of an achieved nobility but also of an inherited one. The dwarf is taken, reveals his lord's ancestry, Gareth follows to rescue him, and in a short time the knight and Lyones declare their love. But the dwarf had already revealed to the lady Gareth's identity and ancestry (233). Despite all the confusion here, the important thing seems to be not that Gareth must prove himself further but that he must suffer the pangs of love before being rewarded with his lady's hand. Once again his patience and humility must dominate; he must, as it were, give his all for love.

Thus, after Gareth sorrowfully leaves Lyones, Malory writes that he is not able to sleep: he "had no reste, but walowed and wrythed for the love of the lady of that castell" (242). As Lynet says, not only is Gareth "curtyese and mylde" but he is also "the moste sufferynge [enduring] man" she ever knew (244). This suffering is presented as a quality, even as a virtue; and as such it is something new to the Arthurian chivalric order seen in Malory. Earlier, in the *Tale of Arthur* Pelleas had suffered for love, but his woe was presented as an excess and something to be avoided. In the *Tale of Gareth*, on the other hand, suffering means enduring and must of necessity be found in a man worthy of both victory in battle and the love of a noble lady.

But both Gareth and Lyones are so much "in hoote love" that they desire "to abate their lustys secretly" before marriage (247). This consummation, another example of *desmesure*, is prevented by the "subtyle craufftes" of Lynet, who suddenly appears possessing magic and being similar to Nyneve, the Damsel of the Lake, seen in the *Tale of Arthur*. She causes armed knights to intrude upon the two lovers as they lie together in bed; and, although Gareth keeps killing them, Lynet keeps bringing them back to life. Although Gareth criticizes her action, Lynet, by acting for Gareth as a kind of conscience based on chivalric and Christian ideals, does succeed in preventing the lovers from rashly consummating their love. She tells Gareth that everything she does "shall be for your worshyp and us all" (249).[37]

The rest of the *Tale of Gareth* (250–73) is primarily concerned with the hero's demonstrating his perfection, primarily his courtesy, to the world and especially to Arthur and his court. Gareth has Lyones call a tournament in which she will be the prize for the best knight. Gareth obviously expects to win the lady, and the tournament may be seen as the specific proof that will rank him among the best knights in the world. In effect, it is really what Lyones had desired when she sent Gareth away, but now it is Gareth himself who suggests the test.

In this tournament Malory seems more concerned with splen-

dor and combat than with Gareth's development. Whereas the
hero's action in declaring this tournament that could theoretically
end in his losing the lady might seem rash, proud, and even
marked by *desmesure*, no such implications are present. Malory
appears to be interested only in the tournament itself, and he glories in his descriptive art. In fact, in the whole *Tale of Gareth*
there is a striking play of color, of a quality found, as Vida Scudder says, nowhere else in the *Morte Darthur*.[38]

The tournament may be regarded as a battle of the greatest
knights in the world, and the list of participants reads like a roll-
call of the most famous of all Arthurian knights. Gareth, receiving
the help of the knights he had formerly defeated, takes on all of
Arthur's forces except Lancelot, who, out of courtesy, will not
fight him. The jousting ends inconclusively, however; for, when
Gareth's identity is discovered, he is so disturbed that he rides off
by himself into the forest. There he performs more acts of prowess
that seem to be largely superfluous and finally, in ignorance, fights
Gawain, his brother. Before either is killed, however, Lynet, now
described as the "lady Savyaige" (268), suddenly appears to stop
the fight. The tale ends with Gareth's receiving fealty from the
knights he has conquered, becoming a ruler in his own right,
and marrying Lyones. Malory also writes that in the future
Gareth draws away from the "evir vengeable" Gawain and comes
closer to Lancelot, who still remains his ideal. The imperfection in
Gareth's brother, specifically the fact that whenever Gawain
hates, "he wolde be avenged with murther" (270), is an imperfection that the good, proved Gareth cannot tolerate.[39]

The closeness of Gareth and Lancelot is not accidental, for this
entire tale is properly seen in conjunction with the *Tale of Lancelot*. The two men make up earthly perfection, and their two stories describe it; one complements the other. Also these two tales
act in conjunction with *Arthur and Lucius*, in which the perfection of Arthur and his Order is seen; and all together these tales
illustrate and create the perfection of chivalry in its various manifestations in this world.[40] All that is lacking is a detailed account of
perfection in terms of love. The subject was briefly seen in both
the stories of Lancelot and Gareth, but the detailed picture is re-
served for the next story, the *Book of Sir Tristram de Lyones*.
Although this romance is not merely a tale—it is longer than the

first four romances together—and although its subject, love, and its main character, Tristram, may be regarded as being apart from the main stream of the action in Malory's Arthur-saga, the story performs a real purpose of illustrating the quality and meaning of earthly love and of analyzing it in relation to chivalric ideals. It thus has a proper place in Malory's story of Arthur and his realm.

## IV  *The Man of Love*

The *Book of Sir Tristram de Lyones* (Caxton's Books VIII–XII) is invariably a disappointment to readers familiar with the story of the love between Tristan and Iseult as told, for example, by Thomas of Britain or Gottfried von Strassburg. Malory's source is not these earlier romances but the first two books of a version of a sprawling thirteenth-century French work called the Prose *Tristan*.[41] Although Malory may be partially exonerated of blame for the lack of organization and inadequate development of the story —his romance is six times shorter than the French—this section of the *Morte Darthur* is, nevertheless, invariably regarded as the weakest. Because of its great length and seemingly haphazard array of adventures, it has been adversely criticized as causing the whole of Malory's Arthur-saga to bog down.

Still, although there are without doubt very real dramatic flaws in this romance—flaws generally in its structure as a story in the modern sense of the word—the work does have an organization that may best be seen by viewing it thematically in terms of the ideas being stressed in the *Morte Darthur* as a whole. Many readers of the tale, however, would probably agree with Eugène Vinaver's criticism, that "in reinterpretating the story in his own way, as each medieval writer had done before him, Malory failed to give it a meaning, a *sen*, capable of supporting its complex and delicate narrative frame. He failed above all to grasp and bring out the tragic theme, essential to any coherent form of the Tristan legend and still discernible in its prose version." [42] These words have truth if one views the romance by itself, but it is necessary to realize, as Vinaver does elsewhere, that the French prose *Tristan* itself shifted the emphasis of the legend "from the original story of tragic love to the protagonist's adventures in the service of the Round Table." [43] It was probably this shift that was important to Malory, for his *Book of Tristram* presents love as one of the qualities necessary to the ideal knight and functions, not merely as Malory's redoing of the Tristan story, but as an integral part of his Arthur-saga and as an essential piece in his picture of the hero.[44]

Earlier, Lancelot and Gareth had appeared as complements of the ideal knight; but it must not be forgotten that Gareth's merit was defined in terms of Lancelot, the prototype of nobility. In a sense then, Gareth's story acted as an objective or detached restatement of Lancelot's own *enfances*, showing in detail the element of personal merit found in Lancelot and, by implication, in all good knights. Such a view is reinforced by an episode in the *Book of Tristram*—which may have a relationship to the *Tale of Gareth*—where a poorly dressed knight, later called La Cote Male Tayle, comes to court and asks to be knighted. Several knights recommend to Arthur that he overlook the man's poor clothing and grant what he asks; for, as they remind the king, "evyn suche one was sir Launcelot whan he cam fyrst into this courte, and full fewe of us knew from whens he cam" (342).

Other courtly qualities found in Lancelot, specifically those relating to him as the lover of Guinevere, become the main subject of the *Book of Tristram*. In it love permeates all the adventures: knights fight for love, quest for love, and even seem meritorious because of love. The pages of this book are, in fact, filled with lovers—Tristram, Lancelot, Lamorak, Palomides, Bleoberys, La Cote Male Tayle, Meliagraunce, Kahydin, Alexander the Orphan, Epinogris, and Bors. Each of these knights has a lady that spurs him on to noble deeds and, consequently, causes his nobility to increase; but the ladies are hardly emphasized at all. The figure of Isode, for example, is, as Vinaver writes, "neither the 'Iseut douloureuse et forte' of the old poems, nor the sophisticated courtly queen of the French prose romance, but an affectionate and ingenious *amie*."[45] Emphasized in Malory in place of characters or story is the courtly idea that love ennobles those who feel its power. Rather than stress the physical acts of love—rarely are a knight and his lady in bed together—the story primarily emphasizes the goodness that results from being in love. Love may then be regarded as something like one's ancestry: it gives the worthy man an additional value, but worth must be there for it to act. The unworthy lover is the lecher, the man interested only in the physical fact and incapable of being influenced by love's virtues.

In obvious contrast to the many lovers in the book are knights who are incapable of loving, who hate, who are ungentle, and who lack mercy. In particular, there is Sir Brewns sans Pité, who is supposedly "at that tyme the most myschevuste [wicked] knyght lyvnge (418). Said to be a great coward, Sir Brewns rides throughout the romance in chase of damsels in order to behead them; but he flees when he is challenged by a strong knight. Another nonlover is King Mark, Tristram's uncle and Isode's husband, presented as "the moste vylaunce knyght of the worlde" (441) and "the shamfullist knyght of a kynge that is now lyvynge, for he is a grete enemy to all good knyghtes" (431). Tristram's love for Isode, wife of Mark, is, as Vinaver comments, "fully justified because Tristram was a true knight and Mark an enemy of knighthood." [46]

Also in contrast to the lovers, as well as to the vicious men, is Sir Dinadan, a humorous cynical knight who, although not the best jouster, is still the "best felawe" and the friend of all good knights. In the Prose *Tristan*, Dinadan functions as a delightful but somewhat misanthropic critic of the chivalric concepts of duty and valor. Perhaps, as Vinaver believes, Malory failed to appreciate the knight's unconventional criticism against this ideal of knighthood.[47] Perhaps Malory may also have felt that Dinadan's words would obscure his theme in the *Morte Darthur*. In any case, he deletes what in the French are Dinadan's most serious ironic speeches against chivalry; he reduces his words to mere *bonhomie* and Dinadan himself to a mere "good fellow."

At the same time, Malory effectively uses Dinadan's words against love, especially in a passage that reduces a long disquisition in the French to less than three lines. When asked by Tristram if he is not a lover, Dinadan exclaims: "Mary, fye on that crauffte!" (511); later he adds, "God deffende me . . . for the joy of love is to shorte, and the sorrow thereof and what cometh thereof is duras [hardship] over longe" (516). But, as Tristram replies to his initial exclamation, "a knyght may never be of proues but yf [unless] he be a lovear" (511). While this brief exchange can hardly give the character portrayal of Dinadan found in the French, Malory has emphasized neither Dinadan nor his criticism but Tristram's words in reply. In fact, the idea in this statement acts as the real, over-all theme of the *Book of Tristram*. Malory is emphasizing that the hero must be not only the man of prowess and of courtesy but also the man of love who possesses all those qualities of inner development that can come from selfless devotion. The lustful and even romantic elements of love do not appear as important; rather, love is a quality closely resembling courtesy, since it develops the interior man.

Just as the *Tale of Gareth* had isolated and emphasized in other terms the quality of courtesy found in Lancelot, so does the *Book of Tristram* show objectively the hero as lover. Lancelot is again to be seen as the figure of perfection to whom Tristram is compared. Illustrating prowess, courtesy, and love—qualities which he contains within him—Lancelot functions as the epitome of earthly perfection. Gawain and other knights possessing only prowess are easily proved inadequate; Gareth, man of courtesy, and Tristram, man of love, incorporate prowess within themselves but possess more than this simple quality. Each figure also has something of the other in him—Gareth is shown as the lover of Dame Lyones, and Tristram is continually portrayed as courteous —but for purposes of theme, Malory uses Gareth primarily to illustrate courtesy and Tristram to show the qualities deriving from love. Although these knights are superior men, they are still not so good as Lancelot, who holds the three qualities in a balance not achieved by the others. Also, Lancelot's perfection is presented as going beyond his specific tale. When Tristram appears in the *Tale of Gareth*, it is as a knight who admires the nobility of Gareth; likewise, when Gareth is seen in the *Book of Tristram*, he is a good man but not half so strong and valiant as when Malory's emphasis was on his acquired nobility. Lancelot, however, possesses a merit that does not appear to fluctuate—at least not in the tales preceding the account of the Grail Quest.

Stressing the nobility that realized love can give to a knight, the *Book of Tristram* also shows what happens when love is unsatisfied or thwarted, or when the lover is, or thinks he is, out of his lady's favor. Sir Palomides, who loves La Belle Isode but who cannot take the place of Tristram in her heart, suffers and weeps throughout the romance. Although he seems in his external actions to be ennobled by love—he fights best when in Isode's presence—he is flawed by an envy of Tristram that he is freed from only in the final pages of the book. Also Sir Lamorak, son of Pelli-nore and one of the best knights in the world, loves Queen Mar-gawse, widow of King Lot; but he is thwarted because of the hatred between his family and the children of Lot, that is, Gawain and his brothers. In fact, when Gaherys, Gawain's brother, comes upon his mother and Sir Lamorak in bed together, he cuts off Margawse's head and, in effect, takes away Lamorak's reason for being. Soon after this incident Lamorak is reported to have been killed at the hands of Gawain and his brothers, a death that indi-cates the continuation of the old family feud; but it is also a death that is necessary since Lamorak's love is dead. Deaths for unre-quited love are also frequent in the book. One of the first episodes reveals how the daughter of the King of France, who had loved Tristram in vain, "dyed for sorou" (282); and later Sir Kahydin is said to have actually "dyed for the love" of La Belle Isode (366).

The episode of Kahydin's desolate love is also important as a transition to the story of Tristram's going mad because of his love. Having seen the letters of Kahydin and Isode, Tristram accuses them of falseness and leaves in sorrow. After grieving for months, he finally runs into the forest and goes mad, and for half a year "than was he naked, and waxed leane and poore of fleyshe" (369).[48] A similar madness is also related in the brief account of Sir Matto le Breune, who had lost his lady to Sir Gaherys (371); and even the great Lancelot himself wanders mad for two years. Tricked to the bed of another woman, Elaine, Lancelot is con-fronted by Guinevere who accuses him of being a "false traytoure knyght" and commands him never to see her again. After waking from a swoon into which his grief has caused him to fall, Lancelot runs away: "he lepte oute at a bay-wyndow into a gardyne, and there with thornys he was all to-cracched [badly scratched] of his vysage [face] and hys body, and so he ranne furth he knew nat whothir, and was as wylde woode [stark mad] as ever was man. And so he ran two yere, and never man had grace to know hym" (594).

As such madness illustrates, not only does the *Book of Tristram* demonstrate the effects of love—requited and unrequited—on good men; it also shows the excesses of love, even the perversions it causes. For example, when Tristram returns with Isode from Ireland, they arrive at the Castle Plewre, "the wepynge castell," where the custom is for the beauty of the guest lady to be compared with that of the lady of the castle. As Sir Brewnor, the lord of the castle, explains to Tristram, "for and [if] thy lady be feyrar than myne, with thy swerde smyte of [off]my ladyes hede, and yf my lady be fayrer than thyne, with my swerde I muste stryke of hir hede. And if I may wynne the, yette shall thy lady be myne, and thow shalt lese [lose] thy hede" (313). To Tristram, this is "a foule custom and an horryble," and he destroys lord, lady, and custom.

There are many other examples of excess in love. Because of her unreciprocated love of Arthur, the sorceress, Aunoure, tries to have the king killed (364). Because of her inordinate love of Lancelot, Morgan le Fay hates Guinevere and tries constantly to shame Arthur and his court (413). For the love of Morgan, Sir Malegryne says that he has killed ten good knights, and "by outerage and orgulyté," excess and pride, has slain ten more (479). Sir Alexander is told that Morgan keeps him prisoner "for none other entente but to do hir plesure whan hit lykyth [pleases] hir" (480). Sir Persydes is "bounden wyth a chayne faste aboute the waste unto a pylloure [piller] of stone" because he had refused to be the lover of an "uncurteyse lady" (600); he is finally freed by Sir Perceval who says that "this is a shamefull custom of a lady" (601). Although these examples may be multiplied, they are sufficient to show the varieties and degrees of love and lust found in the book.

Indeed, love in all its good and bad manifestations may be seen as the subject of everything in this romance, and it must be emphasized that it is love and not one lover that Malory is writing about. As Vida Scudder notes, Tristram, "splendid and famous knight though he be, is purposely and systematically degraded, in order that the high light may fall steadily on Lancelot." [49] However, this emphasis is made, not because Malory wants to reduce Tristram, but because Tristram exists in this romance only to show objectively and in concrete form one aspect of perfection: one aspect of Lancelot, who has been and still is the ideal figure. Likewise, the love between Tristram and Isode functions as a parallel to the love between Lancelot and Guinevere and prevents it from seeming anomalous. Had Malory told the story of the love between Tristram and Isode for itself, bringing out its "tragic theme," he would have presented something not integrally associated either with the Arthur-saga he was writing or with love as one of the qualities—not as *the* quality—a knight must possess. In his romance, Tristram is the prototype of the lover; but he is by no means the only lover—nor can he be if the book is to have any real unity.

Several critics of Malory's story, noticing that he has a tendency to push the love-intrigue into the background, have berated the author for showing what they consider a distaste for love, or at least for sophisticated courtly love. For these critics the romance shows, primarily it seems," "Malory's moral disapproval." [50] But, as Vinaver has perceptivly noted, Malory "wants Tristram to be more consistently and more deliberately concerned with knight-hood than was his French prototype, and to look upon the 'service of love' as yet another form of his self-assertion as a champion of the 'high order.' " [51] This statement expresses precisely the intent, for Malory has used the Tristram story for its presentation of love, but he has used love itself as one of those qualities compos-ing the ideal knight.

While the book, then, may be regarded as awkward in narrative structure, and while it is difficult, because of the principle of *entrelacement,* to read as a developing story with a beginning, middle, and end, all the episodes making up the work serve a thematic purpose. They exist to illustrate the idea that the hero must be the lover, that all men may receive a nobility through love as well as through prowess and courteous conduct. The repetitive nature of the episodes, which annoys many readers, serves to drive this point home.

Still, Malory is concerned with narrative, with story; and many details in the *Book of Tristram* are concise and complete in them-selves. One of the best tales is that of Alexander the Orphan, which recounts in a few pages the birth, *enfances,* maturity, and death of this knight and is what Vinaver calls "a characteristic example of a biographical novel interpolated in a cyclic ro-mance." [52] In particular, this tale—first appearing in a thirteenth-century prose romance called *Les Prophécies de Merlin* and later added to the Prose *Tristan*—stresses the courtesy and love of Al-exander, a young knight whose father has been murdered by King Mark and who is himself hated by this evil king.

Having made a vow to remain a year and a day in a certain

castle, Alexander is dismayed when he finds that he is, in effect, a prisoner of the lust of Morgan le Fay. Nevertheless, even when this castle of Morgan is razed to the ground, Alexander remains for his appointed time, defending a plot of ground that had been within the castle. This "pyce of erthe" becomes the setting for the main action of the tale and a microcosm of the outer world of tournaments and adventures. Here he jousts with both good and bad knights, including Mordred; and he proves himself a truly noble man: "for every day in that twelve-monthe he had to do wyth one knyght owther wyth another, and som day with three or four, and there was never knyght that put hym to the warre [defeated him]" (484). He also meets a lady whom he loves. At the end of his year, he departs with the lady but never has the "grace ne fortune" to get to Arthur's court. Rather, he is later murdered by Mark; but, in a passage appearing only in Malory, his son, Bellengerus, is said to avenge him. Malory ends this tale by emphasizing that, even though he existed apart from the court, Alexander was "one of the strengyste knyghtes that was in kynge Arthurs dayes" (484). In relation to the rest of the *Book of Tristram,* this episode reinforces the evil associated with Mark and also gives another picture of love joined to prowess and courtesy. In a developed form the story could easily exist by itself, but here are emphasized only those parts of it that are relevant to the theme of Malory's romance.

The framing device or, more precisely, the starting point for the various tales and adventures in this book is the story of Tristram and Isode, the most famous lovers of the Western world. Although the first section of the book shows the development of this love, the love itself remains static throughout most of the book and is not the center of the action. It is the point of origin of Malory's theme, but, after it appears, other tales and adventures intertwine with it. Together, all develop the picture and theme of love found in the book. Although it is impossible in this study to analyze all the episodes in this romance, which is one-third of the length of the entire *Morte Darthur,* one thread may be followed to show something of Malory's method.

Throughout the book, in contrast to Tristram appears the figure of Palomides, a good knight so tormented by his unsatisfied love of Isode that he envies and hates his rival, Tristram. In fact, Palomides, invented by the prose romances as a foil to Tristram, may be regarded as the Lover Hopeless. Although Palomides is a man of prowess, Tristram is a better warrior; and throughout most of the romance Palomides feels frustrated and shamed. For him, earthly fame and love appear to be everything; and, even though he realizes how envy can jeopardize his conduct and his reputation, he cannot rid himself of this sin. As Guinevere says, if Palomides is envious, his other merits lose their value: "Than shall he never wynne worshyp . . . for and [if] hyt happyn an envyous man onys [once] to wynne worshyp, he shall be dishonoured twyse therefore. And for this cause all men of worshyp hate an envyous man and woll shewe hym no favoure, and he that ys curteyse and kynde and jantil hath favoure in every place" (567). Besides making him envious, Palomides' frustration also causes him to appear at times almost schizophrenic. At one moment he admires Tristram, but at the next he tries to shame and even kill him. Once when complaining that he can "never wyn worship where sir Trystram ys," Palomides is asked by Tristram in disguise what he would do if Tristram were present: " 'I wolde fyght with hym,' seyde sir Palomydes, 'and ease my harte uppon hym. And yet, to say the sothe, sir Trystram ys the jantyllyste knyght in thys worlde lvynge' " (394).

Described as following the "questyng beste"—an adventure given to Pellinore in the *Tale of Arthur*—Palomides is also presented as the continual searcher. When a boat appears that contains the body of a knight and a letter asking some noble knight to journey across the water and avenge him, it is Palomides who requests permission to take the adventure. Moreover, a great point is made that Palomides is a Saracen. Although he believes in Christ and in the Christian life, he refuses to be baptized, as he explains, "tyll I have done seven trewe bataylis for Jesus sake" (496). In the last few pages of the tale, Tristram meets Palomides in what is his final battle "for Jesus sake"; the two knights become reconciled; and the *Book of Tristram* concludes with Palomides' being baptized and continuing to follow the questing beast.

The final battle and the reconciliation between Tristram and Palomides, which do not appear in the French, have a very important function in Malory's whole tale. They give a dramatic climax to a conflict that has run throughout the whole romance; consequently, they suggest that something has ended, that the knights have arrived at a level that makes further jousting unnecessary.[53] It is important to note that at the end of this tale Palomides' character has strikingly changed. No longer is he flawed by envy or by an inordinate desire for earthly honors and love. As Vida Scudder remarks, the "pure ennobling power of love is shown through him in its perfection." [54] As he changes, so, significantly, does the whole tone of the action. Everything concludes on a note of happiness that is not found in the prose *Tristan*, which ends with the death of the lovers, Tristan and Iseult. The unhappy ending, found in the third part of the French romance, is omitted by Malory because, as D. S. Brewer perceptively points out, in Malory the "central tales of Lancelot, Gareth, Tristram, and a number of minor characters, are all devoted to the glory and success of the knights of the Round Table." [55] At the same time, Malory's omission of the unhappy ending is similar to his change at the end of the *Arthur and Lucius*. Not yet ready for the final disasters, he still shows the world of the Round Table as developing; and at the end of his *Book of Tristram*, he prepares for the final step of the development.[56]

At this point in his story, in the last few episodes of this tale, Malory presents a glimpse of the world above the transitory. The emphasis now is on the Holy Grail, the object and ideal of holiness in the next romance for which the knights of the Round Table search *en masse*, and also on the fact that one must be good in order to come into contact with the Grail and pure in order to see it and its bearer. At King Pelles' castle, before tricked into lying with Pelles' daughter, Elaine, and into thus conceiving the future Grail hero, Galahad, Lancelot is actually fed by the Grail. There appears to him a "lytyll senser of golde" from which came "suche a savour as all the spycery of the worlde had bene there. And furthwythall there was uppon the table all maner of meates and drynkes that they coude thynke uppon." Then "there came in a damesell passynge fayre and yonge, and she bare a vessell of golde betwyxt her hondis" (583–84). Sir Bors also sees the Grail and has many strange adventures in the Grail Castle (588); Perceval and Ector, having fought and being almost dead, are healed by the Grail (603); and Lancelot, having run mad for two years, is made sane by it (610). The excesses resulting from war and love are thus shown corrected, as it were, by the Grail. It has the power to control the human and, through its presence, to raise man's actions from a gross earthly level.

The new emphasis on the Grail parallels the change in Palomides' way of life. This change, emphasizing that Palomides is no longer bound by his passion or to his worldly desire, is significantly in accord with the holiness and the new kind of perfection stressed at the end of the *Book of Tristram*. Palomides becomes, in fact, something of a model for the Order of the Round Table. Just as he is able to turn from earthly love and fame, so must all the knights be more than men of prowess, courtesy, and love. The perfect knight—the hero perfect in *every* way—must also be pure; and this purity the noble Knights of the Round Table, including the great Lancelot, do not have. All have been shown as lovers— as men delighting in and striving for things of this world.

Now, as love changes from the earthly to the spiritual, it is necessary that God as the object of love replace the mutable earthly objects. The Knights of the Round Table must now go on a spiritual quest that gives meaning to all their previous worldly quests. The prowess, courtesy, and love that the knights have attained are to be only steps up a ladder; and, although through these qualities the knights may reach a perfection of sorts, there is yet something more for which they must strive. The Order of the Round Table and its individual knights have set up on earth a kingdom and a way of life approaching that of the heavenly Jerusalem, but they must understand more of the actual City of God. Their undertaking is shown in the next tale, the *Tale of the Sankgreal*.

As before, Lancelot is the fount of perfection; and, although he is impure because of his affairs with Guinevere, he is still the logical father of the pure knight, the Grail Hero. Like Gareth and Tristram, Sir Galahad, the central figure of the next tale, stems from Lancelot; but, unlike these knights, who demonstrate in their characters virtues possessed by Lancelot, Galahad goes beyond his father. It is significant, and it shows something of the control Malory is exerting over his material, that Galahad appears at Arthur's court and sits in the Sege Perelous at the same feast celebrating the christening of Palomides.

CHAPTER 4

# Holiness and the Quest for Perfection

## I   The Quest and the Pilgrimage

MALORY'S source for his *Tale of the Sankgreal* (Caxton's Books XIII–XVIII) was a version of the thirteenth-century French prose work, the *Queste del Saint Graal*.[1] Although part of the Vulgate Cycle of romances, the *Queste* is concerned less with matters of chivalry than with matters of grace. On the surface it is also very different from other works in the Cycle, for it is filled with religious allegory and theological didacticism. In its spiritual concepts the *Queste* seems to follow Augustinian ideas as seen particularly in the twelfth-century mystic, St. Bernard of Clairvaux, and the work may have been written by a thirteenth-century Cistercian monk.[2]

According to Eugène Vinaver, Malory entered in the *Queste* "a totally unfamiliar sphere"; he found himself "more out of his element than ever before"[3] and could consequently approach the work only by trying to deprive the French story of its religious significance: "Malory the man was certainly not a believer in the supernatural: the simple method of collation shows how consistently he cut it down in adapting his French books. And he was certainly not interested in the complexities of the Grail doctrine, as the same method amply demonstrates."[4] Specifically, according to Vinaver, instead of interpreting the material in his own way, Malory "simply 'reduced' all doctrinal comment, shifted the emphasis from theological disquisitions to poetical representation, and so made the Grail quest appear as a mere pageant of picturesque visions."[5] In his criticism of Malory's romance, Vinaver has even gone so far as to write that "Malory's *Quest* is indeed a confused and almost pointless story, a beautiful parade of symbols and bright visions";[6] but, at the same time, he grants that it is through Malory's version "that the symbol of the Grail has reached in our imagination that degree of reality without which no symbol can live." [7]

Recently C. S. Lewis has pointed to what he appropriately terms a paradox in this view. Although, as he says, "a case can be made out for the view that Malory evaded the religious significance" of the French and that he "ignored or severed" the connection between the Grail story and the final downfall of Arthur and the Round Table, his handling of the Grail story still "sounds deeply religious" and gives the impression that it is "profoundly connected" with what finally happens. For Lewis, Malory's Grail story is "ethical, as against mystical. But we must not say 'ethical, as against religious.'" [8] Recently, Vinaver has restated his position; he says of Malory that, "much as he tries to cut down the religious exposition and even substitute the worldly for the divine, he produces a work which makes a more deeply religious impression on one's mind than the strictly orthodox original upon which it is based." [9]

In Malory's *Tale of the Sankgreal*, the action moves beyond earthly perfection, and the knights are concerned no longer with matters of this world. The tournaments, battles, quests, and loves that have played such a significant part in the action of the previous tales are not only negated but shown as wrong. The call is to a new cause, that which Paul refers to in the words, "Let Christ Jesus himself be the armour that you wear; give no more thought to satisfying the bodily appetites." [10]

C. S. Lewis has perceptively pointed out that "The recall is not from knighthood to the cloister but from knighthood as it has come to be (full of 'sin and wickedness') to knighthood as it was intended to be, grounded in 'patience and humility.'" [11] As P. E. Tucker writes, knighthood represented for Malory "the highest excellence in a man," and in the *Morte Darthur* terms like "chivalry" and "worship" take on "a moral significance." Although throughout his first five tales Malory had presented chivalry as an ideal in itself, in the *Tale of the Sankgreal* he begins "to distinguish between good chivalry and bad—the good consisting in 'knyghtly dedys and vertuous lyvyng,' . . . the bad in Lancelot's devoting his service to Guinevere." [12]

At the same time, things of this world are now portrayed as only shadows of realities beyond the flesh; and it is presumptuous for the knights to think that they can accomplish anything of consequence either in worldly matters or by themselves. Although one hundred and fifty knights leave Arthur's court and go on the Quest of the Holy Grail, only a few attain it. These few succeed not because of their individual efforts, but because they are the chosen heroes: they have divine grace. At the same time, it is necessary that these knights—Galahad, Perceval, and Bors—be worthy of success. But being worthy now means being holy and pure, and it is no accident that these three knights had played little or no part in the earlier adventures of the Round Table. No impure man—no matter how much he excels in prowess, courtesy, and earthly love—can fulfil the Quest of the Grail. The most such a man can get is what Lancelot receives—a tantalizing glimpse of the holy vessel, a glimpse into the eternal world.

Not only must one be clean, one must also possess firm faith and hope in God. When Lancelot approaches the Grail Castle, he sees two lions guarding the entrance. Behaving like the valiant knight he is, he draws his sword and prepares to fight. An invisible force, however, knocks the sword from his hand; and a voice says to him, "O, man of evylle feyth and poure byleve! Wherefore trustist thou more on thy harneyse [arms] than in thy Maker?" (726). Lancelot then returns his sword to its scabbard, crosses himself, and passes the lions without harm. The point is that one with belief in God can achieve everything; without this belief, one accomplishes nothing.

One can hardly agree with Vinaver that the Quest of the Holy Grail was for Malory merely "an *Arthurian* adventure, . . . an opportunity offered to the knights of the Round Table to achieve still greater glory in *this* world," and that Malory was "primarily concerned with 'erthly worship,' not with any higher purpose." [13] The values of the world that Malory has been describing in his Arthur-saga have without doubt changed. Earlier, the qualities associated with prowess, courtesy, and love—valor, strength, skill in arms, *gentillese, mesure,* and obedience to lord and lady—were presented as sufficient for one to be great; but, now that a world beyond that of chivalry has been explicitly revealed to the knights, their own values must change. The knights are shown the direction their lives must take; and, if they do not follow this direction, they will be wasting their lives. Christ has, as it were, now been revealed to the Arthurian world; and, after the revelation, there is no excuse for not following in his path. The past good of Arthur's court is not the present good, for the knights are now required to move beyond this world.

It is not even a question here of fighting or of questing for perfection in the world, for, as Malory reveals concerning Gawain, who is presented as an imperfect knight lacking grace, he "rode longe withoute ony adventure, for he founde nat the tenthe parte of aventures as they were wonte [accustomed] to have" (679). When Gawain meets Ector, he finds that the same is true of this other imperfect knight. Both men are "wery" of searching for the Grail, and Ector furthermore states that he has met "twenty knyghtes that be felowys of myne, and all they complayne as I do" (679). These knights regard the Grail Quest as an adventure in this world, but such quests are now insignificant, as are the skills the knights have used to attain their goals. The only important adventures occur now as part of the Quest of the Grail and when the chosen knights are acting as agents of God. When, for example, Galahad, Perceval, and Bors find themselves in Scotland fighting the enemies of Arthur, they slay, before they know it, a "grete multitude" and think they themselves are, as a consequence, "grete synners" (716). But, as a holy man tells them, they have killed false, unchristened men, and have "ben avenged on Goddis enemyes." As Galahad realizes, "and [if] hit had nat pleased oure Lorde, never sholde we have slayne so many men in so litill a whyle" (717). Like Arthur and his army in the *Tale of Arthur and Lucius*, these knights are agents or representatives of the divine force of right.

Generally speaking, however, external adventures are no longer important, as is indicated by the paucity of fighting in the tale. In fact, the whole conception of the meaning of *quest* is re-evaluated in this *Tale of the Sankgreal*. On the basis of the previous tales, *quest* may be defined as the search for external adventures, one involving the knight as a man in the world outside himself. This meaning is very different from that found in the present tale, where the search is symbolically beyond the world and within the individual. The previous quests now appear to have been mere wanderings that illustrated the restlessness of man and that did not give him ease. Although the quests of the earlier tales had been regarded as necessary for knights-errant, as something to counter-act inactivity and to demonstrate the knights' worthiness, these former searches for adventure are now seen in a new way. Through them, the knights have not gained anything lasting; the questers are no better off than the unhappy knights wandering mad in forests as in the *Book of Tristram*.

As St. Augustine says, addressing God, "Thou hast created us for Thyself, and our hearts know no rest until they find repose in Thee." Man may search in the world forever; but, as is implied, until he finds the Way that leads him beyond this world, he must be regarded as merely a "vagabond, straying through wooded places, and rough places, torn in all his limbs." [14] In this view man cannot find rest until he finds the Truth, God; but in this world "the best man is he who makes his whole life a journey toward the immutable life, and adheres to it with all his affections." [15] In Malory, this journey appears particularly as the Quest of the Holy Grail.

In fact, the search for the Grail may be regarded more as a pilgrimage than as a quest, and the knights who go on it must remove their earthly garments and put on new clothes. To redeem himself of his past misdeeds and to purify himself, Lancelot, for example, is told to wear a dead man's hair shirt and to "ete no fleysshe as longe as ye be in the queste of Sankgreall, nother ye shall drynke no wyne, and that ye hyre [hear] masse dayly" (673). Bors is told to wear a "scarlet cote" instead of a shirt "in sygne of chastisemente" and to eat only bread and water until he sits "at the table where the Sankgreal shall be" (687).

Another impure knight, Sir Gawain, is told he must do penance for his sins; but he replies, "Nay, . . . I may do no penaunce, for we knyghtes adventures [adventurous] many tymes suffir grete woo and payne" (651). For Gawain, earthly prowess is every-thing; he cannot imagine a search that does not value this quality. Told that he must do more than regard the superficial active life as an end in itself, Gawain does not comprehend and appears almost like a buffoon. Again, when told later by a holy man that he is like a barren tree and must repent, Gawain says, "and [if] I had leyser I wolde speke with you" (686); but the adventures in this world are so pressing tht he cannot take time out to be saved. Gawain errs in thinking that he can achieve anything while he is impure. Again, in St. Augustine's words, "whosoever supposes that he can know truth, while he is still leading a wicked life, is in error." [16] Gawain is, in fact, so much in error that he is warned twice to repent; he may be viewed, therefore, as similar to the kind of man Paul spoke of when he wrote, "A heretic should be warned once, and once again; after that, have done with him, recognizing that a man of that sort has a distorted mind and stands self-condemned in his sin." [17] It is not that Gawain is a priori bad, though Charles Moorman feels that Malory has made him "an almost totally bad character." [18] Instead, as Eugène Vinaver points out, Gawain has "earthly virtues and is very much loved and honoured. . . . But since God has no part in his career," Gawain can end only "as a vile criminal." [19]

Opposed to Gawain and knights like him are Galahad, Perceval, and Bors for whom the Quest of the Holy Grail is really a search for spiritual realities, for perfection, and for salvation; and the adventures of these knights prepare them for receiving the Grail. These men—at least Perceval and Bors—are like initiates who must be instructed, tested, and made whole. Only then will they be fit to be the earthly guardians of the Grail and to receive its blessings.

Furthermore, the adventures of the Grail Questers are presented for the edification of the reader, and the various episodes must be seen as containing a meaning beyond the surface narrative. Here explicitly the content exists wholly to reveal a *sententia,* a symbolic meaning, behind it. It is, therefore, necessary to comprehend the various adventures and the signs revealed to the knights so as to get at the peculiarly Christian meaning that is the reason for the existence of the episodes. Speaking of these episodes, that may seem at first to be monotonous, Vida Scudder says: "The colors are faint, the visible world is seen as if through a blur of pallid moonshine, the knights pass through ghostly and unconvincing adventures, explained in far-fetched allegories." [20] These "far-fetched allegories" are the specific truths revealed in the tale; to deny them is to miss the point of the Quest of the Holy Grail in Malory's Arthur-saga.

Though presented by Vinaver in the form of nine parts, the *Tale of the Sankgreal* may be viewed as divided into three over-all sections—the first relates the preliminary adventures before the actual Quest, along with the initial miracles of Galahad; the second emphasizes the adventures of Perceval, Lancelot, Bors, and Galahad in particular, with special emphasis given to the purification and testing of Perceval, Lancelot, and Bors; and the third shows the achieving of the Grail and the adventures of Galahad, Perceval, and Bors after they bear the holy vessel to Sarras.

Within this general division, however, is another more subtle one that serves to explain the order of episodes, an order that may at first seem strange. The main character in the tale is without doubt Galahad, the perfect knight, though Perceval and Bors are of equal importance in terms of the action. But the work is not merely their story, for, interspersing accounts of them are the adventures of several other knights, such as Lancelot, Gawain, Ector, Lionel, Bagdemagus, and Melyot. In what is Vinaver's third chapter, the explicit testing and proving of Perceval are seen; but then in the next main actions, corresponding to Vinaver's fourth and fifth chapters, the narrative emphasizes Lancelot and Gawain respectively. Only with chapter six does the narrative come to the explicit testing and proving of Perceval's peer, Bors. Because Bors' adventures parallel those of Perceval in their emphasis on initiation and redemption, it would seem that the stories of these two knights should appear side by side and not be separated by two accounts of lesser figures.

If, however, the *Tale of the Sankgreal* is viewed as falling into three groups, each having three main episodes (corresponding to Vinaver's chapters), an interesting order appears. The first three episodes, or chapters, show the departure of the knights on the Quest of the Holy Grail, the initial wonders, and finally the perfection of Perceval, which acts as the culmination of this first section. After his perfection, Perceval must wait apart from the world for his two other comrades to join him. The second group of episodes, Vinaver's chapters four through six, shows imperfect knights making various attempts to succeed in their adventures; and the section culminates, like the first group, in the testing and proving of a special knight, Bors, who then joins Perceval to wait for Galahad. But Galahad needs no proving or perfection, for he has been shown as perfect from the beginning. Consequently, the third group of three episodes or chapters begins with his joining Perceval and Bors, who are now fit to receive his company; and it ends with their achieving the Grail and leaving the world of Arthur's realm.

Before proceeding to an analysis of the Grail Quest as it is detailed in Malory, it is necessary to pause over the scene in which the Grail appears to Arthur's court. Although the description of this appearance has often been quoted, it deserves to be repeated:

Than anone they harde crakynge and cryynge of thundir, that hem thought the palyse sholde all to-dryve [burst apart]. So in the myddys of the blast entyrde a sonnebeame, more clerer by seven tymys than ever they saw day, and all they were alyghted of the grace of the Holy Goste. Than began every knyght to beholde other, and eyther saw other, by their semynge, fayrer than ever they were before. Natforthan [nevertheless] there was no knyght that myght speke one worde a grete whyle, and so they loked every man on other as they had bene doome [dumb].

Than entird into the halle the Holy Grayle coverde with whyght samyte [silk], but there was none that myght se hit nother whom that bare hit. And there was all the halle fulfylled [filled full] with good odoures, and every knyght had such metis and drynkes as he beste loved in thys worlde.

And whan the Holy Grayle had bene borne thorow the hall, than the holy vessell departed suddeynly, that they wyst [knew] nat where hit becam. Than had they all breth to speke, and than the kyng yelded thankynges to God of Hys good grace that He had sente them.

(634)

At this "mervayle" the knights vow to quest for the Grail, seconding Gawain's pledge to search for it "a twelve-month and a day or more if nede be," and never to return to court until they have "sene hit more opynly than hit hath bene shewed here" (635). The knights soon find that this special quest needs virtues other than prowess and courtesy. Now the questing knights must excel in prudence, fortitude, temperance, justice, faith, hope, and charity—the Cardinal and Theological Virtues—and must exercise these virtues in the search for Truth. They must choose the right way, persevere and avoid succumbing to excesses or to pride, and they must put their faith in God.

As the knights set out, Guinevere and other ladies are in "grete sorow." In fact, "many of tho ladyes that loved knyghtes wolde have gone with hir lovis." But a messenger from Nacien the Hermit, presented as the driving force behind the Quest and as the Christian replacement of Merlin, says women do not belong "in so hyghe a servyse" and adds, "he that ys nat clene of hys synnes . . . shall nat se the mysteryes of oure Lorde Jesu Cryste." It is also significant that this messenger is described as "an olde knyght . . . in relygious clothynge" (636). All the knights must, as it were, change their worldly garb for God's armor, but only the serious Grail Questers actually make this change.

## II  *Lancelot*

If the quests of Galahad, Perceval, and Bors form the main plot of the tale, then the quest of Lancelot must be viewed as a subplot. At the same time, however, this quest is very important in the structure of the Grail story as it exists in Malory. The noblest knight of this world is not merely being replaced by the successful Grail Questers. His story parallels the main action of the tale but —although his quest for perfection may in fact be even more appealing to readers than those of Galahad, Perceval, and Bors— Lancelot, earthly sinner that he is, cannot achieve perfection. It is not that Lancelot is singled out as a notable sinner; rather, as R. H. Wilson has noted, he is "a representative *par excellence* of the worldly knighthood which needs to be rebuked."[21]

The actual *Tale of the Sankgrael* begins with Lancelot's being taken from the Feast of Pentecost at Arthur's court by a damsel in the service of King Pelles, the father of Elaine, and the king who, as Pellam in the *Tale of Arthur*, received Balin's Dolorous Stroke. Significantly, Lancelot is removed from the court to "an abbey of nunnys," and with this shift in place comes a change in the whole setting and atmosphere of Malory's Arthur-saga. The change from the courtly to the religious suggests that the halcyon days of the Round Table as an earthly order are over. In the abbey Lancelot is asked to knight the youth, Galahad, who he does not know is his son. Significantly, the knighting of Galahad takes place on the morning of Pentecost, the feast at which Arthur was declared king and the Order of the Round Table was created. And on this day of the knighting of Galahad several miracles occur. In particular, on the Sege Perelous, the one seat at the Round Table still remaining empty, are found "lettirs newly wrytten of golde," which say that the seat will be filled four hundred and fifty years "aftir the Passion of oure Lorde Jesu Cryst" (628). The knights compute that the day referred to is the present day of Pentecost.

More marvels appear as a sword is seen held in a "grete stone" floating in the water. On the sword are golden letters announcing that only "the beste knyght of the worlde" may remove it from the stone. This is, as Malory says, the sword of Balin that Merlin had caused to be placed in the rock—an episode found in Malory's first tale. The sword now appears in a fashion that parallels the choosing of Arthur as king, also seen at the beginning of the *Tale of Arthur*. In both instances a sword is found in a rock, and in both it is pulled out by a Fair Unknown, who is thus revealed as the new hero. Significantly, Lancelot, who knows that this adventure is not his, says that "who that assayth [tries] to take hit and faylith of that swerde, he shall resseyve a wounde by that swerde that he shall nat be longe hole afftir" (629). It is here not a matter of every knight's having a chance at a prize; to accept the test means to presume that one is the "beste knyght of the worlde." To fail indicates that one has presumed, and this presumption is a sin which will be punished. Lancelot, acting in part like a seer, also predicts that on the same day "shall the adventure of the Sankgreall begynne, that ys called the holy vessell." Arthur asks both Gawain and Perceval to try the adventure for his sake; and, although neither knight wants the test, each tries and fails. After their failure, writes Malory: "Than were there no mo that durste be so hardy to sette their hondis thereto" (629).

Following this scene, many more wonders appear. All the doors and windows of Arthur's palace shut by themselves, and an old man enters, bringing Galahad with him. Galahad is presented as a young knight "in rede armys, withoute swerde other shylde sauff [except] a scawberd hangynge by hys syde." Also he is described as being "of kynges lynage and of the kynrede of Joseph of Aramathy, wherby the mervayles of this courte and of stronge [strange] realmys shall be fully complevysshed [achieved]" (630). Joseph of Arimathaea is the man who, according to legend, brought the Grail out of the Holy Land into the Western world.

Galahad sits in the Sege Perelous, pulls the sword from the rock, and is now an important member of Arthur's court; in fact, he replaces Arthur and Lancelot as hero. Although Galahad is literally Lancelot's son, he may in a sense be seen as more than this.

Originally at baptism Lancelot himself was called Galahad, and the change of his name to Lancelot is taken as related to the change in his "levynge" when he turned to worldliness. In these terms, Galahad may be regarded as a personification of the perfection in Lancelot at baptism, the perfection that has become stained and corroded by the world. Lancelot, like Adam, has been superseded by Galahad, who may be seen as Christ. Furthermore, Galahad may be viewed as Lancelot's alter-ego; for, as Guinevere notices, "never two men resembled more in lyknesse" (633–34).

As soon as Galahad draws Balin's sword, a lady, sent by Nacien the Hermit, appears and weepingly addresses Lancelot: "A, sir Launcelot! How youre grete doynge ys chonged sytthyn [since] thys day in the morne" (632). Although Lancelot had been the best knight in the world, his failure to draw the sword indicates that there is now a knight better than he. Humbly, Lancelot replies that he "was never none of the beste"; but the damsel contradicts him, saying he was and still is the best "of ony synfull man of the worlde" (633). Lancelot is still good, but now his perfection is qualified. He is no longer the noblest in every respect.

Throughout Malory's *Tale of the Sankgreal* Lancelot appears as both great and imperfect. For example, as the knights prepare to leave on the Quest, and as Arthur sorrows that the fellowship of the Round Table is lost forever, Lancelot says that the Quest "shall be unto us a grete honoure, and much more than[than if] we dyed in other placis" (635). This is the noble Lancelot speaking, but the fact of his imperfection and lowering is soon made manifest when Galahad jousts with him and easily knocks him from his horse. What is most important, however, is that Lancelot takes his imperfections to heart. When they are revealed to him, he wants to repent and change his ways.

Coming to a stone cross, he sees a closed chapel in which appears "a clene fayre candyllstykke whych bare six grete candyls therein, and the candilstyk was of sylver; and whan sir Launcelot saw thys lyght he had grete wylle for to entir into the chapell, but he coude fynde no place where he myght entir" (652). Not yet worthy to enter the holy place, he remains outside. Falling asleep, or rather, "half wakyng and half slepynge," he sees a sick knight borne in a litter near the cross. Soon the candlestick from the chapel appears before this knight, but Lancelot "saw nobody that brought hit. Also there cam a table of sylver and the holy vessell of the Sankgreall." These cause the sick knight to be healed, but Lancelot is powerless to rise or even to awaken fully since, as Malory writes, "he was overtakyn with synne" (653). This state in Lancelot is explained both by the now-whole knight who leaves, taking Lancelot's horse with him, and by a voice that says: "Sir Launcelot, more harder than ys the stone, and more bitter than ys the woode, and more naked and barer than is the lyeff of the fyggetre! Therefore go thou from hens, and withdraw the from thys holy places!" (654). This episode is in contrast to that of the Chapel Perelous in the *Tale of Lancelot* in which Lancelot demonstrated his merits and was praised as the best knight in the world; now, however, Lancelot reveals only imperfections and is cursed.

Lancelot, now "passyng hevy," weeps, curses the day he was born, and realizes how he has sinned. As he says, "whan I sought worldly adventures for worldely desyres I ever encheved [always achieved] them and had the bettir in every place, and never was I discomfite in no quarell, were hit ryght were hit wronge" (654). His misapplied valor and love, along with his undiscriminating exploits, have led him into a state of spiritual imperfection—specifically, spiritual sloth, as is indicated by his inability to rise before the Holy Grail and the "holy bloode" it contained. Still, in spite of his new consciousness, Lancelot is human and imperfect; for, as Malory writes, "So thus he sorowed tyll hit was day, and harde [heard] the fowlys synge; than somwhat he was comforted" (654). But this is a false comfort, for the song of birds is traditionally a sign of worldly pleasures. Lancelot appears to be in danger of being deceived by his pleasant surroundings. His dark night is not yet past; and, when he misses his horse, "he wyst [knew] well God was displesed with hym. And so he departed frome the crosse on foote into a fayre foreyste" (654–55).

The knight-errant has now become the pilgrim; and, when Lancelot enters the forest, it is not to find adventures but purification and salvation. Arriving at a hermitage, he "kneled downe and cryed on oure Lorde mercy for hys wycked workys," and is instructed by a holy hermit who says that, because God has given Lancelot "more worldly worship than ony knyght that ys now lyvynge," Lancelot should thank him. By suggesting the potential greatness of Lancelot, the hermit's words have also, as Charles Moorman points out, deepened Lancelot's awareness of his sin; for his greatness is seen as that "which, were it not for sin, might have saved the Round Table civilization." [22] Furthermore, the hermit instructs that, unless God is with the knight, his "strengthe" and his "manhode" are of little help. Lancelot then confesses everything, especially "how he had loved a quene unmesurabely and oute of mesure longe" (655). He comments further on his desires for earthly honors and love, saying that he never fought "all only for Goddis sake, but for to wynne worship and to cause me the bettir to be beloved" (655–56). Such a statement reveals how Lancelot and his values have changed since the beginning of his quest.

Earthly honors and love are, furthermore, here seen as inadequate; no longer are they held up as the things one should desire most. Delight in things of this earth is now seen as an excess and a misuse of them. At the heart of the medieval attitude toward life is the idea that one must go beyond the surface of things, beyond the beauty of the created world, to the ultimate source of the beauty. In St. Augustine's words, "All sins are contained in this one category, turning away from things divine and truly enduring, and turning toward those which are changeable and uncertain." And further: "The will that turns away from the unchangeable good common to all and turns toward its own good, or to anything exterior or inferior, sins. It turns toward its own private good when it wills to be its own master; toward what is exterior good when out of curiosity it strives to know what belongs to others, and not to itself; toward inferior good, when it loves the pleasures of the body." [23]

Lancelot in his way of life turned specifically to an inferior good; and, in turning away from the immutable good, he had changed from Galahad to Lancelot, becoming a man marked by *amor sui*, self-love. For all his selfless devotion to his lady and to his code of honor, for all his courtly nobility, Lancelot must be viewed as a creature lacking in *caritas*, the ideal of the Christian good life, and marked by *cupiditas*, self-love and avarice. The meaning of the words that Lancelot is harder than the stone, more bitter than the wood, and barer than the leaf of the fig tree, is, as the holy hermit reveals, that Lancelot in his state of sin is like someone in a shell; for he is impervious to God's goodness and to the warmth of the Holy Spirit. Although Lancelot has received from God "fayrenes with semelynes," "wytte and discression to know good frome ille," "prouesse and hardinesse," he is still foul inside, "defouled with lechory," and may be "lykened to an olde rottyn tre" (656–57). Lancelot seems to understand the meaning of the hermit's words, agrees with the interpretation, and says, "frome hensforewarde I caste me [resolve] by the grace of God, never to be so wycked as I have bene." But, although Lancelot intends to do good, his understanding is shown still to be slight; he has far to go before arriving at a state when he is fit even to come to the Grail Castle. His inadequacy is, in fact, immediately evident when he says that he intends "to sew [pursue] knyght-hode and to do fetys of armys" (657). Lancelot has yet to learn that external prowess and victories cannot be the basis of his moral rise.

Rather than move at a consistent rate, Lancelot's development is uneven. At this point in the *Tale of the Sankgreal* there is a pause in the action, as Lancelot remains three days with the hermit, presumably being instructed by the man. Then, riding out, Lancelot comes to a chapel, sees a dead man dressed in white, and hears of the worthiness of the deceased from one of his friends. Lancelot is commanded to wear the dead man's hair shirt and to live without flesh or wine. Next, riding into a forest, he meets a lady who asks him where he is going. Lancelot's reply is significant: "I wote [know] nat whothir I ryde but as fortune ledith me" (673). Fortune is here seen as being wholly under divine command, and Lancelot's words show that he realizes he is no longer his own master. He too, like Fortune, is being directed, and he accepts whatever is in store for him. He is thus like Balin, who earlier made a point of accepting that which came his way; unlike Balin, however, Lancelot is developing as a spiritual man, and the adventures that come to him are further means of his development.

Falling asleep, Lancelot dreams of seven kings and two knights praying to God. He sees an old man come out of the clouds and say to one of the knights, "I have loste all that I have besette in [bestowed on] the, for thou hast ruled the ayenste me as a

warryoure and used wronge warris with vayneglory for the pleasure of the worlde more than to please me, therefore thou shalt be
confounded withoute [unless] thou yelde me my tresoure" (674).
As Lancelot later learns, this dream is of his ancestors and himself; and the words of the old man, a restatement, added by Malory, of the holy hermit's earlier criticism, are actually being ad-
dressed to Lancelot himself.

Waking, Lancelot then meets the knight who took his horse and
easily defeats him, an action suggesting that Lancelot's progress is
not continuous. His regaining the horse seems to be a sign that he
is being allowed to come back to and gain success in the world,
but he still relies on his arms. This victory is, however, temporary;
for he fights soon afterward in a tournament on what is—as he
discovers—the wrong side; is captured for the only time in Malory's Arthur-saga; is shamed; and, as he says, is "sure that I am
more synfuller than ever I was" (677). In a dream, the meaning
of the tournament is explained to him; he is told in words not in
the French that he must leave "bobbaunce [boasting] and pryde
of the worlde" and gain "truste and good beleve" (678). After
Lancelot awakens, he fights a knight who intentionally kills his
horse, causing Lancelot to be again on foot. Once more, apparently because of his lack of understanding in the tournament, he is
humbled; but, instead of lamenting his condition, Lancelot now
"thanked God of hys adventure" (679).

Again there is a pause, and the story returns to Lancelot after
Galahad has joined Perceval and Bors but before these three pure
knights reach the Grail Castle. Like them, Lancelot is commanded
to enter a ship, this one containing a dead lady, Perceval's sister,
who may be regarded as a pure counterpart of Guinevere. In the
French, before Lancelot enters the ship, he is urged to be chaste
in thought and deed; but in Malory the episode is used in a
slightly different way. The flesh and earthly beauty must die, and
this episode, with Perceval's sister functioning as a *momento mori*,
drives the point home to Lancelot. Also he reads a letter in the
lady's hand, detailing the adventures of Galahad, Perceval, and
Bors; and he is thus able to act later as chronicler and interpreter
of the success of these pure knights. Here, with the dead lady, he
stays "a moneth and more" (723), "susteyned with the grace of
the Holy Goste," until one night, "he wente to play hym by the

watirs syde, for he was somwhat wery of the shippe" (724). This very human response certainly shows Lancelot's inability to live apart from the world—to be, like Perceval's sister, dead to the world—but more important is the fact that the knight goes only to the edge of the water. Apparently the ship he is on has remained at the shore for the duration of his sojourn. The opportunity to leave and return to the world has been constantly present for him, but his only aberration is "to play hym by the watirs syde."

Furthermore, this act of Lancelot may be seen as having something of a causal relationship to his next adventures. At the side of the water he hears approaching a knight whom he finds to be his son, Galahad. Lancelot has been tested, but it is not merely this testing that makes him worthy of the company of the pure knight, Galahad. Rather, Galahad's arrival at the moment Lancelot was playing "by the watirs syde" is almost as though it were to keep him from falling. Lancelot has been tested, and up to a point he is successful; not wholly perfect though, he finds divine aid necessary. The further significance of this episode, where Lancelot and Galahad remain together for six months, is that the spiritual man, Galahad, and his earthly father, Lancelot, are no longer separated. They are brought together for the first and last time in the *Morte Darthur*, and through this meeting it is possible to understand the extent of both the instruction Lancelot receives and the purification he attains.

After Galahad, the perfect man, leaves, the ship takes Lancelot to the Grail Castle; and, after the episode in which he is afraid of the lions, Lancelot enters the Castle and approaches a chamber containing the Grail. He prays to be allowed sight of the Grail, and immediately "the chambir dore opyn, and there cam oute a grete clerenesse, that the house was as bryght as [as if] all the tourcheis of the worlde had bene there" (726). Although not allowed to enter the room, Lancelot is able to see "a table of sylver, and the holy vessell coverde with rede samyte [silk] and many angels aboute hit," also a priest holding up what appears to Lancelot to be a young man. Desiring to help the priest, Lancelot enters the forbidden room, again committing the sin of presumption, again showing a lack of faith; and he is immediately punished: "he felte a breeth that hym thought [it seemed to him] hit was entromedled [mixed] with fyre, which smote hym so sore in the vysayge [face] that hym thought hit brente hys vysayge. And therewith he felle to the erthe and had no power to aryse, as he that was so araged [frenzied] that had loste the power of hys body and hys hyrynge and syght" (727). In this state between living and dying Lancelot remains for twenty-four days, a period of time thought later by the knight to be "ponyshemente for the four-and-twenty yere that he had bene a synner" (728). When he awakens, he is told that he has seen all of the Grail he ever will; but, instead of emphasizing Lancelot's failure here as does his source, Malory is much more conscious of the knight's relative success. He shows Lancelot thanking God for his mercy and justice and, before he returns to Arthur's court, being fed once again by the Grail.

Lancelot has now apparently been weaned from the food of this world and is profitably able to be fed by God. He has reached understanding, and his pilgrimage as such is over. Lancelot has now seemingly arrived at what is traditionally called the seventh stage of the ages of man, and he should now have "everlasting rest and peace." [24] Furthermore, Lancelot's change of character and the feast given to him act as an apt comment on the traditional Christian concept that, just as the child cannot be taken away from milk as long as he is at his mother's breast, so man cannot completely give up physical nourishment before he is ready for spiritual feeding. The danger of perishing from hunger is real in both cases. As St. Augustine instructs, one must believe, "do works of mercy," and "place not your hope in man." He continues: "grow; your powers will be strong; and you will see what you could not, and will understand what you did not understand." [25] Now that Lancelot has arrived at a state approaching perfection, he has progressed to what appears to be the completeness of his life.

Throughout the Quest of the Holy Grail, Lancelot's adventures parallel those of Perceval and Bors; and, just as these knights are joined by Galahad after they are purified, so does Lancelot enjoy the company of the perfect knight. As he was in the *Tale of Gareth* and in the *Book of Tristram,* Lancelot remains the object in terms of which everything else is seen. Just as Malory shows the worth of Gareth and Tristram by comparing these figures with Lancelot, so here the worthiness of Galahad, Perceval, and Bors is seen in comparison with that of Lancelot. Furthermore, Lancelot's partial success with the Grail—more than that achieved by any other imperfect knight but less than that accomplished by the holy knights—acts as a prelude to the final attainment of the Grail. Although the Grail adventure is not concluded by Lancelot, the worth and the meaning of this holy object are revealed through him.

It can be shown that Malory has added to the Grail story several passages which praise Lancelot and exalt his supremacy over all other knights. While these passages may be meant, as C. S. Lewis says, "to blunt for us the edge of the abasement which Lancelot undergoes in the French text," and whereas they may emphasize that the best and greatest by the common standards of the world are not enough,[26] they also show that in a very real sense Malory's *Tale of the Sankgreal* is Lancelot's story. In Charles Moorman's phrase, Malory has made Lancelot "the protagonist of the quest without making him the Grail knight." [27] In both the French and Malory, Lancelot may be seen as succeeding and failing; in the French, however, Lancelot is systematically degraded. As P. E. Tucker writes about the French *Queste*, Lancelot's "partial success is a reward for the penance he has undergone, and his failure (which is much more strongly marked) is due to his lack of absolute faith." In Malory, on the other hand, the emphasis is completely different: Lancelot fails because "in spite of his desire his will is not strong enough"; he is marked by an instability which "undoes all his submission and penance." For Malory, what seems most important and most central in his romance is the experience of Lancelot, who, as Tucker points out, "strives and falters as an ordinary man, laboring in a discipline that he does not completely understand, but knows to be good." [28]

To summarize, the *Tale of Sankgreal* is filled with the presences of both Galahad and Lancelot. Galahad stands as the ideal for man, but Lancelot through his development shows what man can do on this earth. His testing also sets the tone for the testing and proving of Perceval and Bors, whose adventures take place within a relatively short space and are not spread out, as are those of Lancelot, from the beginning to the end of the tale.

### III  *Perceval*

In many versions of the Quest of the Holy Grail, the successful quester is Sir Perceval. In the relatively late version that Malory follows, however, Perceval is relegated to a position subordinate to Galahad and appears as "little more than an extra and slightly soiled Galahad." [29] Malory apparently does not know what precisely to do with him, and so reduces his role in the story. At any rate, the most extensive cuts Malory makes in his source are in the sections of the romance dealing with Perceval. But, in terms of the degrees of perfection which Malory presents in his tale, Perceval is very important. Whereas he appears as a pure knight, it is emphasized that he is not so good as Galahad, a fact shown early in the adventures when he is not able to pull the sword from the rock (629) and when he is soon afterward struck out of his saddle by Galahad (652). Furthermore, Perceval significantly begins his adventures searching not for the Grail but for Galahad, originally to avenge himself on him. As Perceval tells a hermit who, he discovers, is his aunt, "I shall never be well at ease tyll that I know of that knyghtes felyship and that I may fyght with hym, for I may nat leve hym so lyghtly, for I have the shame as yette" (658).

Perceval, obviously still concerned with earthly prowess and marked by pride in external adventures, is admonished by his aunt for this pride. She tells him who Galahad is, that "he shall never be overcom of [by] none erthly mannys hande" (658), and instructs him that the Round Table was created by Merlin to honor the greatest knights in the world. Still, as she says, this honoring was not the whole of the Order's function; for, to the Knights of the Round Table, "the trouth of the Sankgreall sholde be well knowyn." She adds that, according to Merlin, "There sholde be three whyght bullis sholde encheve [achieve] hit, and the two sholde be maydyns and the thirde sholde be chaste." When the holy lady also tells Perceval of Galahad's worthiness, Perceval replies: "I woll never have ado with sir Galahad but by wey of goodnesse. And for Goddis love, fayre awnte, can ye teche me where I myght fynde hym? For much I wolde love the felyship of hym" (659). Perceval reaches a new understanding, and with it he acquires a new purpose in his life. Now, turning away from self-love, Perceval desires to be with Galahad and to acquire the purity and goodness seen in him.

Perceval's search for perfection is first of all a search for Galahad, who will be the Way for him. Perceval, with Bors later, needs a guide; and he must find this guide before he can find "the trouth of the Sankgreall." The situation here is similar to that found in the fourteenth-century English poem, *Piers Plowman,* in which Will's search for Truth takes in this world the form of a search for Piers Plowman, who will be his guide. Perceval is now marked by love of Galahad, a love that may be called *caritas,* as opposed to the *cupiditas* formerly seen in him. Furthermore, one can reach a love of God through a love of man. In St. Augustine's words, "By loving thy neighbor thou purgest thine eyes for the seeing of God." [30]

To find Galahad, Perceval sets out on a journey that makes him worthy of Galahad's company. He views King Evelake of Sarras, who, converted by Joseph of Arimathaea, was the first quester of the Grail (660). Because of his sinful life, Evelake was unable to attain his goal; but he was allowed to remain alive until his descendant should attain the Grail nine generations later. Four hundred years old, blind and full of wounds, Evelake waits for victory, healing, and death. He serves to instruct Perceval as to the nature of his quest and as to what will occur at its fulfilment.

Following this episode, Perceval is attacked by twenty knights, his horse is killed, and he escapes only because of the intercession of Galahad, who then rides off (661). This scene is important not only because it shows Perceval more of the merits of Galahad and not only because it demonstrates to Perceval that he must put his faith in God rather than in his own prowess, but also because it serves to humiliate him. As was the case with Lancelot, Perceval must be put on foot, made lowly before he is able to be raised up. With this lowering, the actual testing of Perceval begins.

Perceval meets a yeoman leading "a grete steede blacker than ony beré [berry]" (662), but is told he cannot ride it for its owner would slay the yeoman. When Perceval says he will not steal the horse, the yeoman leaves. Soon, however, the man returns, lamenting that the black horse has been stolen from him;

and he asks Perceval to take his own horse and assist him. Perceval finds the thief, only to have his own horse killed; and, again on foot, he throws away his shield, helmet, and sword, and laments that he is "a verry [undoubted] wreche, cursed and moste unhappy of all other knyghtes," one who is able to do "nother good nother grete ille" (663).

The knight on the horse "blacker than ony beré" is an important motif in the *Tale of the Sankgreal*, for he rides through the story killing the horses of other knights. For example, at the "ryver that hyght [is called] Mortays" Lancelot's horse is killed by a man described as "an armed knyght, horse and man all black as a beré" (678). Although all the editions of Malory before Vinaver's innocently misinterpret "beré" as bear, the correct reading of the phrase may be understood by the French "plus noir que meure," *meure* meaning berry. Perhaps, however, because of a homophonic similarity, "beré" may also mean bier (Middle English *bere*), the dead or death. The armed figure with a horse described this way is the adversary of the Grail Questers and, in effect, a force hostile to all men searching for salvation and perfection.[31]

On foot again and without the arms of a warrior, Perceval laments his state throughout the day until he finally falls asleep. He awakens at midnight, the witching hour, and sees a woman who says that if Perceval will do what she asks, she will give him her own horse. Perceval happily agrees and mounts a great black steed, so fast that "within an owre and lasse he bare hym four days journey thense untyll he com to a rowghe watir whych rored, and that horse wolde have borne hym into hit" had not Perceval "made a sygne of the crosse in hys forehed" (663–64). This action causes the horse, now described as a "fende," to shake off Perceval and, "cryynge and rorynge and makyng grete sorowe," to rush into the water (664). Although this demonic horse is not necessarily the same one mentioned before, he serves to indicate how the other black horse should be interpreted.

Perceval now finds himself "in a wylde mounteyne whych was closed with the se nyghe all aboute" (664). In the wilderness, alone except for "wylde bestes," he experiences the temptations that mark his final testing. Seeing a great lion fighting a serpent that had attacked its young, Perceval helps the lion, "for he was the more naturall beste of the two," and kills the serpent. Perceval is here shown as the traditional Knight of the Lion, the man who, like Chrétien de Troyes' Yvain, is master of two worlds, the physical and the spiritual. Perceval's journey to this wilderness and his escape from the fiend have, as it were, resulted in his existing in a kind of limbo prior to being reborn as the new man of God and the achiever of the Holy Grail.

Throughout medieval romances knights are helped by lions, but the lion here is not properly a Helpful Animal. Although he is friendly to Perceval and goes "allwey aboute hym fawnynge as a spaynell" (664), the lion seems to be used more as the symbol of a right cause. While the devil is often symbolically presented as a lion, it is as a "roaring lion" who "prowls round looking for someone to devour." Christ, on the other hand, is seen in Christian symbolism as the lion who becomes the lamb. [32] It is probably this meaning of the lion which functions here in Malory; for, although apart in an island wasteland, Perceval is not alone. The animal protecting him seems to be a manifestation of divine aid.

When Perceval falls asleep again, he dreams that two ladies appear before him. The first, a young lady riding upon a lion, announces that her lord, "the grettist lorde of the worlde," says he must prepare himself to fight the next morning with "the strongest champion of the worlde." This fight is not to be an ordinary combat between knights; it is one in which defeat means not merely to be maimed but also to be "shamed for ever to the worldis ende" (665). The term "shamed" is here ambiguous; for, as Perceval discovers, his foe is the Devil himself and defeat means existing in a state of sin, perhaps even in a state of damnation. The other figure in the dream is an old lady sitting upon a serpent. She says that, by killing the serpent that was fighting the lion, Perceval has injured her and that he should in retribution become her man. Perceval refuses whereupon the lady threatens him, saying that, if she ever finds him "withoute kepynge," in a state of spiritual weakness with his moral defenses down, she will take him "as he that somtyme was my man" (665). This loathly lady is apparently to be identified with the woman who appeared to Perceval at midnight and who offered him her horse on the condition that he do her will.

The next morning brings Perceval two more visitors. The first is "an olde man clothed in a surplyse, in lyknes of a pryste," who comes to him in a white ship. He interprets Perceval's dream and repeats that Perceval is to fight "the moste douteful [formidable] champion of the worlde" (666). Next comes a ship "coverde with sylke more blacker than ony beré," which contains "a jantill-woman of grete beauté." Although the reader might see the connection between this black ship and the black horses described earlier, and although he might realize that this beautiful lady is really Perceval's adversary, the knight himself fails to make any connection between this adventure and the warnings he has received.

The damsel, a fiend in disguise, begins her temptation by asking Perceval what he is doing in that wilderness "where ye be never lyke to passe hense, for ye shall dye here for [out of] hunger and myscheff [distress]." In reply, Perceval says that he serves "the beste man of the worlde," who will protect him (667). The lady then says that, if Perceval will be her servant, she will take him to Galahad, the object of his quest. Perceval agrees to her terms; but, before she carries out her part of the bargain, she asks if he has eaten lately. Perceval says that he has not but that a "good man" fed him "with hys good wordys and holy." The lady claims that this man was "an inchaunter and a multiplier of wordis" whom Perceval should not follow. Also, she presents herself as "a jantill-woman that am diseryte [dispossessed]" because she had "a litill pryde" in her "grete beawté." Rather than properly see the damsel's story as a disguised account of the fall of Lucifer from heaven, Perceval, blinded by her beauty, has "grete pité" for her and, like Lancelot, who earlier fought in the tournament on the wrong side, promises her "all the helpe that he myght" (668).

Perceval then sleeps in a pavillion that the lady has set up—a sleep symbolic of the state of his spirit. Like Lancelot before the holy objects, Perceval is not able to rise and act as he should. Lacking clear sight, he is not able to see the lady as she is; he fails to look beyond the outward show and chooses to believe her, forgetting the old man and his words of warning. Speaking of man in relation to signs, St. Augustine writes the definitive word for the Christian Middle Ages: "He is a slave to a sign who uses or venerates any significant object without knowing what it signifies." Perceval is like the man who cannot see beyond the surfaces. Not that it is necessary for every man to be a seer, for, also according to Augustine, "He who does not know what a sign means, yet knows it is a sign, is not in bondage." [33] Perceval, however, is so asleep that he does not even realize that the lady is a sign. His spiritual torpor indicates that he still does not have the purity necessary to reach Truth.

Waking, Perceval asks for food and is presented with "all maner of meetes that he cowde thynke on. Also he dranke there the strengyst wyne that ever he dranke." Finishing this earthly food and falling farther into a torpor, he begins to desire the lady and "profird hir love and prayde hir that she wolde be hys." The lady refuses, but Perceval continues "to pray hir of love." When he is "well enchaffed," inflamed with passion, she agrees to let him make love to her on the condition that he become her "trew servaunte" and do only what she commands (669). Perceval, having become immersed in sin—specifically, the sins of sloth, gluttony, and lechery—agrees. As he lies in bed naked with the temptress, he sees "by adventure and grace"—by chance and fate—the sign of the cross in the pommel of his sword. Thinking immediately "of hys knyghthode and hys promyse made unto the good man tofornehande," he crosses himself. At this action "the pavylon turned up-so-downe and than hit chonged unto a smooke and a blak clowde" (669). Astonished, Perceval awakens from his torpor, prays to Christ, and in sorrow draws his sword and punishes his flesh: "he rooff hymselff thorow the thygh, that the blood sterte aboute hym, and seyde, 'A, good Lord, take thys in recompensacion of that I have myssedone ayenste The, Lorde!'" (670).

This act of castration is Perceval's way of detaching himself from the world and the flesh. Now he may be considered the theological *eunuchus Dei,* the man pure in both heart and body who exists not for this world but wholly for God. Perceval has been tempted by the world, the flesh, and the devil; in fact, as he discovers from the old man who returns in his ship, the beautiful temptress was "the mayster fyende of helle" himself. Through the grace of God, Perceval has been saved; his temptation in the wilderness is now over, and he is ready to attain the Grail. The old man disappears; and Perceval, the *novus homo,* the Christian new man, enters the ship to await the final adventure. Before this occurs, however, he must be joined by Bors and Galahad.

## IV  *Bors*

Because of what has gone before, the quest of Bors proceeds straight to essentials. Consequently, his adventure begins: "Whan sir Bors was departed frome Camelot he mette with a religious man rydynge on an asse," who asks him what he is. Bors replies, speaking of his search as that which will bring "much erthly worship" to him who succeeds. The holy man then stresses the "clennes" (here "pure confession") that is a prerequisite for success on the Grail Quest (686). There had been no emphasis on the need of chaste Perceval to confess—though his chastity was severely tested—but for Lancelot and Gawain, in their adventures immediately preceding that of Bors, confession and penance were necessary for the knights even to begin to develop and to be proved. Like Lancelot and Gawain, Bors is shown as imperfect; for, as is revealed in the *Book of Tristram,* he had loved a lady and conceived a son. Bors' imperfection, however, is said to be less than that of the other earthly knights; for "he was never gretly correpte in fleysshly lustes" except for the one act that resulted in the conception of Elyan le Blanke. On the whole, Bors has led a life "mervales" and "stable"; and, because of grace, he is able to overcome his one sin (687).

This "slight imperfection" in Bors is mentioned at this time not merely because it referred to an incident found in an earlier tale. Rather, Bors must of necessity be less than Galahad and Perceval so that he may return to the world of Arthur's court and relate the adventures of the three successful Grail Questers. Were he as perfect as his two comrades, he would remain apart from the world as they do and be transported to Paradise with them. As a main character Bors is, in Vida Scudder's words, "neither a strong knight nor a fascinating one; he has no accomplishments either in love or war; even in matters spiritual, two others at least surpass him." [34]

Throughout the earlier tales in the *Morte Darthur,* Bors played a role that, though limited, was special. For example, in the *Tale of Arthur,* he was listed with several important knights as one who was able to overcome Gawain; and in the *Arthur and Lucius* he was "very actively present," at least in comparison to Malory's source, the alliterative *Morte Arthure,* where he does not appear at all. From the beginning then, "it is plentifully clear that Malory conceives of him as one of Arthur's most trusted, important, and valiant knights." In the *Book of Tristram,* Malory significantly deepens Bors' character, identifying him as Lancelot's chief support, as "the patient bearer of protective responsibility for Lancelot." [35] There is also what may be termed a human note in Bors, one greater than that found in Perceval and Galahad but not so great as that seen in Lancelot. Bors succeeds on his quest because, unlike Lancelot, he is able to "substitute the celestial standard for the courtly." [36]

Following his confession, Bors, "in sygne of chastisemente," dons "a scarlet cote" in place of a shirt. Then, promising to take only bread and water until his quest is finished, he is shown as fit to begin his adventures. These occur immediately with his seeing a tree on which is seated "a passynge grete birde" which "smote hymselffe with hys beke which was grete and sherpe," and fed with his blood young birds "whiche were dede for hungir" but which "toke lyff by the bloode" (687). Though unable to understand this sight, Bors "wyste well hit was a grete tokenynge," thus showing that he at least is able to recognize the existence of signs.

Next, Bors promises to fight for the cause of a fair young lady who is being persecuted by an old woman who had been driven out of the land. These two women may be viewed as paralleling the young and old ones that came to Perceval in a dream. Bors then falls asleep and dreams of two birds, "one whyght as a swanne and that other was merveylous blacke" (688–89). The dream seems very similar to Perceval's previous vision of the two ladies, but now the meaning of the two creatures is much harder to ascertain. The white bird says that, if Bors serves him, he will make Bors "as fayre and as whyght" as he is; but the black bird says only that Bors should serve him and hold him "in no dispite" even though he is black (689). As is later revealed, the white bird is pure only on the surface and is really gross and black within; but the black bird, like the Church, says he is black though Christ is fair (697). Before awakening, Bors has still another vision. Now he sees "a worme-etyn and fyeble tre" beside two flowers looking like lilies. Although one flower seems to want to touch the other, they are separated by "a good man" who asks, "Sholde nat he do grete foly that wolde lette thes two floures perishe for to succoure [help] the rottyn tre?" (689). As with Perceval's dream, this vision symbolically suggests what Bors should do to succeed the next morning in his fight against the forces of evil.

The stated conflict is to be with the lady's adversary, Sir Prydam le Noyre, who is regarded as "the moste douted [feared] man of thys londe" (688). In this fight, though wounded by Sir Prydam, Bors defeats him but shows mercy and spares his life. The old lady, whom Prydam was representing, then flees from the land. This fight, however, is only preliminary to Bors' main fight, which will be within himself and which will be against a form of pride contained within him. Riding off, Bors is soon presented with a problem. He sees his brother, Lionel, who, "all naked, bowndyn uppon a stronge hakeney," is led off, being beaten all the while, by two knights. At the same time, however, Bors sees a knight abducting "a fayre jantillwoman." There are thus two alternatives for Bors: he may save his brother who is likely to be killed, or he may save a lady who is obviously going to be raped. Weeping, Bors lifts his eyes and says, "Fayre swete Lorde Jesus Cryst, whos creture I am, kepe me [protect] sir Lyonelle, my brothir, that thes knyghtes sle hym nat, and for pité of you and for mylde Maryes sake, I shall succour thys mayde" (691).

After Bors frees the maiden, he finds he has acted correctly; for, as the maiden tells him, if she had been raped by the knight, her cousin, who was "enchaffed" (inflamed) by the devil, the cousin would have been "shamed and dishonoured for ever" and, furthermore, "fyve hondred men sholde have dyed therefore" (692). But Bors then meets "a man clothed in a religious wede," who says that Lionel is dead and that Bors did wrong in not helping him. This man also interprets Bors' vision as meaning that he should show *pité* to a lady who has loved him for a long time. Although Bors tends to accept what the man says, the reader is able to see the suggestion that the man is false and that he falsely construes Bors' vision; for the horse he rides is described as "a stronge blacke horse, blacker than a byry." This devil says that, in helping a lady, Bors has caused the death of Lionel; and, if he does not help another lady by making love to her, this lady will die and so too will Bors' cousin, Lancelot. The devil also makes the point that Bors should not think too highly of his own chastity (694). In reply, Bors says he will do nothing to hurt Lancelot; but, nevertheless, when tempted by the lady to whom the old man brings him—"the fayryst lady that ever he saw"—Bors still refuses to break his vow of chastity.

Bors' predicament is intensified as the lady, lamenting that Bors will not love her, goes with her twelve women to the top of a high battlement with the intent of killing herself and her servants. Bors has great *pité* but still will not give in to the lady's wishes, for he refuses to lose his soul. The lady and her servants fall to the ground, and Bors, "all abaysshed," crosses himself. With this action he sees that he has been almost led into "wanhope [despair] and lechery," and that his tempters have been devils: "And anone [at once] he harde a grete noyse and a grete cry as [as if] all the fyndys of helle had bene aboute hym. And therewith he sawe nother towre, lady, ne jantillwomen, nother no chapell where he brought hys brothir to. Than hylde he up both hys hondis to the hevyn and seyde, 'Fayre swete Lorde Fadir and God in hevyn, I am grevously ascaped!'" (695).

Following this adventure, an abbot correctly interprets for Bors the signs he had previously seen. Now the knight understands how the great bird that bled is like Christ, how the white bird is really black within, how the rotten tree in his dream is like his brother, Lionel, "whych ys dry withoute vertu. . . . he ys a murtherer and doth contrary to the Order off Knyghthode," and how the white flowers in his dream are the knight and lady he had correctly kept chaste. The abbot says that Bors would have been "a grete foole and in grete perell" had he caused the two flowers to perish at the expense of the rotten tree (697).

It would seem that Bors has succeeded in passing his tests, but there is yet one to come: Bors must cope with the wrath of his brother, Lionel, who is found alive and who says that, in not helping him, Bors acted unnaturally and did a great "untrouthe." But Bors refuses to fight his brother. All he will do is kneel before Lionel and ask his forgiveness. Lionel, said to be possessed by a fiend, is determined to fight Bors; he knocks him over with his horse and prepares to kill him with his sword. Though likely to lose his life, Bors still cannot fight his elder brother. At this point a holy hermit intercedes only to have his head cut off by Lionel. Then a knight of the Round Table, Sir Collegrevaunce, tries to help; but he too is killed by the enraged Lionel. Weeping and wounded, Bors at last realizes that he must fight Lionel; but, as he raises his hand, God intercedes: "Ryght so alyght a clowde betwyxte them in lykenes of a fayre and a mervaylous flame, that bothe hir two shyldis brente. Than were they sore aferde and felle both to the erthe and lay there a grete whyle in a sowne. And whan they cam to themselff sir Bors saw that hys brothir had none harme. Than he hylde up both his hondys, for he drad last God had takyn vengeaunce uppon hym" (702). Bors is commanded by a voice to depart; and only at this point does he obtain, in lines not in the French, Lionel's forgiveness. Bors has now received divine grace and his testing is over. He has moved from earthly love and an interest in "erthly worship" to the service of God. His testing has also shown that unlike Lancelot, who rises and falls throughout the romance, Bors is stable. Consequently, he is taken aboard a ship where he joins Perceval in waiting for Galahad.

## V  *Galahad and Fulfilment*

In the *Tale of the Sankgreal* Galahad is comparable in function to Lancelot, for he too appears throughout the book to give meaning to the various adventures. A main difference between the two figures is that Galahad is the spiritual ideal, the new man of Christ, and therefore reveals within him that which Lancelot, the old Adam, lacks. As Eugène Vinaver has aptly remarked, Lancelot's begetting of Galahad is "an irretrievable offence against courtly love. . . . It symbolizes the failure of Lancelot's earthly endeavour—the tragic end of his love for Guinevere. The birth of the pure knight brings about 'a catclysm and a deliverance.' The same tragic event defiles the purity of earthly love and inaugurates the realm of divine grace. It is a link between earthly error and the truth of religion, and through the final phase of the threnody of the Round Table runs the liturgical chant of Galahad." [37]

In the first part of the romance Galahad is seen in the role of champion of God. Here he puts on, as it were, what Paul calls "the armour which God provides" so that he "may be able to stand firm against the devices of the devil." Paul's words about the Christian's fight may be applied to the Quest of the Holy Grail, for the struggle of the Knights of the Round Table is not against an earthly enemy, or rather, not against a human adversary. Now they must meet and conquer the world, flesh, and devil. To do so, they must explicitly become knights of Christ. They must, in other words, follow Paul's directions:

Put on all the armour which God provides, so that you may be able to stand firm against the devices of the devil. For our fight is not against human foes, but against cosmic powers, against the authorities and potentates of this dark world, against the superhuman forces of evil in the heavens. Therefore, take up God's armour; then you will be able to stand your ground when things are at their worst, to complete every task and still to stand. Stand firm, I say. Buckle on the belt of truth; for coat of mail put on integrity; let the shoes on your feet be the gospel of peace, to give you firm footing; and with all these, take up the great shield of faith, with which you will be able to quench all the flaming arrows of the evil one. Take salvation for helmet; for sword, take that which the Spirit gives you—the words that come from God.[38]

Galahad serves as model for the followers of Christ; he is first represented gaining spiritual armor, the kind every knight must possess who intends to search for the Grail. It should be emphasized, as Charles Moorman has done, that Galahad is "a heavenly knight, sent to Arthur to accomplish only this one mission, and, by example, reveal the inadequacies of the other knights and of the secular civilization which they represent." While he is, to be sure, "a supernatural object lesson in heavenly chivalry, . . . whose deeds do not in any way affect the fate of the Round Table," he and the perfections he represents are also needed by the world of the Round Table.[39] Whereas Perceval, Bors, and Lancelot are types of the Christian character, Galahad represents the ideal and the whole. Perceval is the type of the Christian soul, simple and full of faith; Bors is the worker in the vineyard of the Lord; Lancelot is the repentant sinner; but Galahad, conceived in the image of Christ, is the realization of all the Christian virtues.[40]

In a sense, the Quest of the Holy Grail may be seen as representing the final apotheosis of the Order of the Round Table.

With Arthur, it conquered the world; with Lancelot, it became the earthly ideal; and now, with Galahad, it is elevated to a spiritual order as it searches for the City of God. This change in direction shows that it is not enough to be ruler of earth or even protector of Christianity. Rather than remain involved with earthly things, one must proceed from the Holy Roman Empire to the Heavenly Jerusalem; and Galahad shows the Way.

Although he is perfect, it is necessary that the Round Table and the reader see his perfection, so several of his early adventures seem designed primarily to reveal his worth as a divinely directed man and as a knight of prowess and courtesy. The several supernatural adventures at the time of his arrival in Arthur's court reveal him as the chosen hero; but, just as Arthur had to be proved in mortal combat, so does Galahad. Before the knights begin their quest, Arthur calls a tournament, primarily "for to se Galahad preved"; and Galahad reveals himself in a way that removes all doubts of his worthiness. Without a shield—he needs only God—Galahad "surmownted all othir knyghtes" (633). This fight is the only courtly tournament at Arthur's court in the tale, for the Grail Quest will now occupy the attention of the Round Table.

At this time Galahad is also asked whether Lancelot is his father, but in reply he says, "nother yee nother nay." The relationship between Lancelot and Galahad may be described in Charles Williams' words as "a kind of imaginative union." [41] Rather than be actually related to any other character, Galahad in reality remains apart from all. In answer to the question about Lancelot, Galahad enigmatically replies: "he that ys my fadir shall be knowyn opynly and all betymys [soon]" (636). Such ambiguity suggests that, although Lancelot may be viewed as Galahad's earthly father, there also exists a divine father whom Galahad serves.[42] The knight may be seen, therefore, as partaking of the highest earthly nobility and of a divine nobility. His earthly lineage may be traced back to Joseph of Arimathaea, as his adventures with a special shield demonstrate (640).

When Galahad rides out, it is not to be proved but to fulfil all the actions preliminary to the final attainment of the Grail. He comes to an abbey containing a white shield with a red cross in the middle "that no man may bere hit aboute his necke but he be myscheved [harmed] other dede within three dayes, other maymed for ever" (638). Galahad's companion at this point, Bagdemagus, first takes the shield; but he is struck down for his presumption by a knight in white armor, who acts here as the heavenly counterpart to the knight on the black horse that tests other knights. Given the shield, which had first belonged to King Evelake, and told its story, Galahad continues his adventures, which take the general form of a series of miracles. From a grave he drives a fiend that says to him, "Sir Galahad, I se there envyrowne [around] aboute the so many angels that my power may nat deare [harm] the!" (642). Also Galahad rescues Sir Melyas, his former squire, who had earlier separated himself from Galahad only to be punished for his pride and presumption. Specifically, Melyas, thinking to strike out on his own, had been conquered by two knights signifying pride and covetousness; but Galahad is able to conquer them since he is "withoute dedly synne" (646). Like Perceval, Melyas says that, as soon as he is able, he will seek Galahad, his means to Truth.

Galahad is next commanded to go to the Castle of Maidens—in the *Book of Tristram* described as the site of a great tournament —and to destroy "the wycked customes." Specifically, the people in this castle are revealed as being in a state of sin, "for all pité ys oute thereoff, and all hardynes and myschyff [audacity and wickedness] ys therein" (647). *Pité* in this context means primarily *caritas*. Before he leaves the world, Galahad must not only show the Way to Truth but also correct the sins of the world. Just as he, Perceval, and Bors later fight God's enemies in Scotland, here Galahad, after defeating seven knights that all attack him at the same time, is given the keys to the castle and is able, like Christ harrowing hell, to release the prisoners and to destroy the evil customs. In an exegesis of the episode, its meaning is clarified: "the Castell of Maydyns betokenyth [signifies] the good soulys that were in preson before the Incarnacion of oure Lorde Jesu Cryste. And the seven knyghtes betokenyth the seven dedly synnes that regned that tyme in the worlde. And I may lyckyn the good knyght Galahad unto the Sonne of the Hyghe Fadir that lyght within a maydyn and bought all the soules oute of thralle" (651).

These adventures of Galahad continue with his defeat of Lancelot and Perceval (651–52), by which he shows them the power of God; with his rescue of Perceval (661–62), by which he depicts the protection and mercy of God; and with his journeys and adventures, which Malory does not detail but which he says Galahad "brought all to an ende" (703). Finally, at the Castle of Carbonec, Galahad is joined by a damsel, later found to be Perceval's sister, who takes him to the ship on which Perceval and Bors are waiting. After their meeting, Bors says to Galahad: "if sir Launcelot, your fadir, were here, than were we well at ease, for than mesemed we fayled nothynge." Galahad replies: "That may not be . . . but if [unless] hit pleased our Lorde" (705). Lancelot is thus explicitly linked to these chosen knights, but his quest is still apart from theirs.

From this point to the end of the tale, the narrative presents primarily a series of signs and miracles. The Questers, along with Perceval's sister, enter another ship, the Ship of Faith, in which only the steadfast may go. There they see a bed, the wonderful Sword with the Strange Girdles—the sword of King David, here said to be responsible for the Dolorous Stroke that caused the Waste Land to come into existence (706 ff.)—and three spindles said to have been made by King Solomon's wife from the Dry Tree, the bough that Eve took with her from Paradise (710 ff). The presentation and exegesis of symbols now become so intricate and confusing that a brief summary can hardly be coherent. But it must be recognized that the exegesis—the stories about these and other relics and the meanings they have—is fundamental to the Questers' final preparation to be proper achievers and recipients of the Grail. Through the exegesis they are instructed in the deep meanings behind human life. The history of the relics they find, especially their association with biblical figures, is now told in detail to the Questers.

Galahad takes the sword, which only the best man in the world can take, and then goes with his companions to fight God's enemies in Scotland. Entering a forest they see a white hart leading four lions. Later at Mass the hart changes into a man who sits on the altar in a rich seat, and the four lions become man, lion, ox, and eagle, the traditional symbols of the four evangelists, Matthew, Mark, Luke, and John (718). The priest celebrating Mass is astonished that the knights are able to see these wonders, and the reader is able to understand vividly the extent of the Questers' purity. Now that they have been instructed in the meanings beyond this life, they are able to see a greater reality more clearly than mere knights of this world can.

One of the most compelling episodes in what may seem to be a jumble of symbolic adventures concerns Perceval's sister and the custom of a castle. As she and her three companions proceed on their way, they are challenged by knights who insist that she fill a silver dish with her blood in order to heal the lady of a castle. This same adventure had earlier appeared in Balin's episode of the *Tale of Arthur* (62), but now it reaches an end. The three Questers refuse either to acknowledge the custom or to allow Perceval's sister to shed her blood. Though threatened that they cannot win even if they were "the beste knyghtes of the worlde," the Questers are able to defeat seventy knights of the castle (719). Finally, however, to save the lady of the castle, Perceval's sister volunteers to give her blood. Warned that she cannot give the required amount of blood without dying, she replies: "and [if]I dye for the helth of her I shall gete me grete worship and soule helthe, and worship to my lynayge; and better ys one harme than twayne" (720–21). Here appears true charity, and the act shows the real function of Perceval's sister in this Grail story. Although all the actual Questers are men, Perceval's sister shows that a woman who is pure may be a follower of Christ. Even though she dies, her body is taken miraculously to the holy city, Sarras.

The presence of Perceval's sister serves, furthermore, to give Perceval a "kinship in spirit" that is not, on the one hand, the worldly love that had been enjoyed by Bors and that is not, on the other, the asceticism of Galahad. As Charles Williams says, the relationship between Perceval and his sister is "a human relationship, but is one known only in the companionship of the quest; it is conjoined love, but love conjoined in the Grail." [43] As such, it is also quite different from the love between Lancelot and Guinevere; and Perceval's sister, like the Virgin Mary in her purity, is the antitype of such worldly lovers as Guinevere and Isode.[44]

Before she dies, Perceval's sister commands the Questers to put her dead body in a boat which will take her to Sarras; and, as she

says, when the three knights arrive there with the Grail, they
should find her and bury her "in the spirituall palyse," the same
place where Perceval and Galahad will later be buried. They
fulfil her wishes and put her in a boat along with a letter telling
her story and that of the three knights. Then "there fylle a tem-
peste suddeyne of thundir and lyghtnynge and rayne, as all the
erthe would a brokyn. So halff the castell turned up-so-downe,"
and everyone in the castle is killed. As explained, "Thys vengeaunce ys for bloode-shedynge of maydyns" (722), and thus represents divine wrath. The knights are then commanded to separate until their final adventure at the Grail Castle.

Inserted now is the story of Galahad's joining Lancelot and of
Lancelot's partial attainment of the Grail. After this episode, Galahad has several adventures which include meeting King Mor-
drayns, who then dies in peace; calming a burning well, signifying the heat of lechery; and, like Christ when he harrowed hell,
descending into a burning tomb, stilling it, consequently releasing the "soulis of erthely payne" and putting them "into the joyes
of Paradyse'" (732). Furthermore, after again being joined by
Perceval and Bors, Galahad puts together a broken sword, something the other knights cannot do; together they view a bleeding
spear, the spear of Longinus which supposedly pierced the side
of Christ on the Cross; and, finally, they attain the Grail and are
fed "with swete metis that never knyghtes yet tasted." From the
Grail comes a man "that had all the sygnes of the Passion of Jesu
Cryste bledynge all opynly," who tells the Questers, described as
"trew chyldren which bene com oute of dedly lyff into the spiritual lyff," that they will see "a parte of my secretes and of my
hydde thynges" (735).

Although this appears to be the climax of the Grail Quest, the
adventures of Galahad, Perceval, and Bors are not yet over. They
must still take the Grail "from the realme of Logrus," where the
people, "turned to evyll lyvyng," do not worship it properly, and
remove it to the holy city of Sarras (735–36). This deed the
knights do, and there they bury Perceval's sister, perform more
miracles, and are imprisoned but kept whole by the Grail.
Finally, Galahad is made King of Sarras. The meaning of Sarras
is not defined explicitly in the tale, but, as is suggested by its
name, which is the same when spelled backward or forward, it

represents that which exists continually. It is also, more specifically, the Holy Land, Jerusalem. When one lives in Sarras, one is in a special land, one partially removed from the world.

This partial removal is not sufficient for Galahad, even though he is ruler; for, perfect knight that he is, he feels the need to leave completely his imperfect state. Thus he asks for actual death. Having known in the Grail something of eternal joy, he wishes to be only in Paradise where his soul "shall be in grete joy to se the Blyssed Trinité every day and the majesté of oure Lorde Jesu Cryste" (737). Galahad's request is granted; he says goodbye to Perceval and Bors; and, in lines not in the French, sends to Lancelot a message that he should "remembir of this worlde unstable" (739), again emphasizing the instability that Malory has associated with Lancelot. Then Galahad "suddeynly departed hys soule to Jesu Cryste, and a grete multitude of angels bare hit up to hevyn evyn in the syght of hys two felowis" (739). With him go the Grail itself and the bloody spear; and as Malory writes, "sythen [afterwards] was there never man so hardy to sey that he hade seyne the Sankgreal" (740).

This death of Galahad presents a significant point. Galahad has been perfect, has served God as his agent, and has ruled the holy city of Sarras. He is a great man, a true servant of God, and certainly more than mere man. He in fact illustrates St. Augustine's words that only those who are "no longer men, but beyond men" may see divinity;[45] but to be beyond man, to be perfect, is to be beyond this world. Perfection cannot exist in an imperfect state, and Galahad longs for completeness. The search for the Grail—a search for spiritual realities, for perfection and salvation—is fulfilled only for a few knights; and society as a whole is not changed. In fact, as is clearly revealed in Malory's next tale, the turning to things of the spirit is only a temporary change of pace. Consequently, those who have known divine perfection see around them an imperfection they find difficult to tolerate. Galahad dies, and Perceval "yelded hym to an ermytayge oute of the cité, and toke religious clothyng" (740). Perceval remains in this hermitage for fourteen months until he too dies, and Bors alone is left to return to Arthur.

There he recounts what has happened and joins his kinsman Lancelot, who also, in a passage not in the French, tells of his adventures with the Grail and says to Bors: "ye and I shall never departe in sundir whylis oure lyvys may laste" (741). It is ironic that the *Tale of the Sankgreal* should end in Arthur's court with Lancelot again at the center of the action. Such a scene emphasizes the exploits of Lancelot, the hero of the whole *Morte Darthur,* and it also suggests that the Grail Quest has ended like any mere worldly quest. A note of foreboding is thus injected that is developed in the next tale.

The Grail Quest, which has been presented by Malory as the reason for the existence of the Round Table and as the most noble pursuit of Arthur's knights, is now over; but it does not conclude Malory's Arthur-saga. Although the Quest should represent the pinnacle of human endeavor, it does not make the City of God and the city of man one and the same; rather, man's old life goes on. The problem now is that this life has nowhere to go; it has no direction, no purpose or action greater than the Quest of the Grail. Consequently, mankind and human society now flounder. Man has had a glimpse of the world of the spirit, but he cannot free himself from the flesh to attain it. The next tale shows man sliding down to his old life.

CHAPTER 5

# The Human Irony

## I  The Pause That Regresses

AT THE beginning of this tale, the *Book of Sir Lancelot and Queen Guinevere* (Caxton's Books XVIII–XIX), Malory presents a world very similar to that seen before the Knights of the Round Table went off on their Quest of the Holy Grail. One's immediate impression, in fact, might be that the Quest never actually took place at all or that the present tale really exists as an account of the knights' adventures before the Quest. But the search for the Grail has occurred, and, realizing this, Malory emphasizes the fact that it has been concluded without ennobling permanently the world of the Round Table. Furthermore, although the world Malory describes seems superficially similar to that found during the halcyon days of Arthur's knights, it has been markedly affected by the facts of the Grail and the Quest. Now, for example, the jousting and love-making of the knights are trivial. Earlier in Malory's whole book, earthly adventures acted as a means of developing within the knights the virtues associated with prowess, courtesy, and love. These virtues functioned to take man beyond external worldly adventures to a quest for perfection and salvation. For man to return to worldly aims after glimpsing higher purposes and values is for man to be either frustrated or deceived into thinking that he is still leading a good and worthwhile life.

Such a return, however, may also be viewed as necessary for imperfect man. As the hermit told Gawain (685), repentance is essential; and the return may exist to enable the knights to repent and to prepare themselves and their society so that they too can achieve what Galahad and Perceval found. Bors is consequently made to return to the Arthurian world as a messenger or prophet of the divine. He is to reveal the Word and the Way so that the other knights may be instructed and achieve for themselves the heavenly kingdom. As in the fourteenth-century English poem, the *Pearl*, the vision has been seen and the way has been shown. Just as there, the dreamer must come back to this world to do penance and make himself worthy of divine grace, so in Malory's present tale the imperfect knights are given a chance to achieve what they now know to exist beyond this world.

Ideally then, the *Lancelot and Guinevere* should act as a continuation of the previous *Tale of the Sankgreal*. The deaths of Galahad and Perceval should herald the end of the courtly Order of the Round Table, release the Arthurian knights and ladies from the imperfect world, and allow them to attain the permanent celestial paradise. In reality, however, the *Lancelot and Guinevere* is anticlimactic, for it provides only a pause between the high point of the Grail Quest and the final disintegration of everything. No penance takes place; instead, the knights, imperfect as they are, make every attempt to take up and hold on to their old life. Although chivalry is stale, it is all they know. The Christian *novus homo* is no more, and the worldly knights are now only spiritual old men. Even the great Lancelot, now that he is back in the world, cannot deny worldly pleasures: "Than, as the booke seyth, sir Launcelot began to resorte unto quene Gwenivere agayne and forgat the promyse and the perfeccion that he made in the queste" (744). Now the love between Lancelot and Guinevere is explicitly revealed in all its physical desire. It is no longer manifested as loyalty or courtesy; now it is desire, even lust; and, as such, it will be the efficient cause of the final conflict and the destruction of the Round Table.

The world of the Round Table is not in itself bad. As Eugène Vinaver writes, Malory, as opposed to the author of the French *Queste,* did not see the Round Table as "forming an antithesis to the Grail ideals." Rather, for him the Round Table "itself became the symbol of all good. And if in the end it must fail, it will fail not because of a religious condemnation, but because of a human tragedy, which rests upon the conflict of love and loyalty." [1] Symbolically love of the world is emphasized in this tale; it is shown as cupidity and as replacing the charity that had been stressed in the previous *Tale of the Sankgreal.* No longer is early love in any way a *fine amour,* a delicate sentiment, seeming to ennoble those who feel it. As long as earthly love is all that the knights know, it can be in itself good; but, when it replaces charity, it must of necessity become gross and bestial, marring rather than ennobling those who love.

This new view of earthly love changes the appearance of the characters in Malory's Arthur-saga, for it makes them and their lives illustrations of *desmesure*. Such a change may be strikingly seen in the figure of Guinevere. In the earlier tales she is merely the consort of Arthur and the queen who appears briefly at several points. Although she at times stands out as a human being—as, for example, in Vinaver's "War with the Five Kings" section of the *Tale of Arthur* when she expresses her gratitude to Kay for saving her and the realm (95)—this is nothing comparable to what is now revealed of her. According to Vida Scudder, Guinevere has changed from being a "queen-in-position," and "has come alive at last." [2] This view, however, is oversimplified; for Guinevere becomes "alive" only when her imperfection is stressed. Now jealousy and pride mark her character, and she begins to act like a spoiled, demanding woman.

When at the beginning of the tale Lancelot joins the company of ladies other than Guinevere, so as "to eschew [avoid] the sclawndir and noyse," the rumors that were spreading about him and Guinevere, she "waxed wrothe" and accuses the knight of no longer loving her (744). Lancelot tries to explain that he cannot forget either "the hyghe servyse" in which he had been on the Grail Quest or the fact that, if he had not thought so much of the queen, he would have seen "as grete mysteryes" as the others. He says that the "boldenesse" of Guinevere and himself will result in "shame and sclaundir" unless he appears more in the company of others (745). To these arguments Guinevere, enraged, replies that Lancelot is "a false, recrayed [cowardly] knyght and a comon lechourere" and forbids him to come into her presence again. Lancelot then leaves, staying away until he has to save the queen's life after she has been wrongly accused of murdering Sir Patryse by giving him a poisoned apple (753 ff.).

The main narrative thread in the *Lancelot and Guinevere* is, as P. E. Tucker says, "the overwhelming of Lancelot which follows his defection from the path of right conduct open to him"—the path symbolized by the Grail Quest.[3] In his relationship with Guinevere, he acts as her champion, defending and rescuing her regardless of the consequences. He in fact says after his first defense of Guinevere that, from the time of his knighting, he had promised to be the queen's knight "in ryght othir in wronge" (755). Lancelot means well but finds himself caught in the middle of a web where it is no longer possible for him to be a good faithful knight to his lady, Guinevere; to his lord, Arthur; and to his God. Earthly love is juxtaposed, therefore, against both feudal loyalty and love of God; but Lancelot does not hesitate to choose the path he must take. In spite of his regret at being an impure knight who could not achieve the Grail and in spite of his sorrow at what he does to Arthur and the Round Table, Lancelot gives his all for love of Guinevere, a love gradually but clearly shown to be destructive. For Malory the ideal "vertuouse love" is when God is first and the lady second (791). This is hardly the order with Lancelot at this point in the story: his lady is everything and his service to her is all that matters to him.[4]

It is certainly right for Lancelot to intercede for Guinevere when she is accused of killing Sir Patryse. In this case the queen is completely innocent, but in Lancelot's next defense of Guinevere matters are more ambiguous. This takes place when, after being rescued by Lancelot from Meliagraunce who has abducted her, the queen is accused of falseness (802 ff.). Because Meliagraunce sees blood covering her bed, he assumes that she has been sleeping with one of several wounded knights who have been in her care, and accuses her of betraying Arthur. Guinevere hotly denies the charge, and she is technically right. The blood on her bed was not from one of the wounded knights in her care but from Lancelot, who had cut his hand while breaking into her chamber. Lancelot again fights for the queen and, because of the technicality, is able to save her. Even though technically innocent of the specific charge leveled at her, she is guilty. If the charge had been phrased differently, that she was false to Arthur by sleeping with another man, Lancelot would not have been able to rescue her so easily. Lancelot's difficulty is, as P. E. Tucker rightly sees, that he is "blinded to questions of right and wrong by the struggle of the moment."[5] Now, rather than show comprehension of what is happening, he seems to rely solely on his prowess, becoming like Gawain in his earlier appearances. These scenes of Lancelot's saving Guinevere are consequently preparatory for the final accusation and rescue which take place in the next tale, and are indicative of Lancelot's faulty judgment.

Actions are now moving from the noble toward the ignoble, and shame is presented as close at hand. Moreover, Guinevere no longer cares about scandal, and with this laxity comes a loss of self-control and the beginning of trouble for the lovers. Also, the action must be regarded as affecting more people than merely the queen: through her excesses and her inordinate actions, Guinevere drags Lancelot down with her and later is partly responsible for destroying Arthur and his Order of the Round Table. It is, however, not Guinevere as a person who does these things. Rather, she must be taken as a symbol of the dangers of excessive earthly love, of what will happen when one puts one's eye wholly on surface attractions. Surface beauties are, like Guinevere, unstable and shifting; and one can never trust them or find a true guide in them. The queen thus may be viewed as representing primarily the wordly alternative to the Holy Grail, and this substitute is, of course, inadequate. Guinevere is also the counterpart of Perceval's sister: instead of saving others through her charity, Guinevere can only destroy through her lust. It is ironic that Guinevere, containing the flaws of Eve, replaces the pure virgin.

To follow the earthly is to destroy oneself, or in St. Augustine's words, "impure love inflames the spirit and causes the soul destined to perish to lust after earthly things and to follow what is perishable, and hurls it into the lowest places, and sinks it in the abyss." [6] As St. Peter writes, "a man is the slave of whatever has mastered him"; and, furthermore, those who have known the Way but have not taken it are condemned to perdition: "They had once escaped the world's defilements through the knowledge of our Lord and Savior Jesus Christ; yet if they have entangled themselves in these all over again, and are mastered by them, their plight in the end is worse than before. How much better never to have known the right way, than, having known it, to turn back and abandon the sacred commandments delivered to them!" [7] The adventures of the Knights of the Round Table, after they have known of the Grail, should have been a continuation of the pilgrimage—the journey beyond self and world—begun by the Grail Quest. But the pilgrims have become questers concerned again with worldly accomplishments and the worship of earthly values. Even Lancelot and Bors, good knights as they are, fall back into the world and are helpless.

The failure of the knights is strikingly seen in the first episode of the tale, that called by Vinaver, "The Poisoned Apple." Sir Pynell le Saveayge, cousin of Sir Lamorak, is angry because Gawain killed Lamorak "by treson"—an episode referred to in the *Book of Tristram* (520)—and because Gawain is "a passyng hote knyght of nature" (747). Consequently, he plans for Gawain to eat a poisoned apple. The plot fails, however, for an innocent "good knyght," Sir Patryse, eats the apple instead. In this scene Malory has, as it were, recalled for the reader the old quarrels among the knights and the plots to destroy the Round Table. The emphasis in the *Tale of the Sankgreal* was on spiritual food that made the eater whole; here, the story returns to physical food, which, conversely, kills the eater. Violence and deception are shown again to be the norm, and the scene anticipates the later plot against Lancelot and the final conflict between the knights.

As a narrative, the *Lancelot and Guinevere* contains several famous, well-told episodes. The story of the Fair Maid of Astolat, who dies for the unrequited love of Lancelot, is—because of Tennyson's rendition—one of the most popular and moving of Arthurian tales. It seems to be used in Malory, however, primarily as an illustration of the destructive power of earthly love, a power that had been in part seen in the *Book of Tristram;* but there love was also presented as good. Now the destruction is, as it were, unrelieved. What is most significant is that Elaine, the Fair Maid, is an innocent girl whose love could have been proper and good. When told by a priest that she should stop thinking of earthly love, she indicates that in her mind she is not wrong to love Lancelot: "Why sholde I leve such thoughtes? Am I nat an erthely woman? And all the whyle the brethe ys in my body I may complayne me, for my belyve ys that I do none offence, though I love an erthely man, unto God, for He fourmed me thereto, and all maner of good love comyth of God. And othir than good love loved I never sir Launcelot du Lake. And I take God to recorde, I loved never none but hym, nor never shall, of erthely creature; and a clene maydyn I am for hym and for all othir" (779).

According to medieval Christianity, Elaine's love for Lancelot is in itself not bad, just as there is nothing wrong with the human body per se and the beauty found in it. But when these are improperly used, enjoyed for wrong reasons, they become bad. While Elaine's love could have stood as an ideal, it appears here more as something excessive and destructive. It must be seen as bad for two reasons: first, it exists wholly for something mortal. In St. Augustine's terms, the loved object is to be used to get to a higher object of love, namely God.[8] Even though Elaine describes her love as a "good love," and even though, when she says she loves only Lancelot "of erthely creature," there is a suggestion that she also has an "unerthely" love, God, this divine or spiritual love is not the dominant one. If it were, she would not have died out of love for Lancelot.

The second reason her love is bad is because it is not received or reciprocated—or "used" in Augustine's sense—and leads to nothing but death. In a very real sense, Lancelot is responsible for the death of the innocent Maid; for, had it not been for his inordinate desire for Guinevere, he could have saved her. Elaine is a good woman, and even Bors speaks of her as "a passyng fayre damesell, and well besayne [good looking] and well taught." Bors, in fact, wishes that Lancelot could love her (773). It must be emphasized that love itself is not being criticized; for, as Paul writes, "To crown all, there must be love, to bind all together and complete the whole." [9] But this love must be charity, that which leads the lover to God and which can never end in destruction.

Arthur's court is saddened by the sight of this dead beautiful damsel floating in her boat down the Thames with a letter to Lancelot in her hand. In defending his refusal of the lady's love, Lancelot says he cannot be "constrayned to love" and, further, that he has not caused her death by his "wyllyng." Instead, he blames Elaine herself who, he says, has loved him "oute of mesure" (781). Although there is a certain truth in Lancelot's words, there is also a point he fails to see. Just as inordinate love has driven the Fair Maid of Astolat to her death, so is it driving Lancelot and Arthur's realm to destruction. It is, furthermore, ironic for Lancelot, ardent lover of Guinevere, to criticize the damsel for loving "oute of mesure."

In dying for love, the Fair Maid resembles Ettarde in the *Tale of Arthur*, who died for love of Pelleas; but a more relevant comparison is with Perceval's sister in the *Tale of the Sankgreal* who died for a different sort of love (and who also floated in a boat). Both ladies may be seen as *exempla* to Lancelot; the Fair Maid in particular shows him the dangers of being ensnared or bound by love. Arthur is certainly right when he says that when love "ys bonden he lowsith hymselff" (781); but what he does not say is that not only is love consequently lost but so is the person. The irony is that Lancelot is beginning to be "bonden" by Guinevere, who more and more jealously suspects and berates him, as she does when she thinks he loves the Fair Maid. Trust and faith are leaving the love.

The episodes of "The Fair Maid" and of "The Poisoned Apple," which precedes it, are joined together but in reverse order in the French *La Mort le Roi Artu,* the last branch of the Vulgate Cycle,[10] and in the English *Le Morte Arthur,* an early fifteenth-century English stanzaic romance derived from the French work.[11] Although Vinaver feels that Malory used only the Vulgate romance, unraveling it and adding links between the passages to present a continuous narrative,[12] other scholars have shown that Malory used both the French work and the English poem, and that the stanzaic *Morte* is, as R. M. Lumiansky writes, "an intermediate step between the complicated interweaving of *Mort Artu* and the simple unified progression of the *Morte Darthur.*"[13] Although the author of the stanzaic poem seems to have done most of the unraveling, Malory made some structural changes. In particular he put "The Poisoned Apple" episode before that of "The Fair Maid," perhaps, as Lumiansky feels, because of a desire to develop a narrative suspense. That is, in "The Poisoned Apple" there is no evidence of Arthur's suspicion of the lovers; but in "The Fair Maid" his suspicion, "though rapidly stilled, is nonetheless present."[14]

Following the story of the Fair Maid is a section called by Vinaver "The Great Tournament," mainly representing the last tournament in Malory's Arthur-saga. After this the fighting is in earnest. For this episode, whose function has never been made clear, no precise source is known. It seems much like the sort of tournament that was a commonplace in the halcyon days of the Round Table before the Grail Quest, and certainly in one sense it serves to suggest further the falling back that occurred after the

Quest.[15] But the episode serves a function more important than this: in it, Lancelot's sinful state is made manifest in at least two ways.

First, while riding in a forest, the knight is ignominiously struck in a buttock by an arrow shot by "a lady that dwelled in that foreyste, and she was a grete huntresse." This anonymous lady with her female companions—Malory emphasizes that "no men wente never with her"—is hunting "a barayne hynde," a female deer that is not pregnant; but her arrow hits the sleeping Lancelot instead (783). Although the symbolism is not transparent, it should not be thought that the episode is without meaning. In a sense the lady is like Diana, Classical goddess of both the hunt and chastity; and the "barayne hynde" is like Guinevere, who has violated both chastity—in not being a faithful wife to Arthur— and the Christian idea of love. For medieval Christianity, the end of love is procreation, and the act of love is justified only if intended to produce offspring. To delight in sexual love for its own sake is a striking example of *desmesure*. Guinevere is, therefore, like the knights who misuse their lives by enjoying quests for adventure as if they were ends: she loves for the sake of loving. A further significance of this allegorical episode is that Lancelot is punished for Guinevere's sins. The arrow, figuratively directed at her, hits him. In this sense the episode ironically forecasts what will happen in Malory's next tale, but more immediate is the possibility that it acts as an *exemplum* to Lancelot who has been spiritually sleeping. Lancelot, failing to see any *sententia*, however, curses the lady: "The devyll made you a shoter!" (784).

The second suggestion of Lancelot's sinful condition appears in the actual Tournament. Lancelot, disguised significantly as a Saracen, a non-Christian, fights for no stated reason against Arthur's side, an action forecasting Lancelot's actual fight against the king in the next tale. Although Gareth fights with Lancelot against Arthur, he does so because, when he saw Lancelot "do so muche dedis of armys," he was "shamed to se so many good knyghtes ayenste hym alone" (790). Arthur approves of Gareth's reason and states in a very significant passage his idea of what should be the actions of the "worshypfull knyght," the ideal man: "For ever hit ys . . . a worshypfull knyghtes dede to helpe and succoure another worshypfull knyght whan he seeth hym in daungere. For ever a worshypfull man woll be lothe to se a worshypfull man shamed, and he that ys of no worshyp and medelyth with cowardise never shall he shew jantilnes nor no maner of goodnes where he seeth a man in daungere, for than woll a cowarde never shew mercy. And allwayes a good man woll do ever to another man as he wolde be done to hymselff" (790). Here *worshyp* is associated not with prowess but with mercy. As in the fight against the old order, seen in the "Merlin" section of the *Tale of Arthur,* the emphasis is on helping others. Here, however, such helping is presented as more than knightly courtesy; it now sounds very much like the Christian idea of charity. Furthermore, one must be, like Gareth, "curteyse, trew, and faythefull to hys frynde"—and not, by implication, treacherous and proud, as Lancelot is. In fact, as P. E. Tucker notes, Malory "magnifies Lancelot's sense of his own prowess until it becomes a fault in his knighthood," a flaw clearly seen in the next tale.[16]

The next episode of the *Lancelot and Guinevere,* called by Vinaver the "Knight of the Cart," begins immediately after this speech of Arthur. This is a version of the twelfth-century romance of *Lancelot* by Chrétien de Troyes, the oldest extant story of Sir Lancelot in world literature. Malory's rendering of this old tale of the abduction of Guinevere by Meliagraunce and her rescue by Lancelot seems, however, to be based on that in the Prose *Lancelot* and is often dismissed as an emasculated account of the adventures.[17] The function of the episode must, however, be understood. As Lumiansky points out, the very act of inserting material from a different source at this point "presupposes a careful plan on Malory's part." Also, because Malory has had Meliagraunce speak twice earlier of his love for Guinevere (359–61), it is most likely that his use of Meliagraunce's abduction of the queen "was not a last-minute or haphazard decision."[18] It functions not to show the development of Lancelot or his overcoming obstacles to rescue Guinevere or even his love for the queen—as was the case in Chrétien—but to act as a preliminary adventure leading to the accusation of infidelity Meliagraunce levels at Guinevere. The episode represents the first tangible threat to the realm since the episodes with Lucius and with the giant of Saint Michael's Mount in Malory's second tale. As such, it anticipates the greater trouble that is coming; but more immediately it serves to lower the quality of the love between Lancelot and Guinevere.

Throughout the *Morte Darthur* this love has been growing more intense as Lancelot serves his lady more completely and more excessively. "The Knight of the Cart" section is marked by physical lust, seen first in Meliagraunce's desire for Guinevere—he will abduct her even though his actions will dishonor Arthur, "all knyghthode," himself, and the queen (793)—and then in the love-making between Lancelot and Guinevere. *Desmesure* marks this episode, and everything is working up to the point of the discovered adultery which Merlin had forecast to Arthur in Malory's first tale (71).[19]

At the beginning of this episode, there appears a digression on love that is surely Malory's own addition. Speaking of the month of May, Malory describes the coming of love into the land, elaborating the theme of the reawakening of nature. In Vinaver's words, this passage represents Malory's "counterpart to the idealistic doctrine of courtly romance, and his most successful escape from the oppressive atmosphere of *courtoisie* into a world of comfortable realities." [20] But Malory is doing more than describing spring and earthly love, for he makes three main points. First, he compares the coming of winter to the turning away from true love: "For, lyke as wynter rasure [mark] dothe allway arace [erase] and deface grene summer, so faryth hit by unstable love in man and woman, for in many persones there ys no stabylité: for we may se all day, for a lytyll blaste of wyntres rasure, anone [immediately] we shall deface and lay aparte trew love, for lytyll or nowght [nothing] that coste muche thynge" (790–91). Because of the lack of "stabylité" in the world, "trew love" is hard to find; and, even when "trew love" exists, it is in danger of being replaced by something less. While describing a human condition, the passage also prepares for the replacement of "trew love" by lust in the "Knight of the Cart" episode.

Following this statement, Malory makes his second point by explicitly speaking of earthly love as secondary to heavenly love: "lat every man of worshyp florysh hys herte in thys worlde: firste unto God, and nexte unto the joy of them that he promysed hys feythe unto. . . . But firste reserve the honoure to God, and secundely thy quarell muste com of thy lady. And such love I calle vertuouse love" (791). The ideal, "vertuouse love," exists only when love of God comes first and human love second. Here Malory, in "his own unsystematic way, impulsive and not reasoning . . . elaborates his very simple reconciliation between romantic love and Christianity." [21]

Malory's third point in this May interpolation is to contrast love as found in the good old days with that of his own time. In the present age, he says, love is "sone hote sone colde. Thys ys no stabylyté. But the olde love was nat so. For men and women coude love togydirs seven yerys, and no lycoures [lecherous] lustis was betwixte them, and than was love, trouthe and faythefulnes" (791). By implication, "vertuouse love" may be described as stable, loyal, not promiscuous or impetuous; and it is also marked by a realization that earthly love must come after love of God. It is "perfectly compatible with the chivalric ideals of honor and loyalty and with marriage," and thus replaces the courtly love found in Malory's sources.[22]

Although this scene begins an episode detailing the love between Lancelot and Guinevere, it should not be thought that their relationship is an example of "vertuouse love." In fact, as Lumiansky says, this description gives "an ironic contrast to the covert adultery" of the two lovers.[23] Although Malory holds up Guinevere as "a trew lover" who had "a good ende," he still thinks of her as something less than ideal; she may be a model because of her "good ende," her years as a religious recluse. Also Malory is not being didactic; rather than judge the queen, he merely states as premise his idea of love and then lets the reader apply it to the action.

Probably the most significant section in the *Lancelot and Guinevere* is that called by Vinaver "The Healing of Sir Urry." In many respects this story, "virtually unknown in Arthurian literature," [24] seems to be out of place here. It is about a Hungarian knight who, after killing a Spanish enemy, is cursed by the dead man's mother, "a grete sorseras": his wounds will not heal "untyll the beste knyght of the worlde had serched hys woundis" (808–09). Although Urry's problem may be comparable to Tristram's and King Evelake's, there is a difference; for, in the earlier actions, the healing was a real part of the narrative and was used to demonstrate the fulfilment of an adventure. Here, however, the story of Urry and his wounds appears as a focal point for the main action, which is to determine the best knight in the world. The story of the Hungarian knight has little narrative function in itself; rather, like the Chapel Perelous episode in the *Tale of Lancelot*, it is the magical or supernatural vehicle for emphasizing that Lancelot is still the best knight.

The difficulty with the episode is that nothing new seems to be discovered. Perhaps the best way of viewing the adventure is as a final surge forward before death. The court and its special hero, Lancelot, shine one final time before the great conflict that destroys everything. Reinforcing this idea is the long list of kings and knights that try to heal Urry. This list acts as a summary of past adventures and past glories. There are, to be sure, some inconsistencies in it; for not every knight mentioned has appeared earlier, and some knights present are supposed to be dead. Nevertheless, in this catalogue of knights Malory allows the reader to recall the real halcyon days of the Order of the Round Table.

At the mention of several knights' names, Malory pauses and reminds the reader of their special merits or adventures. For example, when speaking of the kin of King Pellinore, Malory mentions "sir Tor, sir Agglovale, sir Durnor, sir Lamorak, the moste nobeleste knyght, one of them that ever was in kynge Arthurs dayes as for a worldly knyght, and sir Percivale that was pyerles, excepte sir Galahad, in holy dedis. But they dyed in the queste of the Sankgreall" (811). Likewise, when listing Sir Bellingere le Bewse, he refers to him as "son to the good knyght sir Alysaundir le Orphelyn that was slayne by the treson of kynge Marke." There also appears Sir Belyaunce le Orgulus "that the good knyght sir Lamorak wan in playne batayle"; and Sir Ermynde, "brother to king Hermaunce, for whom sir Palomydes faught at the Rede Cité with two brethirn" (812). Also from other earlier tales are Sir Ironsyde, "that was called the noble knyght of the Rede Laundis, that sir Gareth wan for the love of dame Lyones"; and Sir Pelleas, "that loved the lady Ettarde (and he had dyed for her sake, had nat bene one of the ladyes of the lake whos name was dame Nynyve; and she wedde sir Pelleas, and she saved hym ever aftir, that he was never slayne by her dayes; and he was a full noble knyght)" (812–13).

This recounting is in effect a curtain call; and, by looking back

Malory suggests that the great days are over. The attempt to heal Urry is the final joint endeavor of all the Knights of the Round Table, and, as such, it is the culminating event in the pause between the fulfilment of the Grail Quest and the final destruction of the realm.

The end of the episode deserves special comment. After all the knights of Arthur's realm—and before them the knights of "all the londis crystynde"—have tried unsuccessfully to heal Sir Urry, Lancelot, who had not been present, approaches and is commanded by Arthur to attempt the healing. Lancelot says that, after so many worthy men have searched the wounds and failed to heal them, it would be presumptuous for him to try. Arthur, however, insists, and Lancelot finally agrees, saying to Sir Urry: "Jesu wolde that I myght helpe you! For I shame sore with myselff that I shulde be thus requyred, for never was I able in worthynes to do so hyghe a thynge" (814). Lancelot seems to realize the symbolic significance of the healing. It is a test that will act as a proof of the knight's worth in the eyes of everyone watching and in those of Arthur in particular, who may be finding in this action a sign of Lancelot's purity. As Lumiansky surmises, should Lancelot fail, the implication will be that he is an adulterer.[25] Also, and more important, Lancelot apparently understands that the healer of the wounds will act as an agent of the divine, that he who heals Sir Urry will be the chosen man, just as they who achieved the Grail were selected by God.

In a very dramatic moment, after praying to the "Blyssed Trynyté" that his "symple worshyp and honesté" be saved, Lancelot searches the wounds which heal at his touch and appear "as they had bene hole a seven yere." Following this action, all the kings and knights present kneel down and give "thankynges and lovynge unto God and unto Hys Blyssed Modir. And ever sir Launcelote wepte, as he had bene a chylde that had bene beatyn!" (814-15). The serious moment that has just passed is more than one merely showing Lancelot to be the best knight in the world. Rather, it is almost as if a miracle has just happened; in fact, this adventure, which has long puzzled readers of Malory, might best be viewed as miraculous. Lancelot has, in effect, been accepted by God; in spite of his inconstancy, he is rewarded.

Specifically, Lancelot appears in the role of the priest who is trying to heal the spiritually sick person, particularly the person cursed—containing a demon within himself.[26] Traditionally, exorcism of devils was a terrifying matter, for the effort of driving a fiend from a human body usually proved too demanding for a mere mortal and usually resulted in the death of the priest. In the *Tale of the Sankgreal* Galahad, the ideal knight, was able to drive a fiend out of a dead body (642); but in that same tale Perceval's sister died when she gave her blood to heal the lady of a castle (720–21). When Lancelot weeps following his success, in a passage which C. S. Lewis has called "perhaps the greatest of all passages peculiar to Malory," his tears are, to be sure, of joy.[27] He is glad he has succeeded, but the tears may also be seen as stemming from relief. Lancelot has healed the knight and has been allowed to live. Still, it must not be forgotten that Lancelot's tears are compared to those of "a chylde that had bene beatyn." Lancelot is worn out from his exertion, but he has also in a sense been punished; for, as with his partial success in the Grail Quest, he understands something of what he would have had and been if it had not been for his instability and earthly love.[28]

Malory thus emphasizes for one final time the greatness of the Knights of the Round Table in general and of Lancelot in particular. When he concludes the *Lancelot and Guinevere*, he even says that he must "overlepe grete bookis of sir Launcelot" and the "grete adventures he ded" (815). The pause, the Indian Summer, following the Grail Quest is finished; now only the end with its barrenness remains.

## II  *Death and Destruction*

This end comes about in the next tale, *The Most Piteous Tale of the Morte Arthur saunz Guerdon* (Caxton's Books XX–XXI) which, according to Vinaver, forms with the *Lancelot and Guinevere*, "a coherent whole." Also, Vinaver feels that in these tales Malory uses his sources "with a degree of freedom and independence unparalleled in his earlier works." The *Death of Arthur* in particular must be viewed as "a work of striking originality." [29]

The end of the Order is both quick and complex though it has been in sight from as early as Malory's first romance, the *Tale of Arthur*. Throughout the seven tales preceding this final one, hints, forecasts, and suggestions have amply prepared the reader for the end of the saga and have, in fact, created the suspense that fills both this last tale and the preceding *Lancelot and Guinevere*. As Wilfred L. Guerin states, without the first seven tales, "the eighth is like a silent, isolated fossil, unable to tell of the forces that have brought it to its final situation." [30] Now in the *Death of Arthur* every reader knows what is to come. What he does not know is when the end will come and precisely how it will come. Because he is prepared and is waiting, every action is important not only in itself but also in terms of the imminent disaster. While Malory may have given a "drastic simplification of the spiritual tangle in which the traditional story of Arthur had become involved," one can hardly agree with Vinaver that he "suppresses every link" between the final destruction and the earlier adventures of the Round Table.[31]

Because of its general inadequacy—its imperfection and worldliness—Arthur's court, along with the Order of the Round Table, must fall. It is relevant to anticipate the narrative and note at this point Arthur's dream before his final battle with his son, Sir Mordred: "So uppon Trynyté Sunday at nyght kynge Arthure dremed a wondirfull dreme, and in hys dreme hym semed that he saw uppon a chafflet [platform] a chayre, and the chayre was faste to a whele, and thereuppon sate kynge Arthure in the rychest clothe of golde that myght be made. And the kynge thought there was undir hym, farre from hym, an hydeous depe blak watir, and therein was all maner of serpentis and wormes and wylde bestis fowle and orryble. And suddeynly the kynge thought that the whyle turned up-so-downe, and he felle amonge the serpentis, and every beste toke hym by a lymme" (865). The dreams that had earlier signaled victory now forecast defeat. Specifically, Arthur's present dream is of the Wheel of Fortune, symbolizing the king's imminent fall. He is revealed as a man who, while at the top of the wheel, has achieved the most and the best he could. But the wheel continues to turn, and the achievement limited to this world must of necessity fall.

Both Malory and the English stanzaic *Morte Arthur*, his source for this scene, are, according to Vinaver, "little concerned . . . with the symbolic significance of this vision." What Vinaver means is that, whereas the French *Mort Artu* uses the Wheel of Fortune vision "to explain the whole course of events leading up to Arthur's death," Malory and the English stanzaic poem deliberately shift the emphasis "from this theme to the human tragedy of Arthur, Gawain, and Lancelot." [32] Still, Arthur's fall in Malory appears as part of the over-all pattern of life in this mutable world. That which is mutable is bound to change, and the change comes that topples even the greatest men and earthly institutions.

Not only is this world mutable, it is also imperfect; and those who realize this imperfection and rise above it, namely Galahad and Perceval, leave it willingly and gladly. Arthur, however, has appeared throughout the *Morte Darthur* as a man who wants to hang on to the world. When his knights set out on the Quest of the Holy Grail, the king laments that such action will ruin his glory, that his great Order is being broken up (635). He fails to see that the Grail Quest is in actuality the whole reason for the existence of the Order. When the Order has reached a stage showing that it is ready for this ultimate adventure, the adventure comes; but it is not welcomed by all the knights. Means are thus confused with ends; and, as Malory writes, after the Quest, "than was there grete joy in the courte" (744), joy especially on the part of Arthur; for that which he had viewed as a danger seems to be past and the realm is still whole.

Furthermore, the specific, efficient causes of the final breaking up of the Order are the various sins and excesses seen in Arthur and in his subjects throughout the previous tales. The lechery of Lancelot and Guinevere, the anger of those knights who are Arthur's relatives, the envy of Mordred and Agravain toward Lancelot in particular, their hatred toward the queen, the pride and insecurity of Gawain, the weaknesses of Arthur—all serve to bring about and continue the final disaster. Evil seems to be in everyone; and, just as Lancelot could earlier do only good, now he is no longer in control of his actions, which appear to be ambiguous. Also, the fine ideals of prowess, courtesy, and love are now more than ever revealed as inadequate; for they too are mutable, ever-shifting, and ever-unsure. Some knights still mean well and try to do what they can to alleviate the trouble, but they are of insufficient power.

In fact, as the *Morte Darthur* hurtles to its end, fate is again seen in relation to human actions, though, as P. E. Tucker rightly says, Malory "so develops the sense of personal choice in his characters that the conception of Fate becomes almost superfluous." The characters are certainly individualized: Mordred, for instance, instead of being merely "the instrument of destiny," is "a traitor whose rebellion is the final instance of the failure of loyalties." [33] Although one may also agree with Vinaver that to Malory the final catastrophe is "a human drama determined from first to last by the tragic clash of human loyalties," [34] the sense of fate does enter, in that actions suggest the presence of forces beyond the human.

At one point, for example, it seems that the ultimate disaster can be avoided. In his dream of the Wheel of Fortune, Arthur is also warned by Gawain, who, now dead, is sent from God to tell the king not to fight Mordred until Lancelot joins him. Only by waiting for Lancelot, says the divine messenger-knight, can Arthur achieve the victory. Arthur does as Gawain tells him, his army and that of Mordred meet to agree to a truce, but then the uncontrollable factor enters, and all is laid waste: "Ryght so cam oute an addir of a lytyll hethe-buysshe, and hit stange a knyght in the foote. And so whan the knyght felte hym so stonge, he loked downe and saw the adder; and anone he drew hys swerde to sle the addir, and thought none othir harme. And whan the oste [army] on bothe partyes saw that swerde drawyn, than they blewe beamys [horns], trumpettis, and hornys, and shoutted grymly [ferociously], and so bothe ostis dressed hem togydirs [advanced toward each other]" (867). Thus the final battle begins, of which Malory says, "never syns was there never seyne a more dolefuller batayle in no Crysten londe" (867), the many negatives emphasizing its significance.

In a sense this struggle may be seen as a manifestation of the archetypal conflict between God and the Devil, represented by the snake; but, just as Fortune acts through the consent of God, so does the Devil. The unnamed knight who strikes out at the adder is certainly Everyman, marked, by nature perhaps, with a desire for self-preservation and vengeance. His action of striking at the snake is not in itself either right or wrong. The knight, a typical human being, instinctively strikes out at that which has hurt him; but, significantly, the action causing the pain is over, and the striking out is only an after-the-fact act of revenge. Although the knight cannot save himself by killing the snake, his action is still understandable. Man, being what he is, will act in certain ways; likewise, the world, being what it is, must be marked by change. Fate appears in the form of a typical human response, and the unnamed knight, as well as man in general, cannot be blamed for the destruction that follows. The destruction, the specific manifestation of change, must follow because of fate and the way things are. The flower of chivalry has blossomed; but, after all, it is only a flower. And, although it lives in the light for a short while, it must fade away.

It is relevant to note again the emphasis on springtime, specifically on May, found in these last two tales. At the beginning of the final tale, the *Death of Arthur*, Malory writes that, now that the "rowghe wyndis and blastis" of winter are over, people "rejoysyth and gladith of somer commynge with his freyshe floures"; now "every harte floryshyth and burgenyth" (818). In "thys season," says Malory ironically, there occurs "a grete angur and unhappe [misfortune] that stynted [ended] nat tylle the floure of chyvalry of all the worlde was destroyed and slayne" (818). When one least expects it, in the freshness of spring and the fulness of life, the fall comes.

Agravain and Mordred, two knights by and large neglected in the earlier action of Malory's Arthur-saga, now become important. Mordred from the beginning of the *Morte Darthur* is singled out as the man who will be the final actual threat to the realm, but Agravain receives a subtler treatment. For example, in the whole of Malory's book he never defeats any other knight; he is involved in the murders of the noble knights, Dinadan and Lamorak; and he hates Lancelot.[35] The evil dormant in him now comes out when he and Mordred—though not supported by their brothers, Gawain, Gaherys, and Gareth—decide to tell Arthur about the love between Lancelot and Guinevere. They accuse Lancelot of being a traitor, but, even though Arthur finally agrees to test the knight, he does not like what he must do, "for sir Launcelot had done so much for hym and for the quene so many tymes" (820). No such sentiment is found in either the French *Mort Artu* or the English stanzaic poem. In fact, even though Malory throughout this tale shows Lancelot as related to and, in fact, as a real cause of the trouble at hand, he tends to excuse him or, at least, to temper his guilt with statements emphasizing his nobility. Even when Malory relates the love of Lancelot and Guinevere, he changes his sources which say they went to bed together, and writes that he does not know what the two lovers did "for love that tyme was nat as love ys nowadayes" (821).

When told of Lancelot's love of the queen, Arthur is apparently willing to forgive being deceived; but, because of worldly concepts of honor, he must take action. Consequently, a plan to reveal in certain terms the unfaithfulness of Lancelot and Guinevere is decided upon. Twelve armed knights, all kinsmen of Gawain, join Agravain and Mordred to surprise and take Lancelot in the queen's chamber. Although Lancelot is at first unarmed, he fights his way free and kills all but Mordred, who flees wounded. Lancelot is still the greatest knight in the world, but again this fact is shown to be irrelevant. The harm has been done; the love between Lancelot and Guinevere, which has long existed as an open secret, is now an acknowledged fact. And, as Guinevere says—in lines not in Malory's sources—when the knights appear outside the chamber shouting for Lancelot, "I dred me sore oure longe love ys com to a myschyvus [shameful] ende" (822).

Although Lancelot has escaped the danger, he has killed thirteen knights; and he knows that Arthur cannot ignore what has happened. It is significant that the episode in Malory is much bloodier than that in either source. The stanzaic *Morte* says merely that, after killing Agravain, Lancelot overcomes the other knights; and the French says nothing about his overcoming anyone except the first knight he meets. Malory's grimmer scene suggests the seriousness of what has happened. Lancelot too feels the seriousness and thus prepares for a fight. He also makes plans for the third time to rescue Guinevere, who he knows will be sentenced to burning because of her infidelity.

Throughout this trouble Gawain appears more noble than at any other point in Malory's Arthur-saga. When he disassociates himself from Agravain and Mordred, he says: "I woll never be ayenste sir Launcelot for [because of] one dayes dede, that was whan he rescowed me frome kynge Carados of the Dolerous Towre and slew hym and saved my lyff" (819). Because of his respect for and loyalty to Lancelot, Gawain will do nothing to hurt him. Even after Lancelot, in his escape from Guinevere's chamber, kills several kinsmen of Gawain, including his brother

Agravain and his sons Florence and Lovell, Gawain refuses to do anything against him. He even advises Arthur not to be "over hasty" in fighting Lancelot and in judging Guinevere, and goes so far as to say that he believes Guinevere to be "both good and trew" to the king (829). Arthur does not understand how Gawain can defend Lancelot after he has killed his kinsmen, but Gawain replies that, although he is sorry for their deaths, they themselves, failing to heed Gawain's counsel to refrain from fighting, are "the causars of their owne dethe" (830). It is ironic that their rashness will later be both Gawain's and Arthur's.

Furthermore, Gawain says he will have nothing to do with the execution of Guinevere and refuses to escort her to the fire. Because of Gawain's refusal, Arthur calls on Gaherys and Gareth, Gawain's two noble brothers, to act as escort for the queen. These knights, who also hate what is required of them, decide to do the task without wearing armor; that is, they intend to be apart from the event, to be present only "in pesyble wyse," in garments of peace. When Lancelot bursts in to rescue the queen, these two knights are in the "russhynge and hurlynge" killed by him (831). Although Lancelot did not see them and certainly did not intend to harm them, his rescue of Guinevere could cause only disaster since he was fighting against the right. This action also changes Gawain, who can act no longer as Lancelot's defender. He becomes the knight's principal accuser, and he must be regarded from this point as the person most actively responsible for keeping alive the hostilities that result in Mordred's ultimate treachery and in the conflict between him and Arthur.

At this point it is necessary to review and reassess the character of Gawain as he appears throughout the *Morte Darthur*. Just as Lancelot contains within himself all aspects and degrees of earthly perfection, so does Gawain have all the different degrees of imperfection. At times he exhibits prowess and courtesy; at others, he is cowardly and vicious. For example, in the *Arthur and Lucius* he is a valiant noble warrior, in the *Book of Tristram* he is condemned as a false knight, and in the *Tale of Arthur* he appears as both good and bad.

Because Gawain's character changes even within one tale, the differences cannot be regarded as merely variations Malory makes from one tale to another. Nor does it seem likely that Malory was unconscious of the variations and contradictions existing within Gawain. According to Vinaver, Malory, rather than attempt to reconcile the opposite views of Gawain's character, "blindly accepts the verdict of each of his sources and so produces a picture full of inconsistencies and contradictions." [36] It can be demonstrated, however, that at times Malory makes Gawain blacker and whiter than his sources indicate; but the main flaw in Vinaver's argument is his implication that inconsistency signifies lack of control on the part of an author. As Barbara Gray Bartholomew has pointed out, Gawain may also be viewed as the one knight who typifies all the knights making up the Order of the Round Table. He is "accorded highest praise and sharpest blame because he combines the best and the worst to be found among Arthur's knights. In him are focused the qualities which propel the Round Table to greatness and the qualities which plummet it to its ruin." Still, one might hesitate to say that "Gawain's inconsistency is the inconsistency of humanity" [37] because, in Malory's view, it is Lancelot who possesses this inconsistency. With Lancelot, this is the one flaw in his noble character; with Gawain, this is the mark of his character.

Probably Gawain's only consistent action throughout the *Morte Darthur* is his loyalty to Arthur and to his own family. Beginning in the *Tale of Arthur,* the sons of King Lot, especially Gawain, are hostile to the other groups of knights at Arthur's court. Gawain, the inexorable foe of King Pellinore and his family, is responsible for the treacherous deaths of both this knight and his son, Lamorak. Gawain is likewise envious of the French knights, Lancelot and his kin; but he respects the worth of Lancelot even though Lancelot replaced him as Arthur's favorite. Furthermore, whatever nobility Gawain possesses is in him largely because it is inherited. Gawain also begins many things that are good, but then stops or changes his mind. The Quest of the Grail is a prime example of Gawain's irresolution and fluctuation. Although he is the first knight to state his intention of going on the Quest, he also is one of the first to cease questing. In other words, Malory in the figure of Gawain has shown a knight good up to a point, but irresolute and imperfect. Gawain is not whole; he sees clearly at times, but there is no pattern or direction to his behavior.

Thus, after hearing that Lancelot has killed Gaherys and Gareth, Gawain cannot be contained. He faints, weeps, and, even though he is told that Lancelot did not intend to fight much less to kill them, he is set on revenge. He says to Arthur: "frome thys day forewarde I shall never fayle sir Launcelot untyll that one of us have slayne that othir. And therefore I requyre you, my lorde and kynge, dresse you unto the warre, for wyte [know] you well, I woll be revenged uppon sir Launcelot" (835). Gawain's hatred causes Arthur to wage war on Lancelot, even to follow him across the channel to attack him in his own land. Gawain daily, in front of Lancelot's castle, insults Lancelot by calling him "false and recrayde [cowardly] knyght," and later challenges him to fight (837). Gawain's wrath is excessive, beyond his control; and in the pages of the *Death of Arthur* it contrasts strikingly with Lancelot's constant courtesy and desire for moderation.[38]

Insulted and attacked, Lancelot withholds his power and re-fuses to harm Arthur. In the first battle between Lancelot's forces and those of Arthur, Bors, fighting on Lancelot's side, strikes Ar-thur down and then asks Lancelot if he wants him to kill the king and "make an ende of thys warre." In reply, Lancelot commands: "touch hym no more! For I woll never se that moste noble kynge that made me knyght nother slayne nor shamed." He places the king on his own horse and addresses him courteously: "My lorde the kynge, for Goddis love, stynte [stop] thys stryff, for ye gette here no worshyp and [if] I wolde do myne utteraunce [utmost]. But allwayes I forbeare [hold back from] you, and ye nor none off youres forberyth nat me. And therefore, my lorde, I pray you remembir what I have done in many placis, and now am I evyll rewarded" (840). Arthur on horseback looks at Lancelot and weeps: "than the teerys braste oute of hys yen [eyes], thynkyng of the grete curtesy that was in sir Launcelot more than in ony other man. And therewith the kyng rod hys way and myght no lenger beholde hym, saiying to hymselff, 'Alas, alas, that ever yet thys warre began!' " (840).

But the war has begun, and it continues until all is destroyed. Not even the Pope is able to bring peace although he does effect the return of Guinevere to the king. Lancelot escorts Guinevere to Arthur and at the court makes another plea for peace. In a speech summarizing his past deeds, a boasting speech, not in the French or the English source, which Vida Scudder points out is typical of epic heroes,[39] Lancelot asks to be remembered to Arthur's knights and especially desires Gawain's "good wyll" and Arthur's "good grace" (845). Lancelot, who repeats his sorrow at having killed good knights of the Round Table, humbly offers to go on a pilgrimage from Sandwich to Carlisle barefoot in his shirt, founding every ten miles "an house of relygions, of what order that ye woll assygne [direct] me, with an holé covente, to synge and rede day and nyght in especiall for sir Gareth sake and sir Gaherys" (846). But not even such a magnanimous and gracious gesture can cause Gawain to change his mind although, as Malory writes, "all the knyghtes and ladyes that were there wepte as they were madde, and the tearys felle on kynge Arthur hys chekis" (846–47). Gawain will show no mercy; now that he feels injured, he will try forever for revenge. Consequently, Lancelot is exiled from the land.

Before departing from Arthur, Lancelot laments his state, regretting that he must leave Arthur's realm, which he calls "Moste nobelyst Crysten realme, whom I have loved aboven all othir realmys!" He laments that he should be "shamefully banysshyd, undeserved and causeles," but consoles himself by thinking of Fortune that is "so varyaunte, and the wheele so mutable, that there ys no constaunte abydynge" (847). Like Arthur later, Lancelot now feels the impermanence of life. The glorious days are over, and Lancelot in another very dramatic scene kisses the queen for the last time and leaves the court forever. All these episodes show what Vinaver has termed the "essentially human plane" of the destruction as revealed by Malory. Here are emphasized those emotions which bring about the final tragedy—"the passionate feudal loyalty of man to man, and the self-denying devotion of the knight-lover to his lady." Also the actions of the characters are deeply related to their inner selves; they arise "not from the accidents of human life, nor from the momentary weaknesses of the protagonists, but from the depths of their noblest passions, from the uncompromising sincerity of their devotion to a chosen aim." [40]

The main battles are still to come. Attacked in France by Arthur, Lancelot still holds back his strength; for he is "full lothe [very unwilling] to ryde oute with my knyghtes for shedynge of Crysten blood" (852). Finally, however, feeling that he has been

"dryvyn thereto as beste [beast] tylle [to] a bay" (855), Lancelot
realizes that he must fight. Like Bors before him, who in the *Tale
of the Sankgreal* finally in desperation realized he had to fight his
brother Lionel, Lancelot knows he can hold back no longer and
answers Gawain's taunting challenge to individual combat. But
the divine intercession that kept Bors from fighting his brother
does not come now, and a fierce battle ensues between these two
great knights.

The fight emphasizes Gawain's miraculous strength, which increases until it becomes threefold at noon. Malory writes that this
magical strength "caused sir Gawayne to wynne grete honoure,"
for only a few people knew of it" (856). Perhaps the strength is
mentioned here by Malory—it is also emphasized in the French
source—because of the dramatic need to have Gawain approach
Lancelot in prowess.[41] In the fight Lancelot holds back and merely
defends himself until Gawain's power is back to normal. Then he
fells Gawain but refrains from killing him, for, as he says, "I woll
never smyte a felde knyght" (857). Although Gawain lies
wounded for three weeks, he again challenges Lancelot, who answers him saying: "I know youre myght and all that ye may do,
and well ye wote [know], sir Gawayne, ye may nat greatly hurte
me" (858). As in the stanzaic *Morte Arthur*, the two knights again
fight—in the French *Mort Artu*, there is only one fight—and again
Gawain increases in strength. Now Malory writes, "ever as sir Ga-
waynes myght encreased, ryght so encreed hys wynde and hys
evyll wyll" (859). When his natural strength returns, Lancelot,
who has again been holding back, addresses him, saying that with
his magical power Gawain has "desceyved many a full noble
knyght" (859).

Throughout the *Morte Darthur* Gawain has been continually
praised for his courage and prowess. Whatever faults he had, he
was at least a man of prowess, but now even his strength is taken
from him. More precisely, his prowess is revealed as something
given to him: a "gyffte" from "an holy man" (856). As such, it is
comparable to the nobility which he inherited from King Lot; it is
not something he demonstrates and controls himself. Moreover,
even if the "holy man" who gave Gawain his strength was really a
holy Christian, and even if the strength is good in itself and not
the product of black magic, Gawain still, as Lancelot says, "des-

ceyved" his opponents and certainly did not use the gift of strength as well as he could. In Lancelot's words one may see the beginning of "a hardening of Lancelot's attitude toward Gawain and Arthur." This change adds to the drama of the fight and also, as Lumiansky says, connects these encounters at Benwick "not only with the preceding deterioration of their relationships in the 'Deth of Arthur' but also with succeeding events." [42]

This second fight is the final one between Lancelot and Gawain. Again Lancelot wounds his opponent and again refuses to kill him although Gawain berates him for allowing him to remain alive. Lancelot repeats that he will not "smyte a wounded man" and departs, with Gawain "evermore callyng hym 'traytoure knyght'" and promising to fight him again (859). The perseverance Gawain shows in his adamant hatred of Lancelot is, aside from his continual family loyalty, the first perseverance associated with him in the whole of the *Morte Darthur*. Ironically, only destruction will be the result; and only his death will release him from his hatred.

The destruction comes in the form of news that Mordred, left by Arthur in command of England, has rebelled and seized both the country and the queen, whom he plans to marry. Although Guinevere is able to escape from him and hide in the Tower of London, Mordred is still ruler of the land. Mordred's rebellion, much more serious than Meliagraunce's abduction of Guinevere in the *Lancelot and Guinevere,* is like the challenge of Lucius in Malory's second tale. Like Lucius, Mordred appears as an antichrist, a figure not only in the wrong but also actively against what is right. Specifically, Mordred defies the Bishop of Canterbury, who excommunicates him in spite of Mordred's threats against his person. Symbolically, Mordred, Arthur's son, may be viewed as a reflection of Arthur at this point in his life. Just as Galahad was in a sense contained within Lancelot, so Mordred symbolizes a side of the king's character. Now that the realm is collapsing, Mordred is able to exist. A shadowy figure throughout the earlier tales, always associated with wrong causes and imperfect knights. Mordred now comes into his own and exists as a challenge to Arthur. When chaos is unleashed, he appears as its symbolic representative as well as its unleasher.

Strangely, most of the people of England join Mordred. Malory writes that, according to "the comyn voyce," with King Arthur there had been "never othir lyff but warre and stryff, and with sir Mordrede was grete joy and blysse" (861). Furthermore, addressing his readers, "ye all Englysshemen," Malory attacks the fickleness of the common people in Arthur's time and stresses that they were "so new-fangill" that, just as now, "there may no thynge us please no terme" (862). Such remarks not only represent contemporary social criticism, but also suggest the instability of this world—the theme emphasized over and over throughout this tale.

In the first battle with Mordred, Arthur's forces win the day, although Gawain is struck on the old wound Lancelot had given him and is found "liynge more than halff dede" (862). Gawain, in Malory's addition to his sources, finally realizes the trouble he has caused in his desire for revenge and says to Arthur: "thorow me and my pryde ye have all thys shame and disease [trouble]" (863). Gawain further realizes that Arthur would never have had trouble with Mordred had Lancelot been with the king. Consequently, again in lines not in Malory's sources, Gawain writes a letter to Lancelot, asking his forgiveness and wishing him to return, to pray at Gawain's tomb, and to help Arthur fight Mordred. At this point Gawain is more noble than at any other time in the *Morte Darthur*.

Before the famous last battle following Trinity Sunday, Arthur dreams of his fall and of Gawain's advising him to delay until Lancelot can arrive and give him assistance. Significantly, Gawain is shown in this dream as surrounded by all the ladies he had helped while he lived (865). Nothing is mentioned of his former sins or inadequacies, and it appears that in the end, perhaps through his repentance and knowledge of what he has done, Gawain finally becomes a good knight and achieves the salvation he failed to get on the Quest of the Holy Grail.

The battle, as was said earlier, cannot be avoided; although Arthur's forces win, it is a Pyrrhic victory; for, as Malory writes, there was never "a more dolefuller batayle in no Crysten londe." The fight itself is but briefly detailed, but, nevertheless, by nightfall there was "an hondred thousand leyde dede uppon the erthe" (867). The only surviving warriors are Mordred, on the one side, and Arthur, with Lucan and Bedevere, on the other. Seeing Mordred, Arthur rushes at him in spite of Lucan's warning to remember his dream. In a conversation probably added by Malory, Lucan counsels Arthur to stop fighting, saying "if ye leve of now, thys wycked day of Desteny ys paste" (868). But Arthur, like his nephew, Gawain, is so intent on revenge that he rushes ahead by himself; and, although he succeeds in killing Mordred, he is himself severely wounded in the head, the traditional seat of pride.

The battle is now over, but the horror is just beginning. In a few striking lines Malory describes the crying of the wounded on the battlefield at night as the looters descend on the dead and dying. Lucan, himself "grevously wounded," looks out upon the scene: "he saw and harkened by the moonelyght how that pyllours [plunderers] and robbers were com into the fylde to pylle [plunder] and to robbe many a full noble knyght of brochys and bees [bracelets] and of many a good rynge and many a ryche juell. And who that were nat dede all oute, there they slew them for their harneys [armor] and their ryches" (869). The Order of the Round Table and its ideals are no longer in control of the land; now that darkness has descended, unknightly behavior goes unchecked and the forces of misrule run rampant.

Finally Arthur prepares for his departure from the realm, and a note of the supernatural again comes into Malory's work with the famous scene of the miracle of Arthur's sword. Bedevere, following Arthur's command, throws Excalibur, the sword, into the nearby water. Immediately "there cam an arme and an honde above the watir, and toke hit and cleyght [seized] hit, and shoke hit thryse and braundysshed, and than vanysshed with the swerde into the watir" (870-71).[43] Arthur interprets this supernatural sign as signifying that he has "taryed over longe," perhaps that he has lived too long on this earth. He began his reign drawing a sword from a rock; he ends with his sword returning to a world beyond the human. Like the Grail, this talisman is taken away from an imperfect world.

Arthur is then carried by Bedevere to the side of the water where, awaiting him, is "a lytyll barge wyth many fayre ladyes in hit" (871). Among the ladies is Morgan le Fay, who now seems merely to represent Arthur's supernatural sister. She asks the king why he has "taryed so longe" away from her. With Morgan on the boat are the great sorceresses of the Arthurian legend, but, significantly, both the good and bad appear. Besides Morgan, there is mentioned the Queen of North Wales, shown three times throughout the *Morte Darthur* as Morgan's confederate; the Queen of the Waste Lands, earlier seen in the *Tale of the Sankgreal* as Perceval's holy aunt; and Nyneve, the good sorceress seen primarily in the *Tale of Arthur,* here called "the chyff lady of the laake" (872). It would seem as though all the manifestations of the supernatural are appearing together in this scene. Goodness and evil are no longer separated; and, as Arthur leaves the world, he is accompanied by the same supernatural forces, for evil and for good, which were part of the events of his life recorded throughout Malory's book.[44]

As the boat, now containing Arthur along with the ladies, sets out on its journey, Bedevere cries out that he is alone among enemies. In his last words Arthur counsels him to comfort himself, saying: "do as well as thou mayste [can], for in me ys no truste for to truste in. For I muste into the vale of Avylyon to hele me of my grevous wounde. And if thou here nevermore of me, pray for my soule!" (871). With the ladies on the boat shrieking and crying, Arthur is taken across the water to the other world from which he originally came into this world as king.

Arthur has changed from the impotent cuckold, the ineffectual man who misunderstood the Quest of the Holy Grail and the purpose of his Order of the Round Table; he again appears as a special being. Like the Grail Questers, Arthur now goes apart from the world to a new life. As Vinaver notes, Arthur must be seen as "a God-sent messenger who has only descended upon earth to reshape the destinies of his chosen country. As a knight, however brave and strong he may be, he is liable to suffer defeat; but as a hero-king guarded by God he triumphs over all adverse circumstances and conquers his 'wyked day of desteyne.'" [45] Even though Bedevere sees the next morning a new grave and hears from a hermit, the Bishop of Canterbury, that "at mydnyght, here cam a numbir of ladyes and brought here a dede corse and prayde me to entyre [bury] hym" (872), and believes it to be Arthur's grave, there is still an ambiguity; for, as many people believe, Arthur is "Rex quondam Rexque futurus," the once and future king, and "he shall com agayne, and he shall wynne the Holy Crosse" (873).

The end is forceful. Great happenings have occurred, events that are dramatically as well as thematically significant. The story here of Arthur is more than an example of how men fall on the Wheel of Fortune. This may be one theme within the story, but the story itself exists as a very powerful, compelling, even tragic, tale. The reader is ultimately left with a feeling of the greatness of the heroes and of the drama of their adventures. But there is still more to be told. Bedevere joins the Bishop of Canterbury as a religious hermit, Guinevere becomes a nun; and, when Lancelot, summoned by Gawain's letter, comes from France, he finds the battle finished and everything changed. He laments his own part in the destruction, saying, "in an unhappy owre was I born that ever I shulde have that myssehappe [misfortune] to sle firste sir Gawayne, sir Gaherys, the good knyght, and myne owne frynde sir Gareth that was a full noble knyght" (874). Then, after praying before Gawain's tomb and offering Masses for the salvation of Gawain's soul, Lancelot sets out to search for Guinevere.

The scene showing the meeting of these two great lovers, the result of an interpolation in a late redaction of the story,[46] is one of the most poignant scenes in the *Morte Darthur* though for F. Whitehead "the handling of the psychological and religious issues is somewhat heavy-handed" when compared to the comparable scenes in Malory's sources.[47] Guinevere, a changed person, now has an understanding of the role she, Lancelot, and their love have played in the general destruction: "Thorow thys same man and me hath all thys warre be wrought, and the deth of the moste nobelest knyghtes of the worlde; for thorow oure love that we have loved togydir ys my moste noble lorde slayne" (876). The queen is now wholly concerned with the salvation of her soul— she has become a "trew lover"—and forbids Lancelot to see her again. She tells him to get married and live "wyth joy and blys" but also to pray for her. In reply, Lancelot says he will never be false to Guinevere but will do as she has done and become a religious hermit: "the selff [same] desteny that ye have takyn you to, I woll take me to, for the pleasure of Jesu, and ever for you I caste me [intend] specially to pray" (876). Guinevere, however, doubts Lancelot's ability to persevere and says she cannot believe "but that ye woll turne to the worlde agayne." Answering her, Lancelot refers to the Grail Quest, saying: "For in the queste of the Sank-greall I had that tyme forsakyn the vanytees of the worlde, had nat youre love bene" (877).

From the beginning, Lancelot had tried to be perfect; but he also had been unable to extricate himself from the queen and the "erthly joye" associated with her. Here he does not renounce the world for the queen's sake; his resolute action is not quite what Whitehead calls "an act of self-identification with his lady." [48] Rather, as P. E. Tucker says, "her renunciation leaves him free at last to make his." [49] One might even say that, rather than be an incongruous end to their love, their decisions to become religious recluses demonstrate that human love, because it has been faithful and sincere in its own way, has prepared them for spiritual love.[50] Still, even now, as Lancelot says, if he had found Guinevere so disposed, he would have taken her with him into his realm; but, since she has renounced the world, Lancelot will follow and "wyl ever take me to penaunce and praye whyle my lyf lasteth." He asks for one final kiss from his love, but, in Malory's variation from the French, Guinevere refuses; and Lancelot rides off to the hermitage where Bedevere is. Throwing down his weapons, Lancelot laments, "Alas! Who may truste thys world?" (877).

At this hermitage Lancelot is joined by Bors and other knights who remain as recluses and in prayer for six years. Finally Lance-lot becomes a priest, and the other former knights remain with him to help him: "they redde in bookes and holpe [helped] for to synge masse, and range bellys, and dyd lowly al maner of servyce. And soo, their horses wente where they wolde, for they [the knights] toke no regarde of no worldly rychesses" (878).

Finally, in an episode that is probably Malory's own, Lancelot is told in a vision that Guinevere has died and that he should bury her beside King Arthur. At her burial Lancelot faints; when re-buked for his sorrow by the bishop-hermit, Lancelot replies that his sorrow is not for "ony rejoysyng of synne" but because it "may never have ende." He continues, explaining the nature of his sorrow: "For whan I remembre of his beaulté and of hir noblesse, that was bothe wyth hyr kyng and wyth hyr, so whan I sawe his [Arthur's] corps and hir corps so lye togyders, truly myn herte wold not serve to susteyne my careful [sorrowful] body" (880). This is the remembrance of things past, so powerfully expressed in the medieval lyric as the *Ubi sunt?* tradition—that which remembers and asks what has happened to the joys of the past.

Lancelot's remembrance is, however, of more than Guinevere's "beaulté" and "noblesse"; for, as he continues, he shows his realization of his past sins and laments what he has done to Guinevere and to Arthur. He realizes how—through his "defaute," his "orgule," and his "pryde"—the king and queen "were bothe layed ful lowe." In Lancelot's eyes, they were "pereles"; and, as he says, "their kyndenes and myn unkyndenes sanke so to myn herte that I myght not susteyne myself" (880). For F. Whitehead, Lancelot's actions here are marked by worldly concerns, laments, inordinate emotion, and broken slumbers "not in keeping with the monastic way of life he has adopted." In fact, according to Whitehead, the whole last tale, far from being "an improving religious work," is marked by "the general theme of thwarted affection and lament for former friends." That is, by ending on a note emphasizing "the power of human affection and the remembrance of the past," Malory "perverts" the theme of the *contemptu mundi* found in the French *Mort Artu*.[51] However, as the following episode shows, Malory is not making a necessary separation between human life and love on the one hand and the salvation of the soul on the other; for Lancelot achieves both.

Soon Lancelot himself dies, and his death is told to the bishop-hermit in a dream. As he relates to the knight-hermits, "I sawe the angellys heve [raise] up syr Launcelot unto heven, and the yates of heven opened ayenst hym [at his coming]" (881). This salvation is so glorious that the hermit, rather than feel sadness, actually laughs. It is a joyful scene, and the hermit's word, "heve," describing how the angels took Lancelot to heaven, suggests its atmosphere. Lancelot has finally achieved his Grail, and has become for the world something of the model his son Galahad was. The main difference between the two men is that Lancelot is of flesh and blood. As the knights are burying Lancelot's body, Sir Ector, his brother, rides up and in a eulogy over the grave gives the final and definitive praise of Lancelot:

A, Launcelot! . . . thou were hede of al Crysten knyghtes! And now I dare say, . . . thou sir Launcelot, there thou lyest, that thou were never matched of erthely knyghtes hande. And thou were the curtest knyght that ever bare shelde! And thou were the truest frende to thy lovar that ever bestrade hors, and thou were the trewest lover of a synful man that ever loved woman, and thou were the kyndest man that ever strake wyth swerde. And thou were the godelyest persone that ever cam emonge prees of knyghtes, and thou was the mekest man and the jentyllest that ever ete in halle emonge ladyes, and thou were the sternest knyght to thy mortal foo that ever put spere in the reeste.

(882)

In this eulogy, which, though perhaps modeled on others, is largely in Malory's own words, Lancelot is presented as noblest of "erthely knyghtes" and "hede of al Crysten knyghtes." All the threads are drawn together. Now the remaining knights, who are Lancelot's kin, live as "holy men"; and Bors, Ector, Blamour, and Bleoberis in particular are described as going into the Holy Land where, as "Crysten knyghtes," they fight and die "upon a Good Fryday for Goddes sake" (883).

The end here, especially Ector's eulogy, represents a definitive statement of Malory's chivalric ideal, the ideal which has been a theme throughout all his tales. As P. E. Tucker says, "The connexions between courtesy and bearing a shield, between fidelity and bestriding a horse, seem irrelevant and illogical unless we realize that for Malory chivalry was the outward and temporal expression of inner and timeless virtues." At the end of the *Morte Darthur* the virtuous life of the chivalric tradition is in harmony with that of Christianity.[52]

## III  *Conclusion*

It is difficult to know how to react to this final tale. Certainly the ending is not the sort one would ordinarily call happy, but it emphasizes more than unrelieved frustration and waste. In fact the *Death of Arthur* does not end with the final destruction and the event described in its title. Rather, there follows the final adventures and death of Lancelot—an episode that is, in effect, the apotheosis of the early knights and a real victory. Lancelot, the main character of Malory's whole work, is here granted what he has been striving for from the time of the *Tale of the Sankgreal* and what was in a sense prefigured in his success at healing Sir

Urry at the climax of the *Lancelot and Guinevere*. Lancelot now has his salvation and has become the truly perfect knight.

At the same time, however, Lancelot's salvation represents an undeniable individual achievement: it, like the successful Grail Quest, is still an exceptional thing. Lancelot and a few knights with him, along with Guinevere perhaps, have attained a victory but not one of the world. Society in general has not entered a monastery or gone to fight the infidel; instead, the men of the world are still busy symbolically looting the dead bodies on the battlefield. Courtliness, along with its concomitant virtues, is literally gone from the land. For a few, it was the way to holiness; but, for most, it was an empty end in itself. Now there is a total return to the way of the world, that of self-love—the opposite of charity and a negation of all that was possible with the coming of Arthur and his Order. As Wilfred Guerin says, Malory has presented "a contrast between what the God-like in man can aspire to, and what his baser self can do." [53]

The final coloring of the *Morte Darthur* is undeniably one of grayness. The reader is neither wholly delighted nor thoroughly disheartened with what has happened. He may feel a sense of regret at the passing of the great age with its great knights, but he probably also experiences a sense of great purposes that remain in spite of the destruction. Malory has been concerned throughout his work with human potential, and his vision of it is still in sight at the end; in fact, one might say that it is present especially at the end. In many ways the conclusion of the *Morte Darthur* is like that of *Paradise Lost* in which Milton describes Adam and Eve leaving Paradise and looking back at the "happy seat" they lost:

> Some natural tears they dropp'd, but wip'd them soon;
> The World was all before them, where to choose
> Thir place of rest, and Providence thir guide:
> They hand in hand with wand'ring steps and slow,
> Through *Eden* took thir solitary way.

Here too the end is mighty; it contains, like Malory's work, a mingling of joy and sorrow. The dominant element in both instances, however, is what might legitimately be termed a sense of hope—a knowledge that a fall has taken place, but also a feeling that it might be a fortunate one, that through it mankind might be able to regain "the blissful Seat" it has foolishly lost. Even if there has as yet been no regaining, one still leaves each work feeling the sense of potential.

# Notes and References

## Chapter One

1. W. H. Schofield, *Chivalry in English Literature: Chaucer, Malory, Spenser, Shakespeare* (Cambridge, Mass., 1912), p. 78.

2. Roger Ascham, *The Scholemaster*, Book I, in *English Works*, ed. W. A. Wright (Cambridge, 1904), p. 231.

3. Sir Herbert Read, "Sir Thomas Malory and the Sentiment of Glory," *Times Literary Supplement*, June 21, 1928, p. 457; reprinted in several collections of Read's work, including *The Nature of Literature* (New York, n.d.), pp. 171–72.

4. M. C. Bradbrook, *Sir Thomas Malory*, Writers and Their Work, No. 95 (London, New York, and Toronto, 1958), p. 7.

5. Eugène Vinaver, "On Art and Nature," in *Essays on Malory*, ed. J. A. W. Bennett (Oxford, 1963), p. 40.

6. All quotations from the *Morte Darthur*, including Caxton's Preface, are according to the one-volume edition, *The Works of Sir Thomas Malory*, ed., Eugène Vinaver (London, 1954), and will be identified in the body of the text. Although this Oxford Standard Authors volume lacks the textual and critical apparatus of Vinaver's magnificent three-volume Oxford English Text edition, which is being brought out in its second edition, it contains the same text as the larger work and is more easily accessible to the general reader.

7. George Lyman Kittredge, *Who Was Sir Thomas Malory?* (Boston, 1897), reprinted from Harvard *Studies and Notes in Philology and Literature*, V (1896), 85–106. See also Kittredge, *Sir Thomas Malory* (Barnstable, Mass., 1925).

8. Edward Hicks, *Sir Thomas Malory, His Turbulent Career* (Cambridge, Mass., 1928); Albert C. Baugh, "Documenting Sir Thomas Malory," *Speculum*, VIII (1933), 3–29. It should be noted that William Matthews in a forthcoming book questions Kittredge's identification of Malory.

9. If, however, Malory was the "Thomas Malery" who accompanied the Yorkist king Edward IV on an expedition to the North in 1462, he probably did not fight on the Lancastrian side. See E. K.

Chambers, *English Literature at the Close of the Middle Ages* (Oxford, 1945), pp. 203–4.

10. T. W. Williams has suggested that in the late 1460's Malory may have gone to Bruges and there may have come into contact with Caxton to whom he may then have given a copy of his romance (*Sir Thomas Malory and the 'Morte Darthur'* [Bristol, 1909]). See Chambers, p. 203. The idea is, if nothing else, certainly pleasant to think about.

11. Roger Sherman Loomis, *The Development of Arthurian Romance* (London, 1963), p. 169.

12. Hicks, p. 52.

13. Loomis, p. 169.

14. Chambers, p. 197. Of the several books on fifteenth-century England, see especially, C. L. Kingsford, *Prejudice and Promise in XVth Century England* (Oxford, 1925); E. F. Jacob, *The Fifteenth Century, 1399–1485* (Oxford, 1961); and Percival Hunt, *Fifteenth Century England* (Pittsburgh, 1962).

15. Chambers, p. 197. See also *The Paston Letters, A.D. 1422–1509*, ed. James Gairdner (London and Exeter, 1904), 6 vols.; and H. S. Bennett, *The Pastons and Their England, Studies in An Age of Transition* (Cambridge, 1922).

16. J. Huizinga, *The Waning of the Middle Ages* (London, 1937), esp. p. 89, but see also pp. 56 ff. and 82 ff. See also the chapter on chivalry in Vinaver, *Malory* (Oxford, 1929), pp. 56–59.

17. Loomis, p. 169.

18. Vinaver, *Essays*, p. 31.

19. R. W. Chambers, *On the Continuity of English Prose from Alfred to More and His School* (London, 1932), p. cxxxix.

20. *Ibid.*

21. Huizinga, pp. 57–58. See also the several statements on the place of chivalry in late fifteenth-century England in Arthur B. Ferguson, *The Indian Summer of English Chivalry, Studies in the Decline and Transformation of Chivalric Idealism* (Durham, N. C., 1960), e.g., pp. xiii–xiv, and 8–11.

22. Vinaver, *Malory*, p. 110.

23. Ferguson, p. 43.

24. Vinaver, *Malory*, p. 55.

25. St. Augustine, *De doctrina christiana*, I, iv.

26. Vinaver, *Malory*, p. 54.

27. Ferguson points out that in fifteenth-century England, chivalry had "to continue to do what it had been doing since the twelfth century, namely to supplement for the purposes of secular life the great

body of Christian ethical teaching" (p. 32). Romances tend to teach chivalry by example.

28. See *The Works of Sir Thomas Malory*, ed. E. Vinaver (Oxford, 1947), 3 vols. numbered consecutively, I, xxi.

29. One of Caxton's texts was also the source of *The Book of the Noble Kyng, Kyng Arthur*, printed by Wynkyn de Worde in 1498. In 1529, de Worde printed another edition which was used by two later editors: William Copland in 1557; Thomas East, *ca.* 1585. A "newly refined" version of East's text, using Caxton and de Worde, appeared at William Stansby's press in 1634. This last black-letter edition of Malory was the source for many later printings. Other important editions of Malory were Robert Southey's in 1817, based partly on Caxton and partly on de Worde; Edward Strachey's in 1868, based wholly on Caxton; and H. Oskar Sommer's in 1889–91, a reprint of the Ryland's copy of Caxton (See Vinaver, *Malory*, pp. 189–96; and *Works*, I, lxxxvi–lxxxvii).

30. The most recent statement by Oakeshott of his discovery is "The Finding of the Manuscript," in *Essays on Malory*, pp. 1–6.

31. Vinaver, "Sir Thomas Malory," in *Arthurian Literature in the Middle Ages*, ed. R. S. Loomis (Oxford, 1959), p. 545; (hereafter referred to as *ALMA*).

32. D. S. Brewer, "Form in the 'Morte Darthur,'" *Medium Aevum*, XXI (1952), 14–24; and "'the hoole book,'" in *Essays on Malory*, pp. 41–63; R. M. Lumiansky, esp. "The Question of Unity in Malory's Morte Darthur," *Tulane Studies in English*, V (1955), 29–39; Charles Moorman, esp. "Internal Chronology in Malory's *Morte Darthur.*" *Journal of English and Germanic Philology*, LX (1961), 240–49; and Robert H. Wilson, esp. "How Many Books Did Malory Write?" University of Texas *Studies in English*, XXX (1951), 1–23. See also the essays in *Malory's Originality, A Critical Study of Le Morte Darthur*, ed. R. M. Lumiansky (Baltimore, 1964); and Charles Moorman, *The Book of Kyng Arthur: The Unity of Malory's Morte Darthur* (Lexington, Ky., 1965).

33. Brewer, *Essays*, p. 41.

34. *Ibid.*, pp. 44–45, 61; see also R. H. Wilson, Texas *Studies in English*, XXX (1951), 4–12.

35. Vinaver, *Works*, III, 1646; see also T. C. Rumble, "The First *Explicit* in Malory's *Morte Darthur,*" *Modern Language Notes*, LXXI (1956), 564–66. Since the discovery of the Winchester manuscript, Caxton has often been berated for interfering with Malory's text and deceiving readers about its true nature. In editing Malory, however, Caxton was doing only what, in a sense, Malory himself did when

he rewrote the romances of his predecessors. Although the work Caxton presented to the world was no longer the eight separate romances Vinaver has found in the Winchester manuscript, Caxton, through his subdivisions, may not have been projecting on Malory's work a semblance of continuity and order but may merely have been emphasizing a unity that he saw already present in spite of the possible existence in his source manuscript of several major divisions. His own twenty-one divisions, in most cases containing a single theme, might be viewed as a presentation of Malory's composition in which are emphasized the themes that give the work unity and that are at the heart of the book. Recently scholars have been reassessing Caxton's achievement. See especially Sally Shaw's perceptive essay, "Caxton and Malory," in *Essays on Malory,* pp. 114–45, along with the general remarks by C. S. Lewis in the same collection, "The English Prose *Morte,*" p. 26. Vinaver has termed Caxton's Preface to his edition "the finest and in many ways the soundest essay ever written on the *Morte Darthur*" (Works, I, cix).

36. Lewis, *Essays,* p. 22.

37. R. M. Lumiansky, however, has made a case for historical or intentional unity (*Tulane Studies in English,* IV [1955], 32 ff.).

38. Brewer, *Medium Aevum,* XXI (1952), 17. In Vinaver's view, on the other hand, Malory "did not try" to write "a single Arthurian epic"; rather, he endeavored to present "a series of short and well-defined tales" (*Works,* I, lvii).

39. E. Talbot Donaldson, "Malory and the Stanzaic *Le Morte Arthur,*" *Studies in Philology,* XLVII (1950), 464; see also R. H. Wilson, "Malory's 'French Book' Again," *Comparative Literature,* II (1950), 172–81.

40. Vinaver, *Works,* I, xxiii, xlix.

41. *Ibid.,* I, l. C. S. Lewis describes this technique as polyphonic and points out that it is not peculiar to medieval prose romances (*Essays,* p. 13).

42. On the principle of *entrelacement,* see Jean Frappier, *Étude sur La Mort le Roi Artu* (Paris, 1936, 1961), pp. 347–51; Ferdinand Lot, *Étude sur le Lancelot en prose* (Paris, 1918), pp. 17–20; and C. E. Pickford, *L'Évolution du roman arthurien en prose vers la fin du moyen age* (Paris, 1960), pp. 186–201.

43. See Vinaver, *Works,* I, lii.

44. Of the approximately 425 characters in the *Morte Darthur,* 182 do not appear elsewhere. See Robert H. Wilson, "Malory's Naming of Minor Characters," *Journal of English and Germanic Philology,* XLII (1943), 377.

45. Vinaver, *Works,* I, lvii.

46. *Ibid., Malory,* p. 31.

47. Lewis, [Review of E. K. Chambers, *Sir Thomas Malory*], *Medium Aevum,* III (1934), 238.

48. *Ibid.*

49. Vinaver, *ALMA,* p. 545.

50. On the many studies of the Arthurian legend and literature before Malory, see especially Loomis, *ALMA;* and J. D. Bruce, *The Evolution of Arthurian Romance from the Beginnings Down to the Year 1300,* 2nd ed. with supplement by A. Hilka (Göttingen and Baltimore, 1928; Gloucester, Mass., 1958), 2 vols. The best current introduction to Arthurian literature is probably R. S. Loomis, *The Development of Arthurian Romance.*

51. Vinaver, *Works,* I, cvii.

52. *Ibid., Malory,* p. 104.

53. *Ibid.*

54. *Ibid.,* p. 100.

55. P. E. Tucker, "Chivalry in the *Morte,*" in *Essays on Malory,* p. 64.

56. Brewer, *Essays,* p. 44.

57. *Times Literary Supplement,* June 7, 1947, p. 274

## Chapter Two

1. The Huth version (British Museum Add. 38,117) was published as *Merlin, roman en prose du XIIIᵉ siècle,* ed. G. Paris and J. Ulrich, Société des Anciens Textes Français (Paris, 1886), 2 vols. The Cambridge manuscript (British Museum Add. 7071, fols. 159–342), discovered in 1945, is at present being edited by Fanni Bogdanow. For a brief summary of the relationship between this manuscript and Malory, see Eugène Vinaver, *The Works of Sir Thomas Malory,* III, 1277–80. A small fragment of the *Suite* has recently been found in the State Archives of Siena. See the discussion of the *Suite* by Fanni Bogdanow in *Arthurian Literature of the Middle Ages,* ed. R. S. Loomis, pp. 324–35, and that of the *Suite* in relation to Malory by Thomas L. Wright, " 'The Tale of King Arthur': Beginnings and Foreshadowings," in *Malory's Originality,* pp. 9–66.

2. Wright, p. 48; see also Wright's unpublished dissertation, "Originality and Purpose in Malory's 'Tale of King Arthur' " (Tulane University, 1960).

3. R. M. Lumiansky, "The Question of Unity in Malory's Morte Darthur," *Tulane Studies in English,* V (1955), 36–38; and Charles Moorman, "Internal Chronology in Malory's *Morte Darthur,*" *Journal of English and Germanic Philology,* LX (1961), 242–248, esp. 248. See also Robert H. Wilson, "How Many Books Did Malory

Write?" University of Texas *Studies in English*, XXX (1951), 10–11.

4. As in the Robin Hood stories. See, for example, Lord Raglan, *The Hero* (London, 1936), pp. 50–53.

5. Vinaver, *Malory*, p. 52. See also E. Vetterman, *Die Balen-Dichtungen und ihre Quellen* (in *Beihefte zur Zeitschrift für romanische Philologie*, LX [Halle a. S., 1918]), esp. 82–83.

6. Laura A. Hibbard, "Malory's Book of Balin," in *Mediaeval Studies in Memory of Gertude Schoepperle Loomis* (New York, 1927), p. 179.

7. Vida D. Scudder, *Le Morte Darthur of Sir Thomas Malory and Its Sources* (London and New York, 1917), p. 196.

8. Vinaver, *Malory*, p. 53.

9. C. S. Lewis, "The English Prose *Morte*," in *Essays on Malory*, p. 12.

10. See Vinaver's comments in *Works*, III, 1304, 1274.

11. Scudder, p. 201.

12. Wright, *Originality*, p. 41.

13. *Ibid.*, p. 45.

14. R. M. Lumiansky, "Arthur's Final Companions in Malory's *Morte Darthur*," *Tulane Studies in English*, XI (1961), 15. See also Henry Grady Morgan, who writes that Morgan becomes in Malory "a symbol of the weakness in loyalty which is the ultimate downfall of the society" brought in by Arthur ("The Role of Morgan le Fay in Malory's *Mort Darthur*," *Southern Quarterly*, II (1964), 166.

15. Vinaver, *Works*, III, 1277.

16. *Ibid.*, III, 1346.

17. See *Die Abenteuer Gawains Ywains und le Morholts mit den drei Jungfrauen* (Bibliothèque Nationale fr. 112), ed. H. O. Sommer (*in Beihefte zur Zeitschrift für romanische Philologie*, XLVII [Halle a. S., 1913]), which carries the narrative beyond where it breaks off in the Huth and Cambridge manuscripts.

18. Vinaver, *Works*, III, 1349.

19. *Ibid.*, III, 1356.

20. F. Whitehead, "On Certain Episodes in the Fourth Book of Malory's *Morte Darthur*," *Medium Aevum*, II (1933), 206.

21. Vinaver, *Works*, III, 1356.

22. This is the view of Whitehead, *Medium Aevum*, II (1933), 202; and Vinaver, *Works*, III, 1356.

23. Vinaver, *ibid*.

### Chapter Three

1. At present the best edition of the alliterative *Morte* is probably that edited by E. Brock, Early English Text Society, OS 8 (London,

1865, 1937). Based on the unique text in the Thornton manuscript in Lincoln Cathedral Library, this version is almost certainly different from the one used by Malory. Mary E. Dichmann feels that Malory may also have used Wace's *Roman de Brut* ("Characterization in Malory's *Tale of Arthur and Lucius*," *PMLA*, LXV [1950], 881; revised as " 'The Tale of King Arthur and the Emperor Lucius': The Rise of Lancelot," in *Malory's Originality*, pp. 70–71).

2. William Matthews, *The Tragedy of Arthur* (Berkeley, 1960), p. 172. See also Eugène Vinaver. *The Works of Sir Thomas Malory*, III, 1363. For general analyses of the tale, see also Tania Vorontzoff, "Malory's Story of Arthur's Roman Campaign," *Medium Aevum*, VI (1937), 99–121; and Helen I. Wroten, "Malory's *Tale of King Arthur and the Emperor Lucius* Compared with Its Source, The Alliterative *Morte Arthure*" (unpub. diss., University of Illinois, 1950).

3. Matthews, pp. 175–76. See also Dichmann, pp. 888–91 (*Originality*, pp. 80–85).

4. Vinaver, *Works*, I, xxiv. See also Dichmann, esp. pp. 888–89 (*Originality*, esp. pp. 80–81). In Caxton's redaction of the tale Arthur is even more a Christian monarch, "unvexed by moral problems or the vices attendant upon an ambition to be ruler of the whole world" (Matthews, p. 177). In fact, as Sally Shaw has noted, "Caxton's selective text enhances rather than detracts from Arthur's glory" ("Caxton and Malory," in *Essays on Malory*, p. 135).

5. Emphasizing the idealized portrait of Arthur here, Vinaver suggests that Malory may have been writing an allegorical tribute to Henry V, the English king who was victor at the Battle of Agincourt in 1415. He argues that Malory has added to his source "several details which make Arthur's expedition against the Romans resemble Henry V's triumphant campaign in France" (*Works*, I, xxv). Also, Vinaver says that by ending his tale on a note of triumph, Malory "is anxious that the story of Arthur's triumph should remain uppermost in the reader's mind as a record of the greatest English victory of his age and that the reader should know how this victory was won" (*ibid.*, I, xxv–xxvi). For persuasive criticism against this idea, see, for example, Dichmann, pp. 887–88 (not in *Originality*).

6. Dichmann, p. 883 (*Originality*, p. 75). She also notes that Bors too is developed here; the knight does not even appear in the *Morte Arthure* (p. 894); (*Originality*, pp. 88–89).

7. Speaking of this short triumphant conclusion, Matthews suggests that it may be related to the *Metrical Chronicle* of John Hardyng, in which a similar crowning of Arthur is planned (pp. 172, 208 n.).

8. Vinaver, *Works*, I, xxxix.

9. See Robert H. Wilson, "Malory's Early Knowledge of Arthurian Romance," University of Texas *Studies in English,* XXIX (1950), 41 ff.; and Matthews, p. 173. This position was also once held by Vinaver (E. V. Gordon and E. Vinaver, "New Light on the Text of the Alliterative *Morte Arthure,*" *Medium Aevum,* VI [1937], 84–85). For a detailed analysis of the idea that the *Tale of Arthur* was designed as part of a longer narrative, see Mary Dichmann, pp. 878 ff. (*Originality,* esp. pp. 72–74).

10. D. S. Brewer, "'the hoole book,'" in *Essays on Malory,* p. 46.

11. Vinaver, however, feels that in placing his *Lancelot* here after the story of the Roman campaign, Malory does not understand the position of this story as it exists in the Vulgate Cycle (*Works,* III, 1398). Vinaver has also stated that in this tale Malory "had as yet developed no ambition except that of telling a good story" (*ibid.,* III, 1402).

12. The Prose *Lancelot* occupies volumes III–V of *The Vulgate Version of Arthurian Romances,* ed. H. Oskar Sommer (Washington, D. C., 1908–16). See also Ferdinand Lot, *Étude sur le Lancelot en Prose,* and Jean Frappier, "The Vulgate Cycle," in *Arthurian Literature in the Middle Ages,* ed. R. S. Loomis, pp. 295–318.

13. Vida Scudder, *Le Morte Darthur of Sir Thomas Malory and Its Sources,* p. 213.

14. See Robert H. Wilson, Texas *Studies in English,* XXIX (1950), 40; and R. M. Lumiansky, "The Relationship of Lancelot and Guenevere in Malory's 'Tale of Lancelot,'" *Modern Language Notes,* LXVIII (1953), 87 ff. (revised as "'The Tale of Lancelot': Prelude to Adultery," in *Malory's Originality,* pp. 93 ff.).

15. See Lumiansky, *ibid.,* p. 88 (*Originality,* p. 94).

16. August J. App, *Lancelot in English Literature, His Role and Character* (Washington, D. C., 1929), p. 58.

17. *Ibid.*

18. Vinaver, *Works,* I, lvi.

19. According to Vinaver, however, the problem here of whether an "adventurous man" should remain wifeless is not suitable to courtly literature and is "entirely foreign to the literary tradition which had produced the story of Lancelot" (*Works,* III, 1403–4).

20. See Robert H. Wilson, "Malory and the *Perlesvaus,*" *Modern Philology,* XXX (1932–33), 13–22; and the parallels in the Cambridge manuscript discussed by Vinaver, *Works,* III, 1414 ff.

21. See Wilson, Texas *Studies in English,* XXIX (1950), 40.

22. Charles Moorman, "The Relation of Books I and III of Malory's *Morte Darthur,*" *Mediaeval Studies,* XXII (1960), 363 ff.

23. Lumiansky, *Modern Language Notes*, LXVIII (1953), 90 (*Originality*, p. 96).

24. Several scholars have suggested meanings for the soubriquet *Beaumains*. One goes back to G. L. Kittredge, who writes that Malory may have added the name to the story of Gareth as a tribute to his old patron Richard Beauchamp, who was for the fifteenth century a contemporary personification of chivalry (*Who Was Sir Thomas Malory?* pp. 5–10; see also Vinaver, *Malory*, p. 3). A second meaning, suggested by R. S. Loomis, equates *Beaumains* with Gawain, making Gareth's nickname a derivative of the French form, *Gauvains*. Loomis points out several parallels between the adventures of Malory's knight and those of Gawain in the romances in which he appears ("Malory's Beaumains," *PMLA*, LIV [1939], 656–68). Vinaver discusses both these ideas and then presents his own view that Gareth should be equated with Gaheret, Gawain's youngest brother in the Prose *Lancelot* and a figure noted for his beauty and modesty. According to Vinaver, Gareth was named *Beaumains* because, as with Gaheret, one arm was longer than the other (*Works*, III, 1419–22; see also Vinaver's earlier statement of this idea in "A Romance of Gaheret," *Medium Aevum*, I [1932], 157–67; for criticism of this idea, see R. H. Wilson, "How Many Books Did Malory Write?" University of Texas *Studies in English*, XXX [1951], 15–16; and D. C. Muecke, "Some Notes on Vinaver's Malory," *Modern Language Notes*, LXX [1955], 326).

25. Maurice Valency, *In Praise of Love, An Introduction to the Love-Poetry of the Renaissance* (New York, 1958), p. 39.

26. For Vinaver, however, Malory was in accord with the idea that "a man of low birth cannot defeat a nobleman except by accident or by guile" and thus "championed the claims of knighthood as an aristocratic institution" (*Works*, III, 1424). Wilfred L. Guerin feels that the *Tale of Gareth* shows the "clearest manifestation" of the courtly principles stated earlier at the end of the "Torre and Pellinore" section of the *Tale of Arthur* (" 'The Tale of Gareth': The Chivalric Flowering," in *Malory's Originality*, p. 108).

27. Valency, p. 48.

28. Vinaver, *Malory*, p. 138. Because the story was probably "not very intimately related to the Arthurian cycle," it may have formed a branch of the huge thirteenth-century French composition called the Prose *Tristan* (*ibid., Works*, I, lvi; III, 1422–24).

29. *Ibid., Works*, III, 1417. A recent study of the *Tale of Gareth* in relation to other medieval romances is found in C. C. D. Schmidz, *Sir Gareth of Orkeney, Studien zum siebenten Buch von Malory's*

*Morte Darthur* (Groningen, 1963). In particular, Schmidz, after reviewing the scholarship on the *Tale of Gareth*, relates the tale to stories centering on the motif of the Fair Unknown—specifically, *Bel Inconnu, Carduino, Libeaus Desconus,* and *Wigalois*—and to the *Erec* and *Yvain* of Chrétien de Troyes. See also Morton Donner, "The Backgrounds of Malory's *Book of Gareth*" (unpub. diss. Columbia University, 1956), and Wilfred L. Guerin's discussion of similarities to the story of Gaheret in the version of the *Suite du Merlin* represented by MS. B.N. 112 (pp. 103–6; see also Vinaver, *Medium Aevum,* I [1932], 157–67). Guerin, however, also suggests that the tale is "Malory's own creation."

30. Vinaver, *Works,* III, 1424.

31. See *ibid.,* III, 1417. Cf. Robert H. Wilson, "The 'Fair Unknown' in Malory," *PMLA,* LVIII (1943), 2 ff.; and Schmidz, pp. 22 ff.

32. Scudder, p. 219.

33. See, for example, Joseph Campbell, *The Hero with a Thousand Faces* (New York, 1949), pp. 101 ff.

34. Five allusions to this act of knighting occur later in the *Morte Darthur* (in the *Lancelot and Guinevere* story) and may indicate, as Guerin suggests, that "Malory intended the episode to be instrumental in the unification of the entire book" (p. 115).

35. This episode with the Green Knight offers, according to Vinaver, "a prima facie parallel to the central episode of *Sir Gawain and the Green Knight*" (*Works,* III, 1425).

36. In pointing out how Gareth's adventures are a curious mixture of literary reminiscences, among which the twelfth-century romances of Chrétien de Troyes figure prominently, Vinaver discusses, in particular, relationships between the Red Knight here and the figure of Mabonagrains in the *Joie de la Cort* episode of Chrétien's *Erec* (*Works,* III, 1418). See also the study of parallel motifs in Schmidz, pp. 67–90. Schmidz gives an interesting discussion of the Red Knight, Sir Ironsyde, emphasizing the stress on red and iron indicative of the evil in him (pp. 106–8). On this knight see also the full discussion by Robert W. Ackerman, "Malory's Ironsyde," *Research Studies* (Washington State University) XXXII (1964), 125–33.

37. For Charles Moorman the love of this tale is "natural, untutored affection, very different from the artificial, conventionalized *l'amour courtois*"; it is one that "works towards the propositions that the true end of love is marriage not adultery" ("Courtly Love in Malory," *ELH* XXVII [1960], 169, 171). See also Guerin, pp. 110–11.

38. Scudder, p. 222.

39. In Guerin's view, however, Gareth "is used to demonstrate the

depth and breadth" of Gawain, especially to show "certain redeeming qualities" in that knight (p. 112).

40. For Guerin, this *Tale of Gareth* "contributes importantly" to the unity of the *Morte Darthur* "through its happy picture of the Round Table at the height of its success, and through its preparation of Gareth for the role he will later play in the collapse of the Round Table" (p. 100); (see also p. 117 and Guerin's unpublished thesis, "The Functional Role of Gareth in Malory's *Morte Darthur*" [Tulane University, 1953]).

41. The Prose *Tristan,* extant in at least 48 manuscripts, is in the process of being printed in full for the first time since 1586. The first part has appeared as *Le Roman de Tristan en prose,* ed. R. L. Curtis (Munich, 1963), vol. 1. On the work in general see, for example, Vinaver, "The Prose *Tristan,*" in *ALMA,* pp. 339–47; *Études sur le Tristan en Prose* (Paris, 1925), and Eilart Löseth, *Le Roman en Prose de Tristan, Le Roman de Palamède, et la Compilation de Rusticien de Pise, Analyse critique d'après les manuscrits de Paris* (Paris, 1891). On the relationship of this work to Malory, see Vinaver, *Le Roman de Tristan dans l'oeuvre de Thomas Malory* (Paris, 1925); and Thomas C. Rumble, "'The Tale of Tristram'; Development by Analogy," in *Malory's Originality,* pp. 118–83; as well as Rumble's unpublished dissertation, "The Tristan Legend and Its Place in the *Morte Darthur*" (Tulane University, 1955).

42. Vinaver, *Works,* I, lxxiv.

43. *Ibid.,* III, 1432. For P. E. Tucker, the fact that "the love story is not placed firmly at the centre of interest" is "one defect" of both Malory's work and the Prose *Tristan* ("Chivalry in the *Morte,*" in *Essays on Malory,* p. 73).

44. Also, as Rumble stresses, it was only in the Prose *Tristan* that Malory could have found "just the parallels and contrasts that he could cause to bear so implicitly, yet so clearly, on the principal matter of *Le Morte Darthur*: the birth and rise to power of King Arthur, the Lancelot-Guinevere-Arthur triangle, the tragic fall of the Round Table, and the dolorous death and departing of them all" (*Originality,* pp. 121–22).

45. Vinaver, *Works,* I, lxxiii. See also Rumble, who points out that, although the character of Isode is "not especially important" to the tale, Malory has "deliberately altered" what in his source showed her to be unattractive (*Originality,* p. 142).

46. Vinaver, *Works,* III, 1435. Rumble emphasizes that, although the Prose *Tristan* blackens the character of Mark, Malory has added to the blackening (*Originality,* pp. 140, 153).

47. Vinaver, *Malory,* pp. 66–67.

48. For a concise statement of the differences between Malory's treatment of this madness and that in the French, see, for example, *ibid., Works,* III, 1460–61.

49. Scudder, p. 241.

50. See, for example, P. E. Tucker, *Essays,* pp. 73 ff., esp. p. 79.

51. Vinaver, *Works,* III, 1436. For Tucker, the effect of Malory's making "the interest in chivalry alone so predominant" is that "the love story—itself inadequately told—loses its essential dependence on its setting" and becomes meaningless (*Essays,* p. 75).

52. Vinaver, *Works,* III, 1485. The French tale has been edited by C. E. Pickford as *Alixandre l'Orphelin* (Manchester, 1951).

53. According to Tucker, however, the reconciliation comes about because, for Malory, "it was the rivalry of two noble knights that mattered, not the cause of it" (*Essays,* p. 74). Such a reading is right as far as it goes, but it fails to concern itself with why Malory is interested in these "noble knights" and with how is he using them and their rivalry.

54. Scudder, p. 244.

55. Brewer, *Essays,* p. 46.

56. Also, as Rumble states, Malory's *Tristram* "seems designed to complement Malory's Arthurian story and to throw into a sharper relief than would otherwise have been possible not only the tragic fall of an almost perfect world but the reasons for that fall" (*Originality,* p. 147).

## Chapter Four

1. *La Queste del Saint Graal,* ed. Albert Pauphilet, Classiques français du moyen age (Paris, 1949). See also Pauphilet, *Études sur La Queste del Saint Graal* (Paris, 1921); Frederick W. Locke, *The Quest for the Holy Grail, A Literary Study of a Thirteenth Century French Romance* (Stanford, 1960); and Jean Frappier, "The Vulgate Cycle," in *Arthurian Literature in the Middle Ages,* ed. R. S. Loomis, esp. pp. 302–7.

2. See Pauphilet, *Études,* esp. pp. 53–83; and Etienne Gilson, "La mystique de la grâce dans *La Queste del Saint Graal,*" *Romania,* LI (1925), 321–47. Eugène Anitchkof has written a series of articles on the relationship between the *Queste* and the teachings of Joachim of Flora, the Cistercian abbot from Calabria. See, for example, "Le Galaad du Lancelot-Graal et les Galaads de la Bible," *Romania,* LIII (1927), 388 ff.; as well as his book, *Joachim de Flore et les milieux courtois* (Paris, 1931). See also Jean Frappier's general analysis of the relationship between chivalry and theology in Grail romances,

## Notes and References

"Le Graal et la chevalerie," *Romania*, LXXV (1954), 165–210. The preponderance of theological material in the *Queste* has led Eugène Vinaver to remark that it is more a treatise on grace than a work of narrative art and that its author was a man "whose mind never grasped the picturesque possibilities of the story, and whose language never extended to imaginative expression" (*The Works of Sir Thomas Malory*, III, 1526).

3. Vinaver, *Works*, I, lxxv.

4. *Ibid.*, "On Art and Nature," in *Essays on Malory*, p. 33.

5. *Ibid.*, *Works*, I, lxxv–lxxvi.

6. *Ibid.*, *Malory*, p. 84.

7. *Ibid.*, *Works*, III, 1528. Also Vinaver says that the *Tale of the Sankgreal* is the "least original" of Malory's tales (*ibid.*, III, 1521).

8. C. S. Lewis, "The English Prose *Morte*," in *Essays on Malory*, pp. 7, 17.

9. Vinaver, *Essays*, p. 32.

10. Romans, XIII, 12–14. All quotations from the New Testament are according to *The New English Bible, New Testament* (Oxford and Cambridge, 1961).

11. Lewis, *Essays*, p. 17.

12. P. E. Tucker, "The Place of the 'Quest of the Holy Grail' in the 'Morte Darthur,'" *Modern Language Review*, XLVIII (1953), 391, 394.

13. Vinaver, *Works*, III, 1522. An opposing view has been given by Charles Moorman, who says that Malory consciously attempted to link the Grail Quest, existing "as an isolated adventure" in the French Vulgate Cycle, "with his unified Arthurian history" ("Malory's Treatment of the Sankgreall," *PMLA*, LXXI [1956], 497; revised as "'The Tale of the Sankgreall': Human Frailty," in *Malory's Originality*, pp. 184–204; this particular passage is omitted).

14. St. Augustine, *Confessionum*, I, i, 1; *Enarrationes in Psalmos*, LXX, ii, 3.

15. *Ibid.*, *De doctrina christiana*, I, xxii, 21.

16. *Ibid.*, *De agone christiano*, XIII, 14.

17. Titus, III, 10–11.

18. Moorman, *PMLA*, LXXI (1956), 507; in *Originality*, this is changed to "an almost totally unsympathetic character" p. 200).

19. Vinaver, *Malory*, p. 73.

20. Vida Scudder, *Le Morte Darthur of Sir Thomas Malory and Its Sources*, p. 264.

21. Robert H. Wilson, "How Many Books Did Malory Write?" University of Texas *Studies in English*, XXX (1951), 13.

22. Moorman, *PMLA*, LXXI (1956), 503 (*Originality*, p. 195).

23. St. Augustine, *De libero arbitrio*, I, xvi, 35; II, xix, 53.

24. See, for example, *ibid.*, *Sermones*, CCXVI, viii, 8.

25. *Ibid.*, *Enarrationes in Psalmos*, CXXX, 13.

26. Lewis, *Essays*, pp. 18–19.

27. Moorman, *PMLA*, LXXI (1956), 504 (*Originality*, p. 196).

28. P. E. Tucker, "Chivalry in the *Morte*," in *Essays on Malory*, pp. 88–89, 91–92.

29. Moorman, *PMLA*, LXXI (1956), 505 (*Originality*, p. 197). On Perceval as Grail hero, see, for example, Chrétien de Troyes' *Perceval*, with its several continuations, and Wolfram von Eschenbach's *Parzival*.

30. St. Augustine, *In Joannis Evangelium tractatus*, XVII, 8; see also 1 John, IV, 20.

31. See Vinaver, *Works*, III, 1541. The homophonic similarity also exists in French, *meure* (mod. French *mûre*), berry and *mort*, death, and in other Romance languages, going back to Latin *morus*, berry, and *mors*, death.

32. 1 Peter, V, 8; and Revelations, V, 5–6.

33. St. Augustine, *De doctrina christiana*, III, ix, 13.

34. Scudder, p. 288.

35. R. M. Lumiansky, "Malory's Steadfast Bors," *Tulane Studies in English*, VIII (1958), 5–8.

36. Moorman, *PMLA*, LXXI (1956), 501 (*Originality*, p. 192). Still, one might hesitate to say with Scudder that "Bors is lovable from start to finish" (p. 287).

37. Vinaver, *Malory*, p. 77.

38. Ephesians, VI, 11–17.

39. Moorman, *PMLA*, LXXI (1956), 504–5 (*Originality*, pp. 196–97).

40. See Frederick W. Locke, *The Quest for the Holy Grail*, p. 17; and Albert Pauphilet, ed., *La Queste del Saint Graal*, p. xi.

41. Charles Williams, "Malory and the Grail Legend," *Dublin Review*, CCXIV, 429 (April, 1944), 146.

42. Vinaver feels, however, that it is wrong to think of Lancelot as surviving in Galahad, for "their 'virtues' are fundamentally different" (*Malory*, p. 77 n.).

43. Williams, p. 152.

44. See Locke, pp. 76–78; and Myrrha Lot-Borodine, *Trois essais sur Le Lancelot du Lac et La Quête du Saint Graal* (Paris, 1919), p. 54.

45. St. Augustine, *De Trinitate*, I, vi, 11.

## Chapter Five

1. Eugène Vinaver, *Malory,* p. 79; see also E. K. Chambers, *Sir Thomas Malory,* English Association Pamphlet, No. 51 (Oxford, 1922), p. 9.

2. Vida Scudder, *Le Morte Darthur of Sir Thomas Malory and Its Sources,* p. 314.

3. P. E. Tucker, "Chivalry in the *Morte,*" in *Essays on Malory,* p. 93.

4. As Tucker writes, Malory's idea that "Lancelot's love for Guinevere mars the perfection of his knighthood" is a notion never proposed by the French ("The Place of the 'Quest of the Holy Grail' in the 'Morte Darthur,'" *Modern Language Review,* XLVIII [1953], 392–93).

5. Tucker, *Essays,* p. 94.

6. St. Augustine, *Enarrationes in Psalmos,* CXXI, 1.

7. 2 Peter, II, 19–21.

8. St. Augustine, *De doctrina christiana,* I, lv, 4.

9. Colossians, III, 14.

10. *The Vulgate Version of the Arthurian Romances,* ed. H. O. Sommer, VI, 263–391; and *La Mort le Roi Artu, roman du XIII^e siècle,* ed. Jean Frappier (Paris, 1936; Geneva and Lille, 1954). On the work, see M. B. Fox, *La Mort le roi Artu, étude sur les manuscrits, les sources et la composition de l'oeuvre* (Paris, 1933); J. Frappier, *Étude sur La Mort le Roi Artu;* and "The Vulgate Cycle," in *Arthurian Literature in the Middle Ages,* ed. R. S. Loomis, pp. 307–13.

11. See *Le Morte Arthur,* ed. J. D. Bruce, Early English Text Society, ES 88 (London, 1903). See also Bruce, "The Middle English Metrical Romance 'Le Morte Arthur' (Harleian MS. 2252): Its Sources and Its Relation to Sir Thomas Malory's 'Morte Darthur,'" *Anglia,* XXIII (1901), 67–100.

12. Vinaver, *The Works of Sir Thomas Malory,* III, 1572–78.

13. R. M. Lumiansky, "Malory's 'Tale of Lancelot and Guinevere' as Suspense," *Mediaeval Studies,* XIX (1957), esp. 114 (revised as "'The Tale of Lancelot and Guenevere': Suspense," in *Malory's Originality,* esp. p. 217). See also R. H. Wilson, "Malory, the Stanzaie Morte Arthur, and the *Mort Artu,*" *Modern Philology,* XXXVII (1939–1940), 125–38; and E. Talbot Donaldson, "Malory and the Stanzaic *Le Morte Arthur,*" *Studies in Philology,* XLVII (1950), 460–72.

14. Lumiansky, *Mediaeval Studies,* XIX (1957), 115 (*Originality,* p. 218).

15. For Lumiansky, the chief function of the episode is "to continue the suspense which has resulted from the two preceding sub-

divisions." Acting as such, it contains "an ostensibly happy view of the Round Table engaged in its favorite pastime and training procedure, a large tournament" (*ibid.*, p. 117; *Originality*, p. 222). For P. E. Tucker, "The Great Tournament" is an "apparently irrelevant and trivial episode"; but at the same time he points out that in it is seen "the fellowship that Lancelot betrays and destroys" (*Essays*, p. 96).

16. Tucker, *Modern Language Review*, XLVIII (1953), 393.

17. See Sommer's edition of the *Vulgate Version*, IV, 154–226; and *Le Roman en prose de Lancelot du Lac: Le Conte de la Charrette*, ed., G. Hutchings (Paris, 1938); also R. H. Wilson, "The Prose *Lancelot* in Malory," University of Texas *Studies in English*, XXXII (1953), 1–13.

18. Lumiansky, *Mediaeval Studies*, XIX (1957), 118 (*Originality*, p. 224).

19. See Lumiansky's summary of the development of this love throughout the *Morte Darthur* (*ibid.*, esp. pp. 109–10; *Originality*, pp. 206–12).

20. Vinaver, *Works*, I, xxii.

21. R. T. Davies, "Malory's 'Vertuouse Love,'" *Studies in Philology*, LIII (1956), 461.

22. Charles Moorman, "Courtly Love in Malory," *ELH*, XXVII (1960), 167. See also Davies, p. 462; and Gervase Mathew, "Marriage and *Amour Courtois* in Late Fourteenth-Century England," in *Essays Presented to Charles Williams* (Oxford, 1947), esp. p. 131.

23. Lumiansky, *Mediaeval Studies*, XIX (1957), 119 (*Originality*, p. 226).

24. Vinaver, *Works*, III, 1578. The statement also applies to most of "The Great Tournament," which, along with "The Healing," is "very probably Malory's own invention." P. E. Tucker however, suggests as source a passage in the Prose *Lancelot* ("A Source for 'The Healing of Sir Urry' in the 'Morte Darthur,'" *Modern Language Review*, L [1955], 490–92).

25. Lumiansky, *Mediaeval Studies*, XIX (1957), 121–22.

26. This idea was suggested to me by Professor James Carney of the Dublin Institute of Advanced Studies.

27. C. S. Lewis, "The English Prose *Morte*," in *Essays on Malory*, p. 20.

28. See P. E. Tucker, who also speaks of the tears as showing Lancelot's "capacity for humility" (*Essays*, p. 99).

29. Vinaver, *Works*, I, lxxx, lxxxii. See also Wilfred L. Guerin, "'The Tale of the Death of Arthur': Catastrophe and Resolution," in *Malory's Originality*, p. 236 ff.; and Guerin's unpublished dissertation,

"The Function of 'The Death of Arthur' in Malory's Tragedy of the Round Table" (Tulane University, 1958). Again Malory's sources are the French *Mort Artu* and the English stanzaic *Morte Arthur*.

30. Guerin, *Originality*, p. 235.

31. Vinaver, *Works*, I, lxxix–lxxx. For views opposed to Vinaver's, see Brewer, *Medium Aevum*, XXI (1952), 14–24; XXV (1956), 22–26; and Guerin, *Originality*, pp. 254–58.

32. *Ibid.*, III, 1633–34. For Vinaver, the addition of the Wheel of Fortune "complicated rather than clarified" the events of the downfall (*ibid.*, I, lxxix). It should be noted that a similar vision appears at the end of the alliterative *Morte Arthure*, the English poem used by Malory as the source of his *Arthur and Lucius;* but there Arthur's fall is explicitly blamed on his pride.

33. Tucker, *Essays*, p. 101.

34. Vinaver, *Works*, III, 1606.

35. Lumiansky, *Mediaeval Studies*, XIX (1957), 111–12 (*Originality*, pp. 211–13).

36. Vinaver, *Works*, III, 1423. Cf. Robert H. Wilson, who feels that Malory tried to harmonize the different concepts of Gawain but was "only partially successful" (*Characterization in Malory: A Comparison with His Sources* [Chicago, 1934], 67–82). See also the comments by B. J. Whiting, "Gawain: His Reputation, His Courtesy and His Appearance in Chaucer's Squire's Tale," *Mediaeval Studies*, IX (1947), 203–10.

37. Barbara Gray Bartholemew, "The Thematic Function of Malory's Gawain," *College English*, XXIV (1963), 264–65. For Guerin, "the bad in Gawain stems from his emotional and instinctual characteristics, the good from the civilizing and Christian influences around him" (*Originality*, p. 265).

38. Cf. B. J. Whiting, who says that in his hatred of Lancelot, Gawain is "mentally unbalanced by cruel grief" (*Mediaeval Studies*, IX [1947], 210).

39. Scudder, p. 346

40. Vinaver, *Works*, III, 1607, 1610.

41. Perhaps, as Lumiansky says, Malory needed "an element of suspense" (*Gawain's Miraculous Strength: Malory's Use of Le Morte Arthur and Mort Artu*," *Études Anglaises*, X [1957], 103).

42. *Ibid.*, p. 107.

43. In Vinaver's words the episode here is told "less circumstantially and therefore more convincingly than in the French *Mort Artu*, and with a finer sense of dramatic preparation than in the stanzaic *Le Morte Arthur*" (*Malory*, p. 99).

44. On this scene, see Lumiansky, "Arthur's Final Companions in

Malory's *Morte Darthur*," *Tulane Studies in English*, XI (1961), esp. 18.

45. Vinaver, *Malory*, p. 92.

46. This redaction is now represented by MS. Palatinus Latinus 1967. See F. Whitehead, "Lancelot's Penance," in *Essays on Malory*, pp. 108–10; and Vinaver, *Works*, III, 1641.

47. Whitehead, *Essays*, p. 110.

48. *Ibid.* For Vinaver, Lancelot repents, not because of "the sins he committed against God," but because of the sorrow he caused Guinevere and Arthur (*Works*, III, 1608).

49. Tucker, *Essays*, p. 99.

50. See R. T. Davies, "Quelques aspects sociaux de l'oeuvre de Malory, en particulier sa conception de l'amour," *Bulletin bibliographique de la Sociéte Internationale Arthurienne*, III (1951), 103.

51. Whitehead, *Essays*, pp. 110, 112. Whitehead here follows Vinaver, *The Tale of the Death of King Arthur* (Oxford, 1955), pp. xxii–xxiii. In Guerin's view, however, Malory "heightens the degree of holiness in the last years of both Lancelot and Guenevere" (*Originality*, p. 247).

52. Tucker, *Essays*, p. 103. See also Arthur B. Ferguson's statement of the necessary relationship between "the knighthood of this world and the demands of life everlasting" (*The Indian Summer of English Chivalry*, p. 56).

53. Guerin, *Originality*, p. 233; see also pp. 271 ff.

# Selected Bibliography

PRIMARY SOURCES:

Sir Thomas Malory. *Le Morte Darthur*. London and New York: Everyman, 1906. 2 vols. Caxton's edition.

*The Works of Sir Thomas Malory*. Ed. Eugène Vinaver. Oxford: Clarendon Press, 1947. 3 vols. Based on Caxton and the Winchester manuscript, with lengthy introduction and notes; second edition to appear soon.

*The Works of Sir Thomas Malory*. Ed. Eugène Vinaver. London: Oxford University Press, 1954. One-volume edition using text of preceding, lacks introduction and notes.

SECONDARY SOURCES:

a. *Books and Pamphlets:*

Bennett, J. A. W. ed. *Essays on Malory*. Oxford: Clarendon Press, 1963. Essays by eight writers, mainly on Malory's themes and artistry; listed separately below.

Bradbrook, M. C. *Sir Thomas Malory*. Writers and Their Work, No. 95. London, New York, and Toronto: Longmans, Green and Co., 1958. Brief introduction to the man and the book.

Chambers, E. K. *Sir Thomas Malory*. English Association Pamphlet, No. 31. Oxford: Oxford University Press, 1928. Brief biographical, critical introduction.

Hicks, Edward. *Sir Thomas Malory, His Turbulent Career*. Cambridge, Mass.: Harvard University Press, 1928. Biography.

Lumiansky, R. M. ed. *Malory's Originality, A Critical Study of Le Morte Darthur*. Baltimore: Johns Hopkins Press, 1964. Critical essays by six writers on Malory's tales, emphasizing the unity of the *Morte;* listed separately below.

Moorman, Charles. *The Book of Kyng Arthur: The Unity of Malory's Morte Darthur*. Lexington, Ky.: University of Kentucky Press, 1965. Mainly a collection of several critical articles by Moorman, emphasizing Malory's art and the unity of his work.

Schmidz, C. C. D. *Sir Gareth of Orkeney, Studien zum siebenten Buch von Malory's Morte Darthur*. Groningen: J. B. Wolters,

1963. Study of the motifs in the *Tale of Gareth* in relation to those in other medieval romances.

Scudder, Vida D. *Le Morte Darthur of Sir Thomas Malory and Its Sources*. London and New York: Dutton, 1917. Critical study of the *Morte* in the light of other romances; old but still relevant.

Šimko, Ján. *Word-Order in the Winchester Manuscript and in William Caxton's edition of Thomas Malory's Morte Darthur (1485)—A Comparison*. Halle a. S.: Max Niemeyer, 1957. Linguistic-stylistic study.

Vetterman, E. *Die Balen-Dichtungen und ihre Quellen*, in *Beihefte zur Zeitschrift für romanische Philologie*, LX. Halle a. S.: Max Niemeyer, 1918. Study of an episode in the *Tale of Arthur* and its various literary appearances.

Vinaver, Eugène. *Malory*. Oxford: Oxford University Press, 1929. Critical study of the *Morte*, emphasizing Malory's method and art; still very useful although Vinaver has since changed many of his critical positions.

————. *Le Roman de Tristan et Iseut dans l'oeuvre de Thomas Malory*. Paris: Librairie Ancienne Honoré Champion, 1925. Source study of the *Book of Tristram* emphasizing Malory's originality.

Wilson, Robert H. *Characterization in Malory: A Comparison with His Sources*. Chicago: University of Chicago Press, 1934. Full study of the characters in the *Morte*.

**b.** *Some Critical and Interpretive Articles and Essays:*

Ackerman, Robert W. "Malory's Ironsyde," *Research Studies* (Washington State University), XXXII (1964), 125–33. Study of a character and various motifs in the *Tale of Gareth*.

Bartholomew, Barbara Gray. "The Thematic Function of Malory's Gawain," *College English*, XXIV (1963), 254–65. Gawain's character and his role in the *Morte*.

Brewer, D. S. "Form in the 'Morte Darthur,'" *Medium Aevum*, XXI (1952), 14–24. Emphasizes the unity of the whole work, challenges Vinaver's views.

————. "'the hoole book,'" in *Essays on Malory*, ed. Bennett, pp. 41–63. Restatement and expansion of ideas found in the preceding.

Chambers, E. K. "Malory," in *English Literature at the Close of the Middle Ages*. Oxford: Clarendon Press, 1949. Pp. 185–205, 229–31. General introduction to the man and the book.

Davies, R. T. "Malory's Lancelot and the Noble Way of the World,"

*Review of English Studies,* VI (1955), 256–64. Lancelot as Malory's hero of the middle way.

———. "Malory's 'Vertuouse Love,'" *Studies in Philology,* LIII (1956), 459–69. Defines ideal love in the *Morte.*

Davis, Gilbert R. "Malory's 'Tale of Sir Lancelot' and the Question of Unity in the *Morte Darthur,*" *Papers of the Michigan Academy of Science, Arts, and Letters,* XLIX (1964), 523–30. Study of the tale's position in the structure of the *Morte.*

Dichmann, Mary E. "Characterization in Malory's *Tale of Arthur and Lucius,*" *PMLA,* LXV (1950), 877–95 (revised as "'The Tale of King Arthur and the Emperor Lucius': The Rise of Lancelot," in *Malory's Originality,* ed. Lumiansky, pp. 67–90). Emphasizes place of tale in the whole book.

Donaldson, E. Talbot. "Malory and the Stanzaic *Le Morte Arthur,*" *Studies in Philology,* XLVII (1950), 460–72. On Malory's handling of sources, especially in the *Lancelot and Guinevere.*

Guerin, Wilfred L. "'The Tale of Gareth': The Chivalric Flowering," in *Malory's Originality,* pp. 99–117. Study of motifs and the place of the tale in the whole work.

———. "'The Tale of the Death of Arthur': Catastrophe and Resolution," in *Malory's Originality,* pp. 233–74. Source study emphasizing Malory's originality and artistry.

Hibbard, Laura A. "Malory's Book of Balin," in *Medieval Studies in Memory of Gertrude Schoepperle Loomis.* New York: Columbia University Press, 1927. pp. 175–95. Critical study of an episode in the *Tale of Arthur.*

Lewis, C. S. "The English Prose *Morte,*" in *Essays on Malory,* pp. 7–28. Consideration of paradoxes about Malory and his book.

Lumiansky, R. M. "Arthur's Final Companions in Malory's *Morte Darthur,*" *Tulane Studies in English,* XI (1961), 5–19. The final episodes seen in terms of the whole work.

———. "Gawain's Miraculous Strength: Malory's Use of *Le Morte Arthur and Mort Artu,*" *Études Anglaises,* X (1957), 97–108. Source study showing Malory's artistry.

———. "Malory's Steadfast Bors," *Tulane Studies in English,* VIII (1958), 5–20. Character study, emphasizing the unity of the *Morte.*

———. "Malory's 'Tale of Lancelot and Guenevere' as Suspense," *Mediaeval Studies,* XIX (1957), 108–22 (revised as "'The Tale of Lancelot and Guenevere': Suspense," in *Malory's Originality,* pp. 205–32). On the function of the tale in the whole work.

———. "The Question of Unity in Malory's Morte Darthur," *Tulane*

*Studies in English*, V (1955), 29–39. Study of sequence of episodes.

——. "The Relationship of Lancelot and Guenevere in Malory's
'Tale of Lancelot,'" *Modern Language Notes*, LXVIII (1953),
86–91 (revised as " 'The Tale of Lancelot': Prelude to Adultery,"
in *Malory's Originality*, pp. 91–98). Study of Malory's third tale
and of the role of Lancelot and Guinevere in the whole book.

——. "Two Notes on Malory's *Morte Darthur:* Sir Urry in England
—Lancelot's Burial Vow," *Neuphilologische Mitteilungen*, LVIII
(1957), 148–53. On episodes in the *Lancelot and Guinevere* and
the *Death of Arthur*.

Moorman, Charles. "Courtly Love in Malory," *ELH, XXVII* (1960),
163–76. Study of Malory's ideas of love.

——. "Internal Chronology in Malory's *Morte Darthur,*" *Journal
of English and Germanic Philology*, LX (1961), 240–49. Study
of the time relationships between episodes in the *Morte*.

——. "Malory's Treatment of the Sankgreall," *PMLA*, LXXI (1956),
496–509 (revised as " 'The Tale of the Sankgreall': Human
Frailty," in *Malory's Originality*, pp. 184–204). Critical study
of Malory's Grail Quest.

——. "The Relation of Books I and III of Malory's *Morte Darthur,*"
*Mediaeval Studies*, XXII (1960), 361–66. On the development
of Malory's chivalric ideas and the relationship between parts of
the whole book.

Morgan, Henry Grady. "The Role of Morgan le Fay in Malory's *Morte
Darthur,*" *Southern Quarterly*, II (1964), 150–68. Uses Morgan to
show the unity of the *Morte*.

Read, Herbert. "Sir Thomas Malory and the Sentiment of Glory,"
*Times Literary Supplement*, June 21, 1928, pp. 457–58 (most
recently reprinted as "Malory" in *The Nature of Literature*. New
York: Grove Press n.d., pp. 168–82. General study of Malory's
view of glory.

Rioux, R. N. "Sir Thomas Malory, créateur verbal," *Études Anglaises*,
XII (1959), 193–97. General appreciative study.

Rumble, Thomas C. "Malory's *Balin* and the Question of Unity in the
*Morte Darthur,*" *Speculum*, XLI (1966), 68–85. On the place of
the episode in the whole work.

——. "Malory's *Works* and Vinaver's Comments: Some Inconsistencies Resolved," *Journal of English and Germanic Philology*,
LIX (1960), 59–69. Shows that many of the so-called inconsistencies in Malory are not inconsistencies at all.

——. " 'The Tale of Tristram': Development by Analogy," *Malory's*

*Originality*, pp. 118–83. Study of Malory's achievement in relation to his source.

Shaw, Sally. "Caxton and Malory," in *Essays on Malory*, pp. 114–45. On the aims and achievements of the editor and the author.

Tucker, P. E. "Chivalry in the *Morte*," in *Essays on Malory*, pp. 64–103. Study of Malory's chivalric ideas in relation to those in his French sources.

————. "The Place of the 'Quest of the Holy Grail' in the 'Morte Darthur,'" *Modern Language Review*, XLVIII (1953), 391–97. Discusses the Grail Quest in terms of Malory's interest in the story of Lancelot.

Vinaver, Eugène. "On Art and Nature," in *Essays on Malory*, pp. 29–40. Restatement and clarification of the idea of the historical disunity of the *Morte*.

————. "Sir Thomas Malory," in *Arthurian Literature in the Middle Ages, A Collaborative History*. Ed. R. S. Loomis. Oxford: Clarendon Press, 1959. pp. 542–52. General introductory essay, though Vinaver stresses his view of separate tales.

Vorontzoff, Tania. "Malory's Story of Arthur's Roman Campaign," *Medium Aevum*, VI (1937), 99–121. Study of the *Tale of Arthur and Lucius* in relation to sources.

Whitehead, F. "Lancelot's Penance," in *Essays on Malory*, pp. 104–13. On Malory's aims in the *Death of Arthur*.

————. "On Certain Episodes in the Fourth Book of Malory's *Morte Darthur*," *Medium Aevum*, II (1933), 199–216. Analyses of the episode of Pelleas and Ettarde and of the quests of Ywain, Gawain, and Marhalt in the *Tale of Arthur*.

Williams, Charles. "Malory and the Grail Legend," *Dublin Review*, CCXIV, 429 (April, 1944), 144–53. On Malory's idea of the Grail and the Grail Quest.

Wilson, Robert H. "Addenda on Malory's Minor Characters," *Journal of English and Germanic Philology*, LV (1956), 563–87. On characters not in Malory's sources.

————. "The 'Fair Unknown' in Malory," *PMLA*, LVIII (1943), 1–21. Discusses the *Tale of Gareth* in relation to stories using a similar folk-motif.

————. "How Many Books Did Malory Write?" University of Texas *Studies in English*, XXX (1951), 1–23. Early criticism of Vinaver's ideas on separate tales.

————. "Malory's Early Knowledge of Arthurian Romance," University of Texas *Studies in English*, XXIX (1950), 33–50. Emphasizes the unity of the *Morte*.

————. "Malory's Naming of Minor Characters," *Journal of English and Germanic Philology,* XLII (1943), 364–85. On Malory's use of minor characters.

Wright, Thomas L. " 'The Tale of King Arthur': Beginnings and Foreshadowings," in *Malory's Originality,* pp. 9–66. Study of Malory's first tale, emphasizing its place in the whole work.

# Index

# Index

[ 219 ]

*Index*

*Index*

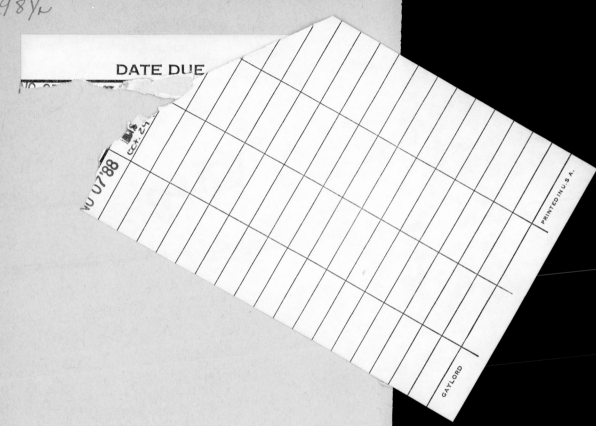